NATO in the Crucible:
Coalition Warfare in Afghanistan, 2001–2014

"As Churchill said, 'There is only one thing worse than fighting with allies, and that is fighting without them.' In this year marking NATO's seventieth anniversary, Hanagan's work shows us that thanks to its political will and organizational ability, it adapted and adjusted to an ever-changing situation while in combat."

— **Tucker Mansager, (Col.-ret.)**, *US Army, International Staff, NATO Headquarters, Brussels*

"Hanagan's superbly researched, comprehensive, and clear-eyed analysis centers on the successful albeit difficult adaptation—political, tactical, organizational, and cultural— that NATO carried out through dialogue, shared experiences, innovation, political will, and military leadership. It is a welcome testament to NATO's foundational value and common principles, and its vitality and relevancy for the future."

— **Gordon B. (Skip) Davis Jr.**, *Deputy Assistant Secretary General, Defence Investment Division, NATO*

NATO in the Crucible

NATO in the Crucible

Coalition Warfare in Afghanistan, 2001–2014

Deborah L. Hanagan

HOOVER INSTITUTION PRESS

STANFORD UNIVERSITY   STANFORD, CALIFORNIA

With its eminent scholars and world-renowned library and archives, the Hoover Institution seeks to improve the human condition by advancing ideas that promote economic opportunity and prosperity, while securing and safeguarding peace for America and all mankind. The views expressed in its publications are entirely those of the authors and do not necessarily reflect the views of the staff, officers, or Board of Overseers of the Hoover Institution.

www.hoover.org

Hoover Institution Press Publication No. 703

Hoover Institution at Leland Stanford Junior University,
Stanford, California 94305-6003

Copyright © 2019 by the Board of Trustees of the Leland Stanford Junior University
All rights reserved. No part of this publication may be reproduced, stored in a retrieval system, or transmitted in any form or by any means, electronic, mechanical, photocopying, recording, or otherwise, without written permission of the publisher and copyright holders.

For permission to reuse material from *NATO in the Crucible: Coalition Warfare in Afghanistan, 2001–2014*, ISBN 978-0-8179-2295-5, please access www.copyright .com or contact the Copyright Clearance Center, Inc. (CCC), 222 Rosewood Drive, Danvers, MA 01923, 978-750-8400. CCC is a not-for-profit organization that provides licenses and registration for a variety of uses.

Efforts have been made to locate the original sources, determine the current rights holders, and, if needed, obtain reproduction permissions. On verification of any such claims to rights in the articles reproduced in this book, any required corrections or clarifications will be made in subsequent printings/editions.

Hoover Institution Press assumes no responsibility for the persistence or accuracy of URLs for external or third-party internet websites referred to in this publication, and does not guarantee that any content on such websites is, or will remain, accurate or appropriate.

First printing 2019
25 24 23 22 21 20 19   7 6 5 4 3 2 1

Manufactured in the United States of America

The paper used in this publication meets the minimum requirements of the American National Standard for Information Sciences—Permanence of Paper for Printed Library Materials, ANSI/NISO Z39.48-1992. ∞

Cataloging-in-Publication Data is available from the Library of Congress.
ISBN: 978-0-8179-2295-5 (pbk. : alk. paper)
ISBN: 978-0-8179-2296-2 (epub)
ISBN: 978-0-8179-2297-9 (mobi)
ISBN: 978-0-8179-2298-6 (PDF)

To Gill and Chris, thanks for your unwavering support.

Contents

List of Figures and Tables

Foreword

I am pleased to write this foreword, not only because it precedes an impressive scholarly work, but also because it means that the Hoover Institution Press has published a book from one of the outstanding alumni of Hoover's Robert and Marion Oster National Security Affairs Fellows (NSAF) Program. Colonel Deborah Hanagan was a member of the 2007–08 NSAF class a few years before I joined Hoover as a senior fellow and became the program's director. The Hoover Institution—once known formally as the Hoover Institution on War, Revolution and Peace—reflects a deeply held commitment to understanding warfare and statecraft to improve the security of our nation and the world. The NSAF program, and this book, are important contributions to that mission.

Colonel Hanagan is a rare breed—a warrior-scholar with impressive accomplishments in both the operational environment and inside the academy. Initially commissioned in the US Army as a military intelligence officer, she later transferred to the Foreign Area Officer functional area. She has served in staff and leadership positions spanning the globe while also earning multiple academic degrees and serving in a number of academic leadership roles, including as a professor of strategy at the US Army War College.

During her time at Hoover, Hanagan distinguished herself, actively engaging in dozens of seminars and conferences and publishing in the *Hoover Digest*, the institution's quarterly journal. My NSAF program predecessor, David Brady, described Hanagan as an "exemplary" fellow and a "good reminder to us at Hoover of the high caliber of individuals who serve in the United States Armed Forces."

Hanagan's latest work grew out of her doctoral thesis at King's College London and reflects the expertise she has garnered as both a scholar and a member of the armed forces. In it, she seeks to explain NATO's involvement in Afghanistan over a thirteen-year period, and the enduring cohesion that existed among coalition members. This work not only provides a comprehensive account of the mission of the International Security Assistance Force but also tackles the question of how coalition cohesion endures in lengthy conflicts. That question is of great and rising importance; data show clearly that both civil and interstate conflicts have grown longer over the past several decades.

Hanagan masterfully uses the existing organizational learning and military adaptation literature—typically used to describe militaries and governments at a national level—to explain a phenomenon at the multinational level. As the international security landscape grows increasingly complex and the challenges confronting multinational security coalitions like NATO continue to diversify, understanding military adaptation and factors of success for coalition cohesion is imperative. This work makes a meaningful contribution to that body of research.

It is made even more special to write this foreword in 2019, as Hoover celebrates the fiftieth anniversary of the NSAF program. For half a century, the program has offered high-ranking members of the US military and government agencies an opportunity to spend an academic year at Hoover to conduct independent research. During their time at Hoover, NSAFs also become essential members of the Stanford University community, attending seminars, participating in workshops, and mentoring undergraduate students. To date, the NSAF program has 158 distinguished alumni, including eleven general officers, two flag officers, twelve US ambassadors, and a former national security adviser. We are proud to call Colonel Hanagan one of our own and to have the opportunity to publish her doctoral research.

Amy Zegart
Davies Family Senior Fellow
Hoover Institution

NATO in the Crucible

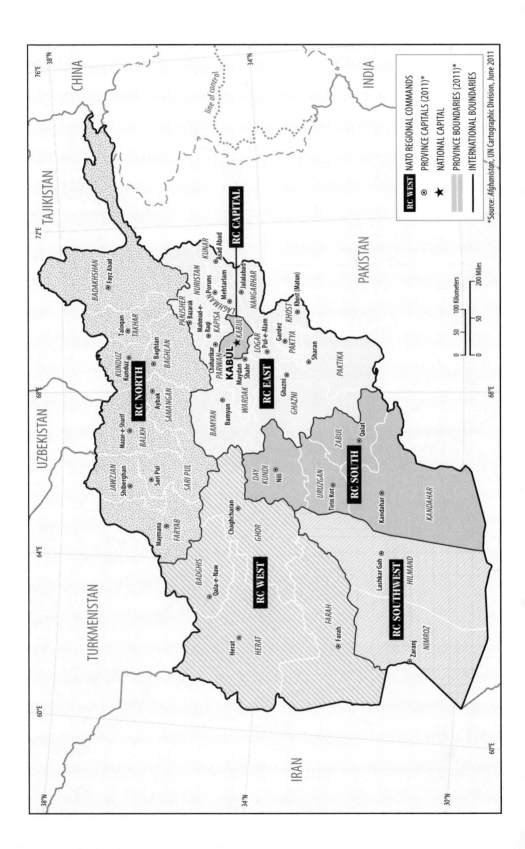

CHAPTER 1

Setting the Stage

The Puzzle

In the annals of North Atlantic Treaty Organization history, 2011 was a banner year. NATO was engaged in ground, naval, and air operations around the world, including the ongoing peace support mission in Kosovo via the NATO-led Kosovo Force.[1] Maritime operations involved two missions: Active Endeavour (launched in response to the Alliance's Article 5 collective defense declaration after the United States was attacked by al-Qaeda on September 11, 2001) and Ocean Shield (a counterpiracy mission operating off the Horn of Africa and in the Gulf of Aden). The NATO Training Mission–Iraq developed Iraqi security forces through training and mentoring activities and contributed to establishing training structures and institutions.[2] The NATO-led intervention in Libya, called Operation Unified Protector, was undertaken under a UN mandate and with the support of the League of Arab States. But despite their wide breadth of activity, these operations were dwarfed by the operations in Afghanistan.

The largest and most significant military activity in 2011, and the only mission in which all twenty-eight of the allies participated, was the NATO-led International Security Assistance Force (ISAF) mission in Afghanistan. Its objective was to ensure the country would never again serve as the base for global terrorism.[3] This year was the apogee of NATO's involvement in Afghanistan and also the year the ISAF coalition reached its maximum size in terms of participating nations (fifty) and number of troops deployed (over 130,000).[4] Over the course of the year, ISAF, in partnership with Afghan security forces, engaged in counterinsurgency and counterterrorism operations against an insurgent coalition that included a reconstituted Taliban and associated groups such as the Haqqani Network (an Islamist organization operating in Afghanistan and Pakistan) and al-Qaeda. ISAF's peace support operations included stabilization and reconstruction activities via twenty-eight provincial reconstruction teams (PRTs). In addition, the NATO Training Mission–Afghanistan (NTM-A), the coalition's main effort, focused on developing the Afghan National Security Forces (ANSF) by training and mentoring the Afghan National Army and Afghan National Police.[5] Finally, ISAF began transitioning full responsibility for security to Afghan forces in 2011. Each major division of the transition was referred to as a tranche. Tranche 1 of the transition began in March, covering Bamiyan Province and the city of Mazar-e-Sharif. Tranche 2 began in November. In the relevant provinces, districts, and cities, ISAF maintained a presence but the troops no longer engaged in direct combat, instead supporting ANSF.[6]

This extensive range of global military activity undertaken with various coalitions was unprecedented for a security organization created more than six decades earlier to defend against Soviet aggression, prevent the reemergence of German territorial ambitions, and keep the United States engaged in Europe. The wide range of coalition warfare—precision combat strikes, peace support operations, humanitarian assistance, counterterrorism, counterpiracy, counterinsurgency, stabilization and reconstruction, and training—indicated that NATO was capable of changing to meet the demands of a changing world. NATO had evolved from a static, defensive alliance focused on deterring conventional and nuclear war to a security organization that could respond to a wide range of challenges.

Of all NATO's activities in 2011, the ISAF mission was the most ambitious (in reality it was trying to help create a resilient Afghan state) and the most extensive in terms of the multinational force contributions involved (ground, air, and naval troops and assets) and the range of missions. The NATO engaged in Afghanistan was almost unrecognizable from the Cold War NATO, just as the ISAF operating in 2011 was dramatically transformed from the ISAF that deployed in December 2001.

NATO was not initially involved in military operations in Afghanistan, but this slowly changed. First, the Alliance decided to take over the ISAF mission in Kabul and expanded the mission geographically and operationally. ISAF then surged, followed by an organized withdrawal. Why did this happen and how did ISAF maintain cohesion throughout the campaign in Afghanistan?

The fact that cohesion endured among the allies and partners in Afghanistan is a puzzle. Many forces were in play that should have frayed the coalition. These forces included intra-Alliance tensions and conflicts over burden-sharing; disagreements about what ISAF should do; concerns about US unilateralism; and reluctance to get involved in combat operations or to remain engaged over the long term. Also, operational inefficiencies (from restrictive national caveats to resource, training, and doctrinal shortfalls) leading to inconclusive battles produced a widespread perception that the international effort was a failure. These problems were exacerbated by major miscalculations about the character of the conflict, underestimations of Taliban resilience, and significant deficiencies among the Afghan partners, including corruption and human capital weaknesses.

This book seeks to address many questions. Why did NATO get involved when the enemy did not threaten the survival of its members? How come the complexity of the conflict in Afghanistan did not fracture the coalition, especially when it was going badly? Why did the missions expand, particularly into the governance and economic domains when that is not what security alliances are traditionally for and why did this not undermine cohesion? Why did no NATO member defect from the coalition, especially considering the Alliance was otherwise globally engaged? Why did partner nations join and stay engaged when they had no formal power in Alliance decision making?

History seems to suggest that alliances and coalitions can be fragile. They have often fractured under combat pressures or when members undergo national political or economic crises. Shouldn't alliances, which result from formal treaties or agreements and have a long-term nature, be more durable than coalitions, which are short term in nature and result from ad hoc and temporary combinations in response to sudden or emerging threats? Logic suggests that when the stakes are high it is more likely allies and partners will stick together, especially in formal alliances, than in cases when the stakes are lower, the situation is opaque, or goals are tenuous. However, actual history seems to indicate otherwise. Alliances have often been as brittle as coalitions, since political, social, economic, or battlefield conditions can fatally undermine the ties that should bind alliances together. For example, in the fifth century BC, the existential threat posed by recurring Persian invasions did not deter constantly shifting alignments among the Greek city-states as they fought each other and against Persia.[7] During the Thirty Years War, despite the invariably heavy costs imposed by war, a number of the protagonists in the Holy Roman Empire changed sides during the conflict due to religious, political, and combat pressures.[8] The six coalitions formed against France during the French revolutionary and Napoleonic wars were a constantly shifting kaleidoscope. The early coalitions in particular were "fragmented by divergent war aims and mutual suspicions" which led to uncoordinated operations, battlefield failures, and disintegration as allies sued for peace individually with France.[9] In June 1940, rather than continuing the war from its territories and colonies overseas, in continued alliance with Britain, the French government decided to defect and surrender to Germany.[10] The subsequent Anglo-American alliance was fraught with rivalries and disagreements from the political level to military operational and tactical levels. Some strategic disagreements were so serious they threatened the alliance's continued cohesion. However, they did not prevent an unprecedented degree of cooperation and the complete fusion of allied strategy and intelligence sharing or the execution of unified operations which ultimately achieved victory.[11] It seems even when allies share a view of the danger they face, as the United Kingdom and France and the United States and United Kingdom did against Adolf Hitler's Germany, a solid and enduring alliance is not necessarily a foregone conclusion. If this applies to cases of extreme danger, then one would expect an alliance or coalition facing lesser risk to fray even more easily. That this did not happen here makes it all the more interesting.

Alliances and coalitions are not necessarily distinct. Since the end of the Cold War, NATO has developed into a formal alliance that can generate discrete multinational coalitions to deal with different security challenges. Its wide range of missions in 2011 demonstrates this point. However, the level of allied participation in them has varied widely and they face different levels of fraying forces. Afghanistan presented a particular challenge since it seemed to represent a synthesis of contemporary threats and challenges. It included a rogue state that was also a failed state, a transnational terrorist group and insurgents, ethnic conflict, ungoverned spaces, and a humanitarian catastrophe. Operations were further complicated by Afghanistan's remote geographic location and its complex cultural context. In fact, given the negative historical experiences of alliances and coalitions, the low stakes involved in the war in Afghanistan, the inconclusive nature of the conflict against the Taliban, the fraying forces identified above, and the fact that today for many European countries war is considered an illegitimate means for resolving international differences, one could argue that the ISAF coalition should have fallen apart and that NATO's involvement in Afghanistan should not have happened or that it should not have developed in the way that it did. However, the fact remains that somehow the Alliance became engaged and ISAF stayed together and maintained an unprecedented level of cohesion in a highly complex conflict, for a long time, in a region far from Alliance territory. Furthermore, ISAF was able to accommodate an ever larger coalition and expand the forms of warfare it undertook as the character of the conflict changed.

This book proposes an explanation for these developments. Its main focus is at the operational level, which entails the command and control structures that integrate multinational military contributions and manage, direct, and coordinate military activities in a specific geographic area—a theater of operations. Operational-level commanders and their staffs translate strategic-level direction into campaigns and major operations (this is known as operational art). As such, the operational level links higher-level direction and objectives to tactical activities. In Afghanistan, ISAF was the operational-level headquarters that provided goals, objectives, and plans which were meant to orient the tactical-level activities of battle groups, PRTs, and embedded trainers. This book examines the decision process in the lead-up to NATO taking over the ISAF mission and then the organizational changes that occurred within the coalition over time, specifically the changes in ISAF's organizational structure and the extensive changes and expansion in ISAF's actual operations. ISAF underwent a dramatic transformation, both structurally and operationally, over the course of its existence. This helped sustain the members' political commitment and enabled the coalition to stay the course in the face of adverse and unexpected conditions as well as to overcome the fraying forces that undermined cohesion. Since ISAF was not an autonomous entity, its examination requires two levels of analysis: the strategic level at NATO and the operational level at ISAF. The levels were inextricably linked. Political authorities in the North Atlantic Council decided whether and when to commit the Alliance in Afghanistan. The Council also issued political direction to ISAF. The military authorities at Supreme Headquarters Allied Powers Europe (SHAPE) and Joint Force Command Brunssum issued strategic and operational direction. While ISAF had wide latitude in translating the higher-level direction into plans and operations, the NATO political and military authorities retained final approval authority over ISAF's successive campaign plans. In addition, the Alliance's various structural elements, such as training facilities, educational programs, and force-generation processes, supported the coalition's activities. Analyzing the ISAF coalition, therefore, requires maintaining an eye on relevant strategic-level developments in NATO.

NATO's eventual involvement in Afghanistan and ISAF's transformation were essentially a case of multinational military adaptation. This book proposes an analytical framework that identifies the main drivers and influences which shaped NATO's initial lack of involvement, its decision to get involved, ISAF's adaptation to the war over time, and the sustainment of cohesion as the conflict changed. The drivers are political will and organizational capacity.

Political will. Security organizations require effort on the part of the member states for action to occur because they are not autonomous. In this case, political will manifests as national policy that is related to NATO. Political will is expressed in public statements and the subsequent activation of Alliance decision forums, persuasion efforts with other members to achieve consensus on an organizational policy or action, and physical contributions, such as defense spending, equipment acquisition, and provision of military forces through the force-generation process for the activation and sustainment of operational missions. Political will must also converge among the members in order for Alliance action to occur. In effect, the convergence of political will generates a decision for operational action and its subsequent sustainment over time.

The national policy positions (political will) of NATO members can vary widely and can shift over time as strategic or domestic conditions change. Political will is therefore shaped or influenced by Alliance politics and domestic politics. Alliance politics has to do with multilateral deliberation, compromise, and constraints, since each member can have different priorities and interests. Working with and depending on allies can slow down decision making, narrow the range of potential actions, and slow the process of adaptation due to burden-sharing concerns and fears of entrapment or abandonment. In addition, allies may be trying to achieve different agendas within the Alliance. The aspirant countries and new members of NATO may have different reasons for supporting Alliance action than the long-standing members. For example, Germany prefers multilateral frameworks for the use of force, so NATO's credibility and survival are important to it as a means to constrain US unilateralism. Some of the aspirants and new members want international protection in the event of Russian aggression so they also want NATO to succeed and endure, but for their own survival.

The tug and pull of domestic politics also influence political will and member state decisions about NATO's operational activities and the level of their contributions. Decisions to employ military force are especially contentious for many European countries for reasons of history. Scholars like John Mueller and James Sheehan have documented the rise of war aversion in the aftermath of the First and Second World Wars such that war is no longer perceived as a legitimate instrument of policy in many European societies.[12] This means national policy makers have to consider the level of public support they may or may not have for a military mission. It also influences what policy makers will commit to an operation and how they will describe their contribution. For example, some countries may only commit forces for humanitarian or stabilization operations and they may emphasize the peace-building aspects of the mission over the more kinetic activities (those involving lethal force). National parliaments may also play a constraining or supporting role, such as approving resources or introducing strict national caveats, depending on their oversight authority. Finally, financial conditions can greatly influence the degree of a nation's contribution. The global financial crisis in 2008–09 and subsequent austerity budgets in many European countries imposed constraints on the resources available for military operations.

Organizational capacity. Organizational capacity provides the ability for a multinational coalition to act once a decision is made and then make adjustments as necessary. This driver has both concrete and abstract attributes. The concrete attributes are primarily structural. They include strategy and planning documents; decision and planning bodies; military resources (compatible forces, military budgets, and/or equipment acquisition plans); unified or compatible doctrine and operating procedures; combined education, training, and exercises; and deployable elements.

The concrete attributes are related to each other. At NATO, the permanent decision body is the North Atlantic Council and it is meant to enable consultation and decision making in the event of a crisis or the emergence of a new threat. Council decisions can activate planning activities, strategy development, and force-generation processes which build the specific force packages needed for a given operation.

The Alliance's published strategy document identifies the purpose and roles of the organization. It articulates the organization's missions and the forms of coalition warfare it will undertake to deal with the threats and challenges facing its members. Strategy influences doctrine, planning activities, force structure (numbers and types of troops and equipment needed), military budgets, and equipment acquisition plans. Regularized Alliance staff planning, educational programs, the execution of periodic training and exercise programs, and the encouragement of national modernization programs are intended to produce compatible and interoperable military forces. They also build trust among the members and can lessen free-riding behavior in the event the organization deploys forces. Finally, the organization's deployable elements can become the command and control structures in operational theaters. Member state force contributions fall in under, and integrate into, these command and control structures. In general, NATO's structural elements would support the operational activities of multinational coalitions like ISAF. When learning occurs in conflict, they could generate strategic-level changes and adaptations that support operational-level actions and changes.

Structural attributes in coalitions like ISAF would include decision and planning bodies embedded in both the headquarters and subordinate commands. Their primary purpose would be to prepare for, plan, conduct, and evaluate operations. They would publish campaign plans that identify the coalition's operational missions and objectives. The plans could also be revised if the coalition concludes that its activities are not having the desired operational effect. That is, campaign plans can change if the coalition has the capacity to learn and subsequently adjust what it is doing. Coalitions like ISAF could also establish common operating procedures and incorporate training programs and exercises to prepare for operational missions and to build trust and increase interoperability; these would contribute to building operational cohesion.

The abstract attributes of organizational capacity are strategic culture, the ability to learn, and experience operating together; they are linked to the concrete attributes. Strategic culture refers to beliefs about the use of force and frames how the organization sees the world and sees itself. As such, the beliefs or norms that the organization and its members share prescribe when and how military force can be used. For NATO, they also prescribe the Alliance's geographic range of action. They are articulated in the organization's strategy documents and campaign plans. Strategic culture is not static—it can change as the strategic environment shifts and as members' conceptions about what constitutes the legitimate use of force evolve—but it can be difficult. NATO's strategic culture during the Cold War encompassed a defensive strategic concept oriented on deterring conventional or nuclear war. Geographically, Alliance activity would occur only within the territory of the member nations. The collapse of the Soviet Union and the emergence of new security threats opened a debate on NATO's purpose and whether it should operate out-of-area. This debate was ongoing, even as the Alliance's strategic culture evolved and NATO undertook a wide range of new missions (peace support, stabilization, and humanitarian) and incrementally shifted from operations on the periphery of member territory to global operations.

Military and security organizations operate in a dynamic environment. To retain their value for their members, they must have the ability to learn and to recognize when they are in a new situation or when they face unprecedented problems. Organizational learning requires a level of self-reflection and open-mindedness since it requires members to acknowledge that their beliefs about the appropriate way to resolve a problem or achieve an objective are wrong. Learning during conflict may also be incremental due to the reciprocal nature of war. Learning is a cyclical process. I rely on a definition proposed by Richard Downie, who argued learning is "a process by which an organization uses new knowledge or understanding gained from experience or study to adjust institutional norms, doctrine and procedures in ways designed to minimize previous gaps in performance and maximize future successes."[13] For NATO and coalitions like ISAF, learning could occur as the Alliance and coalition recognize that the character of the conflict has changed or that operational activities are not achieving the desired effect. Learning could result in new or adapted plans and activities and as such would be reflected in revised strategies and campaign plans; organizational structures; resources; operational missions, operating procedures, and ways of fighting; doctrine; and education, training, and exercise programs.

Experience operating together in multinational missions can increase a coalition's effectiveness since the member states' military forces are more likely to become interoperable over time. This is because they establish common operational procedures, overcome language barriers, and develop a measure of trust in each other. In addition, successful action by an organization (demonstrated capacity) can generate more impetus for its use in other situations. For example, NATO seemed to demonstrate in the 1990s that it had the combat power and expertise to deal with the conflicts in the Balkans, particularly the challenges associated with complex peace operations. This prior experience was a factor in the Alliance's deliberations about whether and how to get involved in Afghanistan.

The two drivers identified above are linked. Political will is critical initially since this driver dictates operational action. Political will can be weak but it can be sustained by organizational capacity. Organizational capacity can either enhance or undermine political will and thus coalition cohesion depending on whether it facilitates or hinders change and adaptation. If the operational coalition can learn (recognize that the character of the conflict has changed or identify that its campaign plan is not achieving the objectives) and subsequently has the capacity to adapt in such areas as organizational structures, operating procedures, or military missions, it is more likely to sustain political will and thus cohesion in the face of potentially destructive fraying forces. ISAF's case represents a bottom-up situation. The multinational operational adaptations helped sustain strategic-level political will and commitment at both the national and NATO levels. As such, ISAF's capacity to adapt generated and sustained cohesion which ensured the coalition did not fracture under the pressure of the multiple fraying forces.

The Genesis of NATO

Alliances and coalitions are generated and exist within the conditions of a given strategic environment. Furthermore, dramatic shifts in the strategic environment can be the precipitating agents for change within military organizations, especially if they possess the capacity to learn and adapt. This means alliances and coalitions can change significantly over time. In the case here, not only did NATO undergo incremental changes after the September 11, 2001, terrorist attacks, but it seems this has been NATO's character since its foundation in 1949. The NATO of the early days of the Cold War looked nothing like the NATO at the end of the Cold War. Similarly, the NATO of 1989 was substantially different from the NATO that became involved in Afghanistan. More important, the changes that occurred in the 1990s—which led to NATO actually undertaking military action for the first time in its history and shifting the type of activities it was prepared to undertake— laid important foundations that were relevant for Afghanistan and for ISAF. Therefore, to explain NATO's involvement in Afghanistan it is necessary to look back in time.

After Hitler's Third Reich was defeated and World War II ended in Europe in May 1945, there was no allied plan for a continuing military alliance. As a consequence, the United States ended the lend-lease program and the allies executed rapid troop drawdowns and demobilizations.[14] Within a year of Germany's surrender, American armed forces deployed in Europe decreased from 3,100,000 to 391,000, British forces decreased from 1,321,000 to 488,000, and Canadian forces decreased from 299,000 to zero.[15]

However, several negative political, economic, and military developments between 1945 and 1948 brought Europe close to collapse.[16] They included the need to deal with tens of millions of refugees and displaced persons.[17] This was exacerbated by severe food shortages and a dollar crisis that undermined the effort to rebuild nations devastated by war. Soviet subversion of politics in occupied Eastern Europe was followed by what the West perceived as aggressive Soviet behavior: the Prague coup d'état, Communist influence in the Italian elections, pressure on Norway to conclude a nonaggression pact, and the Berlin blockade.[18] This significant shift in the strategic environment led to the creation of the Marshall Plan, the provision of new US grants and loans, and negotiations among the Western allies to create a new security pact. Western European leaders not only felt militarily, socially, and politically threatened by the Soviet Union—they feared for the very survival of their nations given their ongoing economic difficulties. They concluded that the only way to stop Soviet expansion and ensure their nations' political stability was an alliance that guaranteed US assistance.[19]

After months of negotiation complicated by US Senate concerns about constitutional obstacles to automatic military commitments, the North Atlantic Treaty was signed in Washington, DC, on April 4, 1949.[20] The initial members were the United States, Canada, and ten European countries: Belgium, Denmark, France, Iceland, Italy, Luxembourg, Norway, the Netherlands, Portugal, and the United Kingdom. (Greece, Turkey, and West Germany joined in the 1950s, Spain in 1982.) The treaty was more than a military pact. It established a community of nations that shared "principles of democracy, individual liberty and the rule of law" and it identified a broad aspiration to safeguard the community's "freedom, common heritage and civilisation." To do this, the various articles of the treaty articulated military, economic, political, and social objectives.[21]

There was initially little permanent substance to the Alliance. Its operating principle consisted of periodic meetings by foreign and defense ministers in various national capitals and the establishment of several planning bodies. The first formal meeting of what came to be known as the North Atlantic Council occurred in Washington, DC, on September 17, 1949.[22] The overwhelming threat posed by the Soviet Union shaped the development of NATO's strategic culture as a defensive alliance and meant the allies initially focused on the treaty's military purpose.[23] While the Council approved a strategy and strategic concept called *forward defense*, implementation of supporting defensive plans was slow and uncoordinated.[24]

The slow pace of NATO meetings and planning changed when the strategic environment abruptly shifted in 1950. After announcing the establishment of the communist German Democratic Republic, the Soviet Union tested an atomic weapon; Mao Zedong established the communist People's Republic of China; and then North Korea invaded the South.[25] As a consequence, the United States decided to significantly increase military aid to help the allies build up their military forces and to deploy additional ground forces and thousands of nuclear weapons on Western European soil.[26] These events led to a new strategic concept: *forward defense and massive retaliation*.[27] They also led to a shift in political will as the allies agreed to make major political and military organizational changes.

The military changes occurred first. The Alliance created a permanent, integrated structure with two strategic military commands. Allied Command Europe was activated in April 1951. It was commanded by the Supreme Allied Commander Europe (SACEUR) who was supported by a new headquarters located in France, the Supreme Headquarters Allied Powers Europe (SHAPE). Allied Command Atlantic was activated in April 1952. Both commands had several permanently operating subordinate commands. The political changes included the creation of the secretary general position and an international staff located in Paris in 1952.[28] These changes meant the Alliance acquired permanent consultation, decision, planning, and command capabilities and arguably gave it the capacity to engage in both conventional and nuclear warfare. The allies signaled the importance they gave to NATO's purpose when heads of state and government began chairing North Atlantic Council meetings in 1957.[29]

A second period of major organizational and strategy changes occurred in the 1960s. In 1966, French president Charles de Gaulle took France out of the integrated military command structure and ordered the removal of all NATO military forces from French territory. Within the next year, SHAPE moved from Rocquencourt, France, to Mons, Belgium. Other NATO elements and US military installations left

France for new sites, primarily in West Germany. The secretary general and his staff moved to a new NATO headquarters established in Brussels, Belgium, in 1967.[30] Other organizational changes included the creation of a small multinational operational force called the ACE Mobile Force.[31] In response to Soviet naval activity in the Mediterranean, the allies created the Maritime Air Force Mediterranean command in Naples.[32] In general, the Alliance continually worked to improve its capacity to plan for and conduct operations. It instituted annual program reviews to monitor the development of national military forces. To improve interoperability, it created educational establishments and began multinational training exercises. The NATO Defense College was established in 1951; initially located in Paris, it moved to Rome in 1966. The NATO (SHAPE) School at Oberammergau, Germany, was established in 1953.[33] The first combined training maneuvers were held in fall 1951.[34] The exercise program expanded rapidly and in 1953 approximately one hundred training exercises were held throughout the NATO area. They ranged from command post exercises at SHAPE headquarters to multinational maneuvers by air, land, and sea forces.[35]

All of the changes were oriented toward strengthening the Alliance's deterrence and defensive capabilities. But at the same time, the Alliance expanded its strategic approach. When the *flexible response* concept was adopted in 1967, the North Atlantic Council also adopted the recommendation of the Harmel Report to encourage détente with the Soviet Union. This was mainly due to a divergence in member threat perceptions as tensions relaxed and relations normalized between Western Europe on the one hand and Eastern Europe and the Soviet Union on the other.[36] NATO accommodated this divergence by balancing defense with détente. Over the course of the 1970s and 1980s, the Alliance endeavored to normalize relations with the Warsaw Pact countries via political dialogue focused on confidence-building measures as well as arms control, disarmament, and balanced force reductions.[37]

Overall, the Alliance seemed to demonstrate it was a learning organization. It proceeded deliberately in creating relevant political and military structures as the strategic environment changed and it was flexible enough to reform or disband subsidiary bodies when it needed to do so. NATO's character was one of constant evolution via new organizational bodies and new strategies to create a credible and interoperable military capability. The efforts were not always successful and members did not always fulfill their commitments. However, the transparency involved in processes like the annual program review allowed the organization and its members to identify weaknesses and seek remedies.[38] The ability to adapt meant the organization retained its value for its members, which influenced their national will to maintain their political and military commitments. This commitment was tested by periodic domestic political opposition and periodic crises.[39] But the deft diplomatic skills of successive secretaries general helped the organization to weather difficult periods such as the Suez Canal crisis, the French withdrawal from the integrated military command structure, the Greek-Turkish conflicts over Cyprus, and disagreements over burden-sharing and nuclear policy.[40] Shared interests and the consultation, decision, and planning bodies assisted the Alliance in sustaining cohesion during the Cold War.

The Alliance's one consistent attribute during the Cold War was a strategic culture which identified a clear adversary and against which it was prepared to conduct defensive conventional and nuclear operations. Thanks to enduring member commitment and a credible deterrent threat, NATO was never called to use military force during its first four decades. This changed after 1989. Fortunately, the long-standing habits of consultation and cooperation, the solid organizational capacities reflected in the military command structures and the planning bodies, and the cultural familiarity developed through education, training, and exercise programs gave the Alliance the ability to survive and adapt in the post-Cold War environment. Its responses to the challenges of the 1990s also laid the foundation for its involvement in Afghanistan.

New Strategic Security Environment

To the surprise of many, the Cold War ended peacefully. Furthermore, between 1988 and 1991, a cascading series of events completely changed the landscape of Europe. The initial impetus for what developed into sweeping strategic changes was the economic crisis in the Soviet Union and Warsaw Pact countries. President Mikhail Gorbachev's actions to revitalize the Soviet Union had unintended consequences which spiraled out of his control, particularly when he made it clear Moscow would not intervene in Eastern Europe.[41] He effectively overturned the Brezhnev doctrine that called for the use of force to prevent Eastern Bloc countries from making economic or political reforms.[42]

NATO leaders recognized that Gorbachev was a different kind of Soviet leader and that his domestic and foreign policy initiatives created an unprecedented strategic opportunity. For example, he withdrew military forces from Afghanistan, took a dramatic step in arms control negotiations by signing the Intermediate-Range Nuclear Forces (INF) treaty in December 1987, and unilaterally reduced the size of the Soviet armed forces by half a million men. His cuts in defense expenditures were part of a broader effort to overhaul the Soviet Union's moribund economy.[43] But even as late as spring 1989, when the communist world in Europe was on the cusp of dramatic change, NATO leaders were hedging their bets, calculating that Gorbachev's reforms would be limited, that the USSR would retain substantial conventional and nuclear capabilities, and that therefore the bipolar nuclear standoff would continue.[44] They could not conceive that Gorbachev's initiatives would lead to political changes throughout central, eastern, and southeastern Europe which would subsequently overturn the security environment.

They miscalculated. Europe's political landscape transformed in 1989 as Poland, Hungary, East Germany, Bulgaria, Czechoslovakia, and Romania successively adopted political pluralism as a result of democratic elections, the collapse of the communist regimes, or an outright coup d'état. The result was a wholesale rejection of communism and a movement toward market economies.[45] These events were accompanied by extensive migration to the West when Hungary opened its borders in September. The opening of the East German border and the Berlin Wall followed in November, at which point the Iron Curtain effectively dissolved.[46] The long-standing goal of German reunification was achieved in under a year.[47] The Soviet Union itself began to disintegrate in March 1990 when Lithuania declared its independence. The other Baltic countries followed with their own independence declarations in 1991. That year, almost every other Soviet republic declared its sovereignty. At the end of 1991, the Soviet Union itself dissolved when Gorbachev stepped down.[48] The Warsaw Pact military alliance disintegrated in 1991.[49]

By 1992, the guiding impetus for the existence of NATO had disappeared. Although the Alliance was not a player in the momentous political events between 1989 and 1991, it had not remained static. It constantly evaluated the security implications of the changing landscape. These included fears of the rise of nationalism and the reemergence of conflict in the transitioning and newly independent countries due to ethnic grievances or border disagreements. Some feared either political instability or internal crisis within the USSR or even the USSR's revitalization.[50] There were also concerns over nuclear weapon proliferation within the area of the Soviet Union.[51] As a consequence, the Alliance held five summit conferences between May 1988 and November 1991 as it grappled with its role going forward.

The May 1988 Brussels Summit recognized Gorbachev's policy changes but it maintained the status quo because of the "steady growth of Soviet military capabilities." The allies reaffirmed the strategy of deterrence and defense, as well as the détente and arms control policies.[52] The May 1989 Summit in Brussels reaffirmed the military strategy, but the allies advanced arms control efforts by proposing significant reductions in conventional forces via the Treaty on Conventional Armed Forces in Europe.[53] However, the underlying context of both summit declarations was the continuing Cold War and a perception of "us versus them." NATO's strategic culture endured as an alliance balanced against the Warsaw Pact. This context changed by the end of the year.

President George H. W. Bush and President Gorbachev announced the end of the Cold War after their summit in Malta on December 3, 1989. In their first face-to-face meeting, they stated they had no intention of fighting each other and agreed to undertake big reductions in military forces.[54] The subsequent communiqué issued by the NATO secretary general announced that Europe was on the threshold of a new era. It no longer referred to two opposing alliances, but rather stated that NATO would seize the opportunity to facilitate and promote democratic reform in the East and thus fulfill the vision of an undivided Europe. While it again affirmed the deterrence and defense strategy, it justified the strategy as a "guarantor for peace" in an environment of "change and uncertainty."[55]

The NATO Summit in London in July 1990 marked a major shift for the Alliance. Because East and West were no longer adversaries, the allies agreed to move away from forward defense, where appropriate, and modify flexible response in order to reflect a reduced reliance on nuclear weapons. The allies also agreed to reduce the readiness levels of active forces and scale back training and exercises. They decided to restructure the active forces, to field smaller, more mobile, but also multinational forces that could be moved to crisis regions within NATO territory.[56] These decisions moved the multinational integration of the military structure from major headquarters down into operational units. These changes laid the foundations for an organizational capacity (deployable, multinational units) that would prove useful in the Balkans and Afghanistan.

The decision to build more mobile and versatile forces reflected the new security concern: instability from political transition or ethnic and territorial disputes. At the time, they were not intended to deploy out-of-area because some member nations still insisted that NATO forces should be used only within NATO territory.

The out-of-area issue had been a long-standing one.[57] The debate had a real-world impact in August 1990 when Iraq's president, Saddam Hussein, invaded Kuwait. The United States led the creation of an ad hoc multinational coalition—under UN mandate, because NATO was not allowed to operate outside member territory, primarily because of French objections.[58] However, the Alliance played a supporting role. It sent AWACS (airborne warning and control system) aircraft to Turkey to monitor the border region.[59] Council representatives gave their political support to the US-led coalition and warned Iraq not to violate Turkey's territorial integrity. The allies logistically supported the deployment and transit of American and European forces. They deployed the air component of the ACE Mobile Force and air defense assets, including Patriot batteries, to Turkey. Additionally, twelve members contributed ground, air, and naval forces to the coalition.[60] In effect, NATO took a very small step toward conducting conventional military operations out-of-area.

The next NATO summit in Rome in November 1991 continued the Alliance's organizational adaptation. The allies unveiled a new strategic concept: *dialogue, cooperation, and defense*. The concept built on the 1990 London Declaration, integrated the political and military elements of Alliance policy, and took a broad approach to security promotion in the new European landscape.[61]

The allies created a virtue out of necessity. In a security environment where military challenges could range from conventional conflict with a resurgent Russia to the spillover of small-scale civil conflicts, terrorism, weapons of mass destruction proliferation, and humanitarian crises, NATO opted to emphasize mobility and flexibility from a smaller pool of multinational military forces. The forces would be trained and prepared to conduct a variety of missions, some of which were new, ranging from collective defense to crisis management, peacekeeping, and humanitarian assistance.[62]

NATO has always been more than a military security pact. It has a political and social vision, as well as military and nonmilitary objectives. However, the nonmilitary side of NATO was relatively invisible during the Cold War. This nonmilitary side became much more visible after 1989. In effect, the end of the Cold War, the transformation of the European political landscape, and the new security challenges provided an opening for the Alliance. Member nations maintained their overall goal of preserving stability and peace on the continent but the Alliance changed what it did to achieve this goal. In particular, NATO's political dimension expanded as it endeavored to achieve an ambitious vision of a Europe whole and free. Ultimately, NATO actions followed

two broad tracks in the 1990s in response to two distinct security challenges: the post-communist transition and war in the Balkans. Both
tracks were oriented toward achieving security and fulfilling the vision.
Both tracks also converged.

NATO's Response to Transitioning
Post-Communist Countries

With the collapse of the Soviet Union and the Warsaw Pact, the
Alliance took its first steps in operating out-of-area as it undertook a
mission to "project stability" in central and eastern Europe. Over time,
its relations with the post-communist countries focused on supporting
their political transition, creating new structures to ensure East-West
cooperation, and encouraging and assisting defense reform, civilian control of the military, and arms control. In general, the Alliance
established an extensive range of contacts with all of the transitioning
countries, to include Russia, that facilitated mutual understanding and
reduced historic suspicions. It also gradually moved the transitioning
countries toward interoperability with NATO military forces.

The deepening relations were accompanied by pressure from many
of the democratizing countries for NATO membership. In 1991,
instability in the Soviet Union and conflict in Yugoslavia raised concerns in central and eastern Europe about a potential wave of refugees from the unraveling Soviet Union or a spillover of violence from
the disintegrating Yugoslavia.[63] However, the allies were not ready for
the political repercussions of enlarging the Alliance toward the east.
Moreover, the defense establishments of the aspirant countries were
incompatible with NATO.

Instead, the Alliance moved toward a structure that institutionalized
regular consultations with the democratizing countries. In October
1991, the US secretary of state, James Baker, and the German foreign
minister, Hans-Dietrich Genscher, proposed the creation of the North
Atlantic Cooperation Council as a forum for East and West to discuss

political and military issues.[64] The forum was established at the Rome Summit in November 1991.[65]

Within two weeks of the first Cooperation Council meeting at which nine central and eastern European countries joined the body, the Soviet Union dissolved. Alliance leaders agreed that membership should be extended to the newly sovereign states.[66] By June 1992, twelve more countries joined the body.[67]

Consultations initially focused on residual Cold War issues such as the withdrawal of Russian troops from eastern Europe. However, in 1992, as conflict in Yugoslavia spread to Bosnia-Herzegovina, the Cooperation Council discussed peacekeeping. In December 1992, the Council agreed members would share peacekeeping experiences and possibly train together.[68] In June 1993, the members agreed to actually engage in peacekeeping operations together under the auspices of the United Nations or the Conference on Security and Cooperation in Europe.[69] However, the Cooperation Council was not the right structure to facilitate the military integration required for NATO and partner nations to operate together.

The introduction of the Partnership for Peace program met this need. Adopted at the NATO Summit in Brussels in January 1994, it complemented the continuing operation of the North Atlantic Cooperation Council.[70] All of the partner nations were invited to join (it was also open to other countries). Besides providing a mechanism for developing convergent and cooperative military capabilities, Partnership for Peace was purposefully focused on strengthening the ability of all nations to undertake multinational operations—in particular, peacekeeping, humanitarian, and search-and-rescue operations.[71]

Participation in Partnership for Peace included specific requirements of partner nations. These included the inculcation of democratic principles and respect for human rights, civilian control of the military, and transparent defense processes. They also had to develop military forces able to operate with NATO, participate in peacekeeping and humanitarian operations, and actively involve themselves in joint planning, training, and exercises with NATO.[72] The program was a concrete way to ensure partners were producers as well as consumers of security. It was so popular that thirty nations had joined it by 2006.[73]

The Partnership for Peace exercise program was robust. From three exercises in 1994, the allies and partners held eighty exercises in 1996.[74] The level of military integration was such that partner nations were prepared to contribute military forces to NATO's first peace support operations in its history. Partner nations deployed forces to Bosnia-Herzegovina and participated in both the 60,000-man Implementation Force, activated in December 1995, and the subsequent 31,000-man Stabilization Force, activated in December 1996.[75]

As partner capacities improved, the North Atlantic Cooperation Council was replaced by the Euro-Atlantic Partnership Council in 1997. Open to all Euro-Atlantic countries, it deepened the NATO-partner relationships by opening consultation to a wider range of security issues and giving partners more decision-making power. By the end of the 1990s, it became the forum in which allies and partners coordinated the continuing Stabilization Force mission and developed a common approach to the Kosovo crisis.[76]

The Alliance eventually decided to admit new members. Between 1999 and 2009, twelve of the post-communist countries joined NATO.[77] Their participation in Partnership for Peace, the North Atlantic Cooperation Council, and the Euro-Atlantic Partnership Council meant that when they joined they were immediately ready to participate in multinational operations, if they had not already done so. However, the road to the use of military force in the Balkans and Afghanistan, as well as the Alliance's engagement in entirely new forms of warfare, was not an easy one.

NATO's Response to War in the Balkans

War in Yugoslavia developed and spread in stages, beginning when both Slovenia and Croatia declared independence on June 25, 1991. The conflict in Slovenia was over almost before it started. After only ten days, the Yugoslav government accepted peace mediations by the European Community. A cease-fire began on July 7.[78] Croatia was different. Fighting between Croatian and Yugoslav federal military forces (the JNA) erupted as the JNA withdrew from Slovenia in July. Fighting was bitter. By the time a UN-brokered cease-fire was announced in December 1991, Serb irregular forces and the JNA had occupied a third of Croatian territory. As the UN Protection Force began deploying into Croatia to monitor the cease-fire in March 1992, war broke out in Bosnia-Herzegovina following its declaration of independence on March 6.[79] The UN Protection Force mission expanded into Bosnia in September 1992 and the United Nations added the mission to protect six safe areas (Srebrenica, Sarajevo, Žepa, Tuzla, Goražde, and Bihać) in spring 1993.[80]

NATO was not initially engaged in Yugoslavia because the member nations did not ask it to get involved. Alliance leaders did not see NATO as the solution for all the problems in the new European security landscape. This was reflected in their support for the creation of conflict prevention and crisis management mechanisms in the United Nations and the Conference on Security and Cooperation in Europe and their support for the development of a European Community/European Union security and defense capability.[81] Furthermore, the European Community stepped forward to help negotiate an end to the conflicts. European confidence was reflected in a statement by Luxembourg's foreign minister, Jacques Poos: "The hour of Europe has dawned."[82] He added, "If one problem can be solved by the Europeans it is the Yugoslav problem. This is a European country and it is not up to the Americans. It is not up to anyone else."[83] The United States supported Europe's role. It was not interested in getting involved in Yugoslavia, as demonstrated in then secretary of state James Baker's famous quote: "We don't have a dog in this fight."[84]

However, mediation efforts were fruitless and violence escalated in Bosnia. Western media reporting of extensive ethnic cleansing and death camps increased the pressure for the international community to act.[85] Since neither the United Nations nor other bodies had the military capabilities required to deal with the conflict, NATO very slowly became involved in 1992 as its members reached consensus on operating militarily out-of-area.[86] It launched three missions: using warships to monitor compliance with the UN arms embargo in the Adriatic, employing AWACS aircraft to monitor the UN no-fly zone over Bosnia, and then actually enforcing the arms embargo (over the seven months of the mission, NATO warships challenged 12,000 ships, inspected 176 of them, and detected nine violators).[87]

NATO's military activity expanded in 1993 and again in 1994 after the North Atlantic Council agreed to actually enforce the no-fly zone over Bosnia and then offered airpower to support the UN Protection Force's mission to protect safe areas in Bosnia.[88] The United Nations accepted its airpower offer, which ultimately led to NATO's first conventional combat operations in its history. On February 28, 1994, two NATO F-16 aircraft shot down four Bosnian Serb fighter-bombers that were violating the no-fly zone near Banja Luka. Over the rest of the year, NATO engaged in limited air strikes (called pinpricks by some) against a variety of targets.[89]

The next year, after repeated Bosnian Serb violations of safe areas, the massacre at Srebrenica, and a mortar attack on a marketplace in Sarajevo, the allies undertook a major air campaign called Operation Deliberate Force. Over ten days, September 5–14, 1995, allies flew 3,400 sorties with 750 attack missions.[90] This NATO show of strength in Bosnia, combined with an independent effort in Croatia by the Croatian army to retake territory occupied by Serbs, induced a shift in Serbian president Slobodan Milošević's war aims that changed the dynamics of the conflict. This enabled the successful conclusion of a peace agreement after years of effort.[91]

After the warring parties signed the Dayton Peace Accord in Paris in December 1995, the UN Protection Force mission ended and NATO deployed ground forces out-of-area for the first time in its history. The 60,000-man Implementation Force, operating under a one-year UN mandate, was also NATO's first peace support operation. All of the allies, sixteen nations, and eighteen partners contributed forces.[92] As the mission's end date approached, the allies and partners agreed to extend the military presence in Bosnia since the security provided by the forces was essential for continued progress on the civil side.[93] The 31,000-man Stabilization Force (sixteen allies and twenty-two partners) was activated in December 1996. It operated for eight years until the Alliance turned the mission over to the European Union.[94]

For the Alliance's peace support mission in Bosnia, the military forces were distributed into three multinational task forces. Thus NATO's first operational employment of land forces was in a purely multinational formation.[95] The command's headquarters element rotated every six months. This NATO mission was part of a larger international effort in Bosnia. The Dayton Peace Accord identified three lines of effort—military, civil, and political—which were mutually supporting and interdependent. To facilitate coordination among the military, governmental, and nongovernmental agencies involved in the country, the Implementation and Stabilization Force commanders created a civil-military coordination working group to synchronize activities.[96] Due to shortfalls in resources on the civil side, the NATO forces ended up undertaking a wide range of nonmilitary activities (humanitarian assistance, election support, reconstruction, and support to police reform) in addition to their specified military tasks.[97] At the strategic level, SHAPE supported the mission by creating a program to train troops in civil-military coordination skills. It also drafted policy and doctrine on civil-military coordination to ensure a proper level of military involvement in civilian tasks.[98]

The resolution of the Bosnia conflict did not end war in the Balkans. The next conflict area was Serbia and its province of Kosovo. The deep roots of the conflict were tied to tensions between Muslim Kosovar Albanians and Orthodox Serbs. Yugoslav federal forces were deployed to Kosovo five times between 1945 and 1990 to quell civil disturbances before Yugoslavia disintegrated.[99] By 1991, Serbian political appointees controlled the executive and administrative institutions in Kosovo and 6,000 Serbian police maintained a fragile calm.[100] But in 1996 the Kosovo Liberation Army began an armed insurrection targeting Serbian police, supposed Albanian collaborators, and Serbian civilians. Kosovo Liberation Army violence escalated in 1997 and 1998. In response, the Serbian army and police launched what were essentially scorched-earth counterinsurgency operations in May and September. By late 1998, some 200,000 Kosovar Albanians were displaced within the province and 98,000 had fled the region.[101] International diplomatic efforts to stop the fighting in 1998 and 1999 were unsuccessful, ultimately leading to a North Atlantic Council decision to intervene.[102]

The NATO air campaign to force Serbia to withdraw police and military forces from Kosovo began on March 24, 1999, and continued for seventy-eight days until June 10.[103] Preparation for the operation had begun long in advance. The NATO ministerial meeting held in May 1998 tasked military authorities to begin planning for a range of contingencies.[104] At the June ministerial meeting, the allies directed the military authorities to conduct air exercises in Albania and Macedonia to demonstrate NATO's ability to project power rapidly into the region and they expanded the range of possible military contingency missions.[105] These two ministerial meetings identified why NATO was concerned about Kosovo: allies feared the violence and instability could jeopardize the peace agreement in Bosnia, the conflict could spill over into Albania and Macedonia, and humanitarian problems involving refugees and displaced persons could balloon.[106]

The extensive advance planning efforts meant NATO military forces were ready to act rapidly when negotiations broke down in March 1999.[107] Operation Allied Force was the largest conventional operation on European soil since World War II. Some 912 aircraft and more than thirty-five ships (from which cruise missiles were launched) participated in the campaign that involved 37,465 sorties with 14,006 attack missions.[108] The air campaign lasted longer than NATO had anticipated, for allied leaders had wrongly expected Milošević to crumble rapidly. But it was ultimately successful in forcing Serbia to meet international demands.[109]

Recognizing the need to stabilize the shattered province while a durable political settlement was sought, the North Atlantic Council authorized the second peace support mission in NATO's history. The Kosovo Force deployed into Kosovo on June 12, 1999.[110] Operating under a UN mandate, it included 50,000 troops from all nineteen allies and twenty partners.[111] Once again, the forces were distributed into multinational task forces and the headquarters element rotated every six months.[112] Since there was no longer any functioning local government in the province, the United Nations created the Interim Administration Mission in Kosovo to execute civil, political, and reconstruction activities. The Kosovo Force commander established a civil-military working group to coordinate and synchronize the military, political, and economic lines of effort. As had occurred in Bosnia, due to short-falls in resources on the civil side, the Kosovo Force ended up undertaking a wide range of nonmilitary activities (humanitarian assistance, medical services, policing duties, reconstruction, and election support) as well as its military tasks.[113]

In general, throughout the decade, NATO demonstrated it was a learning organization, although adaptation was often incremental and reluctant. It recognized it was in a new strategic environment and it grappled with the best way to respond. The Alliance's strategic culture significantly changed when its members reached consensus on operating out-of-area. It not only employed force for the first time in its history, albeit very incrementally and only after it became evident other international bodies were not capable of dealing with the conflicts in Bosnia and Kosovo, it also adopted new military missions and created new bodies (such as the Euro-Atlantic Partnership Council) and new programs (Partnership for Peace) as it slowly got to grips with the character of the emerging security challenges. With each air, naval, and ground mission, the Alliance gained experience in deploying multinational military formations and developed the habit of integrating partners. The various NATO leaders also gathered lessons learned and updated doctrine, education, and exercise programs as they sought to improve what the Alliance did and how it performed. NATO's experience in the democratizing countries and the Balkans would prove relevant in Afghanistan.

CHAPTER 2

September 2001–July 2003: NATO Absence

As the twenty-first century dawned, NATO had settled into conducting peace operations in the Balkans. No one would have predicted the Alliance would soon be leading a large, multinational coalition in a shattered country deep in the heart of Central Asia. The 1990s had seen a number of firsts for NATO: first use of military force in conventional combat operations, first out-of-area interventions, and a shift to entirely new activities, including peace and humanitarian operations. But the organization and its member nations were not prepared for the sudden shift in the strategic security environment caused by the attack of a nonstate actor against the most powerful state in the international system.

The attacks on the United States on September 11, 2001, by al-Qaeda, the militant Islamist organization led by Osama bin Laden, took almost everyone by surprise. It was also a prime manifestation of the dangers posed by the combination of transnational terrorist groups, failed states, and ungoverned spaces, for the interests of Afghanistan's Taliban government converged sufficiently with al-Qaeda's to give this Islamic jihadist movement a base from which to launch terrorist attacks around the world.

NATO's initial response to the attacks was another first. Alliance members invoked Article 5 (an attack against one member is an attack against all) for the first time in history. Ironically, the members rallied to the aid of the United States, when for more than fifty years they had expected it would be the United States who would come to their aid. NATO's activities in the Balkans had laid the groundwork for eventual operations in Afghanistan. But this did not lead automatically, or easily, to the organization's involvement in Afghanistan after the initial statement of solidarity. As with the Balkans in the 1990s, NATO's involvement in Afghanistan was incremental and occurred only after significant shifts in political will and strategic culture.

NATO's strategic culture did not initially encompass fighting a transnational Islamic terrorist movement and did not envision the Alliance operating thousands of miles outside NATO territory. In addition, there was no political will on the part of the members to utilize the Alliance against either the Taliban government or al-Qaeda and the Alliance lacked the capacity to deploy and sustain coalition forces in a distant theater of operations. As NATO grappled with its role in the new security environment, the two drivers identified in the analytical framework began to change, which ultimately led to NATO assuming command of an adaptive multinational coalition. However, NATO's strategic evolution was gradual. It was also often halfhearted, contradictory, and ineffectual.

A Shattered State and Terrorist Sanctuary

Afghanistan in 2001 was politically, economically, and socially shattered far beyond what Kosovo had been. This, along with its austere environment—a high mountainous desert with scattered and isolated fertile valleys—and geographic remoteness made it a particular challenge for international intervention. Before the 1978 communist coup, it had been self-sufficient in food production and had undergone halting political, social, and economic development.[114] However, more than twenty years of war, between 1979 and 2001, destroyed much of that progress. In addition, the wars and associated massive refugee population movements damaged the traditional tribal authority structures. This opened a power vacuum into which the Taliban and al-Qaeda moved.[115]

Afghanistan's destruction occurred in two phases. It began with the Soviet Union's invasion in December 1979. At the war's height, 115,000 Soviet troops occupied the country. This Soviet-Afghan war was waged primarily in rural areas where the Russians executed a methodical strategy to depopulate the countryside and destroy rural infrastructure.[116] By the end of the occupation in February 1989, Afghanistan was awash in abandoned Soviet military equipment, from small arms and ammunition to rockets and heavy weapons such as tanks, artillery, and Scud missiles.[117] The country was also flooded with land mines. According to the United Nations, between five million and seven million mines were scattered across the country by 1989.[118]

The various mujahedin movements that had formed to resist the Soviet occupation turned against each other in 1992 when the government led by President Mohammed Najibullah collapsed after Soviet sponsorship ended. The Afghan civil war in the 1990s completed the destruction begun by the Soviets as cities became the new primary battlefields between rival groups vying for power. Kabul, in particular, which had survived intact in the 1980s, was practically destroyed.[119] In effect, the "rubblization" policy of the Soviets was duplicated in the cities. A new actor joined the conflict in 1994 when the Taliban, a Pashtun phenomenon, emerged. (The word Taliban comes from *talib*, "student" in Arabic, as the movement began among students in madrassas, or Islamic religious schools.) The civil war never entirely ended, even though the Taliban movement consolidated power over much of the country by 1996, since it was still fighting Ahmed Shah Massoud's Northern Alliance forces in the Panjshir Valley in summer 2001.[120]

By September 2001, Afghanistan was a shattered state.[121] It was internationally isolated (only Pakistan, Saudi Arabia, and the United Arab Emirates formally recognized the Taliban government) and it depended on international humanitarian assistance.[122] The Taliban government did not act like a conventional government. It did not rebuild traditional state political, economic, and security institutions—in fact the leader, Mullah Muhammad Omar, remained largely isolated and interacted with only a small circle of advisers in Kandahar. Ministries in the capital, Kabul, were excluded from decision-making processes.[123]

The fractured nature of the Taliban's failed state served the interests of al-Qaeda, which moved into the country in 1996.[124] The lack of governance structures and the ongoing conflict gave al-Qaeda freedom to maneuver. It reinvigorated the jihadist training infrastructure that had endured since the 1980s. Al-Qaeda trained, according to estimates, tens of thousands of jihadists between 1996 and 2001 and continued world-wide terrorist attacks with no interference.[125] In addition, it made itself useful to the Taliban government by contributing money and troops (Arab fighters) and supporting it in its fight against the Northern Alliance.[126]

Both the Taliban movement, which emerged from radical Pash-tun madrassas in Afghan refugee camps in Pakistan, and al-Qaeda were founded on similar ideologies. They draw on ultraconservative Wahhabist, Muslim Brotherhood, and Deobandist interpretations of Islam.[127] Both are *Salafist* and *takfiri* movements. *Salafi* movements, in general, are dedicated to purifying Islam and Islamic society.[128] *Takfiris* hold that Muslims whose beliefs are different from theirs are heretics and thus infidels. They advocate violent jihad to fight all infidels, to overturn apostate Muslim states and establish pure Islamic regimes, and to reinstate the Caliphate, or Islamic empire.[129] Al-Qaeda saw itself as the vanguard of an Islamic movement that was fighting to create a new world order based on this Caliphate and which would eventually defeat the West.[130] The Taliban considered Afghanistan to be an emir-ate in this new order.[131]

Over time, through such activities as intermarriage, charities, and funding networks, plus imposition of order through dispute settle-ments, al-Qaeda embedded itself into tribal authority structures and the Pashtun social and geographic terrain.[132] This terrain included areas in both Afghanistan and Pakistan, as Pashtun tribal areas spill over both sides of the Durand Line (a boundary between Afghanistan and Pakistan drawn by the British colonial government in 1893 but which the Afghan government has never recognized as its international border with Pakistan).[133] This cross-border al-Qaeda sanctuary was like a natural fortress due to the austere conditions of the high mountain area, reinforced by the Pashtun social code of *Pashtunwali*. *Pashtunwali* shapes Pashtun identity, culture, and social organization. Based on the concepts of hospitality (*melmastia*), honor (*nang*), revenge (*badal*), manhood (*meranah*), bravery (*tureh*), the right of asylum (*nanawati*), and the defense of the honor of women (*namus*), it was the cultural basis for the safe haven provided to al-Qaeda (and the Taliban) both before and after September 2001.[134] As a consequence, the Taliban and al-Qaeda were linked by ideology, shared networks, and ties of marriage and blood within *Pashtunwali*.

Geography and ideology, the endurance of radical madrassas which continued to turn out *talibs* in the 2000s, the deeply embedded logistical, training, and funding networks that crossed the Afghan-Pakistan border (and which overlapped with criminal networks), and *Pashtunwali* created a complex mix that influenced the character of the conflict after 2001. These complicated religious, social, cultural, political, and economic factors were often unappreciated, or underappreciated, by the international coalition, but they had implications for coalition strategy. As the international community came to grips with the interconnected dimensions of the conflict, the coalition strategy slowly expanded. International intervention needed a spark, however, and that spark was the attacks of September 11, 2001.

New Strategic Environment: The West Goes to War

According to one scholar of al-Qaeda, its attacks in New York and Washington, DC, were intended "to cripple the economic, military and political power of the United States and critically weaken its capacity for retaliation."[135] They had the opposite effect, since one of the first results was the rallying of NATO around the United States. On September 12, the North Atlantic Council invoked Article 5, which triggered the Alliance's mutual defense guarantee.[136] Similarly, the Australian government invoked the mutual defense guarantee of the Australian-US security alliance.[137] Also on that day, the UN Security Council, via UN Security Council Resolution 1368, declared a response by the United States would be legitimate under the terms of the UN Charter. This led to a declaration of solidarity from the

European Union (EU).[138] It was followed by a call for regime change in Afghanistan.[139] The declarations had political and military significance, since they indicated the United States had the political backing of a large number of allies to form an antiterror coalition. It also meant al-Qaeda and the Taliban would not just face a US response. NATO's Article 5 activation turned into concrete actions on October 4 when the United States requested eight specific individual and collective actions.[140] However, none of the actions involved military operations in Afghanistan. Instead, they supported US-led action in Afghanistan and the wider war on terrorism.

NATO did not undertake action in Afghanistan because its members did not ask it to do so. The organization was not prepared for such an unexpected strategic challenge and, in effect, strategic-level drivers blocked the generation of a decision for action due to factors related to organizational capacity which resulted in an absence of political will. The main inhibitor was strategic culture—that is, the Alliance's security role as conceived by its members and its beliefs about the use of force (when, how, and where it could employ military forces), as articulated in the Alliance's strategic documents. In short, it was not a global security organization and the conduct of such an unusual antiterror and regime-change mission was outside the parameters of what was considered legitimate military activity. Although the 1991 and 1999 strategic concepts had mentioned "acts of terrorism" as risks in the evolving security environment, this was not translated into military activities within the context of the Alliance.[141] Before September 11, fighting transnational terrorism was not something that NATO's members thought the organization should do. Before 2001, therefore, the Alliance's military planning bodies had not developed any contingency plans to deal with problems like al-Qaeda and the Taliban government. Existing NATO operational plans also did not envision an unusual campaign like the one waged in fall 2001: the use of several hundred covert agents and special operations forces to coordinate a bombing campaign and to organize more than 20,000 indigenous forces to fight against the Taliban and al-Qaeda.

Furthermore, no member besides the United States had the means to deploy combat forces thousands of miles from NATO territory and logistically sustain them for a prolonged time. The United States possessed the vast majority of the necessary strategic assets: airlift, refueling, strategic bombing, intelligence, secure communications, and precision munitions. The US government had no interest in allowing its allies to constrain operational decisions through political conditions tied to military contributions.[142] This lack of strategic-level organizational capacity influenced the US position, but domestic politics also influenced it. The Bush administration wanted quick action and an unprecedented form of combat action. The Alliance could not have planned and executed such an innovative operation fast enough to suit Washington.[143] Leading an ad hoc coalition maximized the US freedom to maneuver.

Indeed, if the United States had asked NATO to lead the international military response, the organization would probably have declined due to the objection of allies like France. (France's subsequent resistance to NATO taking over the International Security Assistance Force and the merger of Operation Enduring Freedom and ISAF substantiates this assumption.) In many ways, the situation was similar to 1990 and Saddam's invasion of Kuwait. The Alliance could not meet the immediate requirements of the new security environment. In recognition of this fact, according to the US permanent representative to NATO, Ambassador Nicholas Burns, the United States asked NATO for actions and contributions that made best use of its existing capabilities.[144]

Just as they had at the end of the Cold War, national governments and NATO had to grapple with how to respond to the changed security environment. Their public statements reflected the uncertain nature of the time. While the allies and the Euro-Atlantic Partnership Council partners repeatedly pledged to work together, the NATO secretary general qualified their support by adding that "members shall respond commensurate with their judgment and resources."[145] In particular, members' positions on the use of force ranged widely and changed over time. For example, in mid-September, the Italian defense minister initially ruled out contributing any military troops to a response to the terrorist attacks but later stated Italy might contribute special forces to a NATO response. The German president and chancellor made opposing statements—the president doubted German troops would be involved in a military response while the chancellor refused to rule it out. The French government pledged its solidarity but also warned against a disproportionate military response. Spain pledged its full support with no reservations.[146] The initial reluctance of some European countries to contribute air, ground, and naval forces disappeared by October as policy positions converged and the European Union legitimized regime change at its summit in Ghent.

The Bush administration did not turn to NATO partly because its conception of the conflict was broader than just a military effort in Afghanistan. It described the conflict as a fight against global networks of Islamic terrorist groups, led by al-Qaeda, and stated the United States would use all its resources to fight them: diplomatic, intelligence, financial, law enforcement, and military. It also saw the conflict as the world's fight, which is why the president called on every nation to join it. While administration officials welcomed NATO's solidarity, it anticipated that the war on terrorism would be fought by several kinds of coalitions.[147]

The allies indicated their support for this US position several times. This suggested all members were more comfortable coordinating military contributions on a bilateral basis, since it increased their room for maneuver, but it also reflected an unspoken agreement that NATO did not have the organizational capacity to undertake immediate military action in a country so far from continental Europe. It also coincided with the consensus of the time that out-of-area for NATO meant regions peripheral to Alliance territory.

Just as in 1990–91 in Kuwait, while NATO did not lead action in Afghanistan, it supported it, as did the allies and partners. For example, countries in Central Asia joined their fellow Euro-Atlantic Partnership Council members in condemning the 9/11 attacks and they pledged their support in defeating terrorism. They subsequently opened their airspace to the coalition by granting blanket overflight clearances and three of them approved Central Command's (CENTCOM) request to establish critical airbases in Manas, Kyrgyzstan; Dushanbe, Tajikistan; and Karshi-Khanabad, Uzbekistan.[148] As Operation Enduring Freedom began on October 7 with targeted bombing raids and the delivery of humanitarian assistance by US and British forces, the other allies reaffirmed their support. Some, such as Canada, France, Germany, and Italy, pledged to contribute military forces in the coming days and weeks.[149] In early November, the French president, Jacques Chirac, acknowledged that 2,000 French troops were already involved in operations and his prime minister told the French National Assembly that the country was ready to do more. Germany's chancellor, Gerhard Schroeder, announced Germany would mobilize 3,900 specialized troops.[150] The first military "boots on the ground" were special forces from the United States and the United Kingdom in October. They were joined by New Zealand in November and Canada, Australia, Germany, Denmark, and France in December.[151] European allies took the new security challenge seriously. They ultimately provided ground, air, and naval support to operations in Afghanistan, including special forces, combat and support troops, combat and refueling aircraft, strategic airlift, and a variety of naval assets, such as frigates, resupply ships, and aircraft carrier battle groups.[152]

Thus, while initially including only American and British forces, the coalition quickly expanded after October 2001. General Tommy Franks, the CENTCOM commander, briefed the president, defense secretary, and chairman of the Joint Chiefs of Staff on his plan for Afghanistan on September 20. An integral part of his plan for what became known as Operation Enduring Freedom (OEF) was building a military coalition whose core was the NATO allies. During the brief, he stated, "America's NATO partners, as well as Australia, were already lining up to contribute forces and logistical support to a coalition."[153]

However, the contributions were accompanied by a delicate political-military negotiation process. The negotiation process went something like this: Ally said, "I want to contribute." CENTCOM staff responded,

"What do you want to contribute?" Ally replied, "What do you want?" CENTCOM, "What have you got?" Since the allied armed forces representatives (liaison officers) did not want to put their entire military on the table, they would then describe the ground, air, or naval assets their governments had indicated they were willing to contribute and the staff officers from the two sides then worked to figure out where they could best be integrated.[154] Unfortunately, the acceptance and integration of coalition forces was frequently not communicated within the contributing nation's government. In his memoir, former undersecretary of defense for policy Douglas Feith described the complaints the Bush administration received, both publicly and through diplomatic channels, from senior government ministers about alleged CENTCOM nonresponsiveness to offers, which fed into an inaccurate perception of American unilateralism. He said they eventually unraveled the mystery: "The messages often weren't flowing clearly or quickly enough from those [liaison] officers to the civilian leaders *of their own defense ministries*—and those officials, in turn, sometimes failed to inform their colleagues in their foreign ministry and prime minister's office." The administration resolved the communications problem by devising procedures to deliver acceptance and coordination messages to allies and partners through Defense Department, State Department, and National Security Council channels.[155]

By February 2002, twenty-five nations were contributing forces to military activities in Afghanistan, including sixteen of the nineteen NATO members.[156] Operation Anaconda in March 2002, OEF's largest ground combat operation thus far and the first major multinational operation, was conducted by more than 2,000 coalition troops from eight nations (Australia, Canada, Denmark, France, Germany, Norway, the United Kingdom, and the United States). Supported by Afghan militia forces, they killed, wounded, or captured hundreds of al-Qaeda and Taliban forces who had concentrated in the Shahi Kowt Valley in Paktia Province.[157] By April 2002, it seemed the allies and partners had stepped up to the plate and were bearing an equal share of the operational burden. Of the 11,000 forces in OEF and ISAF, about 6,000 were from allies and the rest from the United States.[158]

With participation came national caveats. For example, Belgium contributed strategic airlift (C-130 aircraft) but only for the delivery of humanitarian assistance.[159] The coordination of national contributions under the terms of various national caveats made everything more complex. It also required new structures and processes, such as the "coalition village" at CENTCOM headquarters where allied and partner liaison teams worked together with the CENTCOM staff.[160] Similar multinational coordination structures and processes were eventually created in the ISAF headquarters to facilitate the integration of diverse national contributions.

International military contributions were only one component of an effort that remained focused on keeping Afghanistan from reverting back to a safe haven for transnational Islamic terrorist groups.[161] This objective was more complex than it at first appeared. It meant the international community had to help create a resilient Afghan state capable of preventing the reconquest of the country by insurgents and terrorists.

This in turn required a strategy with three mutually supporting lines of effort in security, governance, and economic development (echoing NATO efforts in the Balkans).[162] Security was the immediate priority, but over the long term, governance and economic development were more important. Initially, the military coalition was faced with defeating the Taliban government, the al-Qaeda terrorists, and the insurgent coalition that formed after the Taliban government collapsed, while it rebuilt Afghan security forces (military and police) which were expected to progressively take over the fight. In principle, increasing security would underpin the rebuilding of functioning state institutions, as well as provide space for economic development. The three domains would reinforce each other. For example, functioning governance structures and capable security forces would increase the government's stability and legitimacy, while a functioning national economy would provide the revenue for a self-sufficient state, all of which would protect the country from again becoming a failed state and a terrorist sanctuary. However, executing a complex strategy with multiple lines of effort over a long time horizon is extremely difficult, if not impossible, as the coalitions found in Afghanistan.

In practice, the OEF coalition became involved in all three lines of effort (as ISAF did later) since the conflict never ended, nonmilitary international efforts were often slow to start and develop, and governance and economic development could not wait until after security was established.[163] Specific elements of the strategy evolved over time. For example, the forms of coalition warfare expanded as the character of the conflict changed. Its implementation was often under resourced, uncoordinated, and ad hoc. The situation was further complicated by the fact that Afghan institution-building was slow and corruption ridden, which undermined Afghan citizens' faith in their government. These weaknesses provided the opportunity for an insurgent coalition to form and for the conflict to continue.

The strategy's three lines of effort relied on the creation of several civilian and military multinational coalitions, initially based on a lead nation-lead entity concept.[164] They also reflected the recognition that the diverse civilian and military efforts were all linked—they depended on each other for long-term success. Under American leadership, annual international coordination meetings began in November 2001.[165] Different nations and international organizations volunteered to take responsibility for various efforts. The United Nations took the lead for the political transition process after the Taliban government collapsed and assisted Afghan representatives in establishing a transitional government and a road map for creating a representative government in the Afghan Bonn Agreement in early December 2001.[166] The United States took the lead for creating and training a new Afghan army. Germany took up police training, the United Kingdom took the counternarcotics mission, and Italy took up judicial reform. Japan funded the disarmament, demobilization, and reintegration (DDR) program, which was a UN effort executed under the auspices of its

Afghanistan New Beginnings Program.[167] However, no single nation or organization took the lead for reconstruction and economic development. This significant weakness seriously undermined the overall strategy. Individual nations and organizations, like the World Bank, United Nations, and Asia Development Bank, pledged funds (which were often slow to be committed) or volunteered for specific projects. This meant the reconstruction efforts were uncoordinated and slow to develop. At times they even conflicted with each other. Even after the UN Assistance Mission in Afghanistan was created in March 2002 by UN Security Council Resolution 1401, it did not become the central coordination point for all economic development, reconstruction, and humanitarian activities. Some initiatives were eventually taken up by ISAF (police and counternarcotics) which further complicated the situation because the Afghan government was forced to deal with conflicting groups of officials from NATO, contributing nations, and international organizations.

In the meantime, OEF's campaign plan for military operations relied on a light footprint. Military planners at CENTCOM kept historical and religious lessons in mind as they built the plan and adjusted it over time. They did not want to repeat the mistakes of the British in the nineteenth century or the Russians in the 1980s. They did not want to be perceived as an occupation force or as infidel invaders necessitating Afghan resistance for religious reasons.[168] The coalition also did not want to create a relationship of dependency.[169] Furthermore, as US attention turned to Iraq in early 2003, there was pressure on CENTCOM to avoid overcommitting resources to OEF. In effect, OEF became an economy-of-force mission for the US government.[170] This concern to keep troop levels low contributed to the creation of a security vacuum that Taliban insurgents exploited.

CENTCOM and OEF commanders and planners benefited from the fact that violence levels were relatively low for a few years, facilitating the coalition's transition in military operations. They adapted to what they thought was the winding down of the conflict. By early 2002, OEF forces began stabilization and reconstruction efforts in conjunction with combat operations. US military leaders had not initially envisioned conducting any nation-building tasks as they built the OEF campaign plan in fall 2001, but after Operation Anaconda they substantially changed OEF's activities. By mid-2002, OEF was engaged in three lines of effort: security operations, stability and reconstruction operations, and training.[171] All of these activities were eventually subsumed into ISAF.

The security operations dealt with Taliban and al-Qaeda remnants.[172] In general, OEF forces conducted pursuit operations, cordon and search operations, and raids to capture or destroy remaining pockets of militants. They destroyed training camps and seized and destroyed arms caches. Many of these multinational operations were small efforts with a limited number of forces, but others were quite large, such as Operation Anaconda in March 2002.[173] Overall, these operations could be considered strategic failures, since coalition forces rarely engaged directly with organized enemy elements for several years after spring 2002 and they never completely eliminated the militants. The operations were not counterinsurgency efforts, since there was not a perception that an active insurgency existed and military forces did not permanently secure the population. Instead, coalition forces launched their operations from bases at Bagram, Kandahar, and a handful of small forward operating bases in southeastern Afghanistan and returned to the bases when operations were complete.[174] The resulting lack of physical control of the Afghan countryside contributed to the security vacuum.

Humanitarian assistance activities were integrated with security operations. For example, during Operation Village Search in October 2002, civil affairs teams assessed medical conditions and identified potential reconstruction projects.[175] Furthermore, since ISAF's initial mandate was limited to Kabul and international reconstruction and economic development pledges were frequently slow to be honored, the OEF commander created a new element to jump-start civil, economic, and reconstruction activities in the provinces.[176] This effort surpassed the civil-military coordination efforts in the Balkans. The

Combined Joint Civil-Military Operations Task Force did far more than coordinate humanitarian, governance, and economic development activities among governmental and nongovernmental organizations (NGOs). It also managed coalition humanitarian liaison cells in ten cities throughout Afghanistan which directly provided assistance on the ground. These popular six-man cells were successful at providing "quick impact" assistance in 2002, especially in unsecured areas where NGOs did not operate but where Afghan needs for development, reconstruction, and humanitarian assistance were massive. Much more needed to be done, and faster. So the humanitarian liaison cells inspired the creation of the provincial reconstruction teams (PRTs), an innovative structure that fully merged the civil and military efforts.[177]

While the idea for PRTs began germinating in spring 2002, the concept was not fleshed out or proposed to then president Hamid Karzai's government until the fall. After the transitional government's approval, the OEF command element, Combined Joint Task Force-180, established three American-led pilot PRTs in 2003 in Gardez (January), Bamiyan (March), and Kunduz (April). The other members of the coalition were encouraged to participate in the effort. As a consequence, in July the United Kingdom established a fourth PRT in Mazar-e-Sharif.[178] New Zealand's government decided to take over the Bamiyan PRT.[179]

The PRTs were intended to make the reconstruction effort more effective by combining representatives from the lead nation's defense, foreign, and aid agencies into one focused team. Team size varied depending on the local security conditions, but in general it ranged from seventy to one hundred personnel, of which the vast majority (sixty to eighty) were military forces who provided force protection and support services to the rest of the PRT. The teams worked directly with local Afghans to coordinate the humanitarian, governance, and reconstruction projects that were most needed in their areas. Since representatives from the Afghan transitional government (such as agriculture and education ministries) were included in the coordination chain, the PRTs were also intended to extend the reach of the new government and enhance its legitimacy.[180] For the OEF coalition, the PRTs represented the beginning of the official transition away from combat operations and toward stability operations.[181]

The training of the new Afghan security forces (ANSF)—army and police—began as part of the expansion of coalition efforts into stability operations. The training efforts were meant to strengthen the new government by building its capability to provide security within the country. As leader of the police training effort, Germany refurbished the police academy in Kabul and began a comprehensive five-year program in mid-2002 that concentrated on traditional law enforcement training for the new Afghan National Police. CENTCOM created the Office of Military Cooperation–Afghanistan to undertake the army training effort.[182]

The Office of Military Cooperation–Afghanistan got to work in an on-the-fly manner necessitated by the CENTCOM commander's desire to quickly build capable indigenous security forces so that the OEF coalition could withdraw quickly. According to Lieutenant Colonel Mark Holler, who worked in the OEF headquarters at the time, the coalition was optimistic it could quickly build sufficient Afghan National Army forces, rapidly turn everything over to the Afghans, and then leave. He described their state of mind in an interview for this book, "We're going to keep the environment secure long enough for the Afghan system of government to kick in through the *loya jirga* process . . . and we're going to start the [army] out on a good footing." He added that the US forces were so convinced they would not be in the country very long they did not build any permanent headquarters or billeting infrastructure for themselves. The OEF command was literally a tent city in Bagram.[183] The OEF coalition was in such a hurry that the first set of Afghan army recruits reported for their ten-week training in May 2002 before funds and resources were in place. Coalition forces began training while the Office of Military Cooperation–Afghanistan was finalizing negotiations with the interim government to use the Kabul Military Training Center as the basic training facility. To further complicate matters, the trainers graduated the first three Afghan army battalions (between July and October) while leaders in ISAF and OEF were still negotiating with the Afghan government over the size and shape of the new Afghan National Army. It was not until December that Karzai approved the plan to build a 70,000-man army.[184]

The training effort was further complicated by the existence of the Afghan Military Forces, the collective term for the mujahedin, Afghan armed forces, and armed groups who had fought with the coalition to remove the Taliban government. The Bonn Agreement declared these groups would come under the control of the interim authority and that they would "be reorganized according to the requirements of the new Afghan security and armed forces."[185] The idea was that some of the officers and soldiers would be integrated into the Afghan National Army and the rest demobilized. However, the Japanese-funded DDR program did not get off the ground until April 2003, many of the troops were unsuitable for the new Afghan National Army, and many of the armed groups proved more loyal to their local leaders and provincial governors (often called warlords) than to the central government.[186] Furthermore, elements of the Afghan Military Forces continued to operate with the coalition in 2002 and 2003 because of the slow growth of the Afghan National Army and the pressure to include Afghan units in security operations.[187]

The Afghan National Army development plan was hugely ambitious. The coalition in effect committed itself to building a national armed force from the ground up. The plan envisioned creating both combat and support units (with their necessary equipment), the bases and infrastructure required for the training programs as well as the operational units, a small air force, and a fully functioning defense ministry and general staff.[188] Coalition members involved in the effort included the British who took over noncommissioned officer (NCO) training, the French who took over officer training, and the Bulgarian, Mongolian, and Romanian armies who agreed to provide specialized training on Soviet-designed weapons and equipment. By fall 2002, the commander of the Office of Military Cooperation–Afghanistan realized his staff was too small for the mission. He convinced his higher headquarters, Combined Joint Task Force-180, to create a new sub-organization, Combined Joint Task Force Phoenix, which stood up in June 2003 to manage the army training program (see appendix 1). It was built upon a US infantry brigade comprised of about a thousand conventional soldiers who took over the training mission from the special forces. Since the basic training only imparted rudimentary skills, Combined Joint Task Force Phoenix created embedded training teams (ETTs) who accompanied the new Afghan battalions after graduation and provided collective training and mentoring to them.[189]

As the OEF coalition undertook humanitarian, reconstruction, and training missions, its leaders believed it was entering a phase of the campaign where combat operations were tailing off while stability operations increased. However, the perception that the conflict was largely over in 2002–03 was premature. The unconventional campaign fought in fall 2001 was spectacularly successful and it killed thousands of Taliban and al-Qaeda fighters. But it did not result in a decisive defeat of either movement. Even though the Taliban government collapsed more quickly than expected, the key leaders of both movements and many fighters fled to Pakistan's cities and autonomous regions, where they found sanctuary.[190] For several years, the Taliban and al-Qaeda primarily focused on regrouping and establishing control of regions within Pakistan's Federally Administered Tribal Areas. The enduring Pashtun tribal, Taliban, and al-Qaeda networks were resuscitated, new insurgent fighters were recruited from the radical madrassas, and *Pashtunwali* provided the cultural foundation for both the reconstitution efforts and the safe haven.[191]

By mid-2002, Taliban leaders had established a base in Quetta and they constituted the Quetta Shura Taliban, a leadership council under Mullah Omar.[192] This organization was different from Taliban rule in Afghanistan as three regional shuras were established under the council in Quetta, Peshawar, and Miram Shah. Together they led and coordinated a loose coalition of former and new Taliban members and groups sympathetic to the Taliban (the new movement was sometimes called the neo-Taliban). Groups that affiliated themselves with the Quetta Shura Taliban included Gulbuddin Hekmatyar's Hizb-i-Islami

Gulbuddin and Jalaluddin Haqqani's Haqqani Network. Altogether they formed a loose coalition that continued to rely on al-Qaeda for mass appeal, funding, resources, and training.[193] Some fighters from these groups infiltrated into Afghanistan to conduct attacks. They were joined by militants hiding in Afghanistan.

Militant activity throughout 2002 and 2003 was limited, which meant violence levels remained relatively low. Afghanistan was still far from peaceful, however. Ongoing violence included sporadic use of improvised explosive devices (IEDs) and car bombs; assassinations of Afghan officials and attacks against Afghan civilians and aid workers; sporadic rocket, artillery, and mortar attacks on Afghan and coalition compounds throughout the country; and some limited organized attacks by militants, such as ambushes.[194] The level and frequency of violence slowly increased during the two years.[195]

Given the disparate violence, OEF's security operations seemed appropriate, although the heavy-handed nature of some search-and-destroy and raid techniques undermined support for the coalition among Pashtun communities who already resented their loss of political power in the new government. This made them ripe for exploitation by the emerging insurgent coalition which had undertaken a new campaign in Afghanistan.[196] The goal of the insurgent campaign was to challenge the authority of the new Afghan government and to counter its state-building efforts. Ultimately the reconstituted Taliban movement wanted to force the international coalition to withdraw and then to reestablish an Islamic emirate.[197] Phase I of the campaign began in late 2002. Phase II began in 2004 and phase III in 2006.[198] With this incremental insurgent strategy, the character of the conflict slowly started to change, just as NATO was adapting.

NATO Starts to Adapt and Gets Involved in Afghanistan

A shift in NATO's strategic culture was the first and most substantial adaptation. The change began as OEF got under way and ISAF was established. The realization that modern civilization gives extremist terrorist organizations potentially enormous destructive power, particularly groups like al-Qaeda that overtly sought weapons of mass destruction, changed Alliance member perceptions about NATO's purpose going forward.[199] By December 2001, allied foreign and defense ministers started thinking about how NATO needed to change and what it should do to combat terrorism. Specifically, military authorities were tasked to develop a military concept for defense against terrorism by the Prague Summit scheduled for November 2002.[200]

A further impetus for the shift in strategic culture was the recognition that Europe already had experience with jihadists. Al-Qaeda's sanctuary in Afghanistan had facilitated attacks in Europe. From the early 1990s, al-Qaeda had established relationships with thirty terrorist groups worldwide. It inspired and assisted them both directly and indirectly. Beginning in the 1990s, Islamic radicals in these affiliated groups opened a second front in their war against apostate Muslim regimes by attacking the United States and its allies. They perceived they could not force change in their home countries without directly challenging Western nations.[201] Europe was attacked repeatedly. For example, the al-Qaeda-affiliated Algerian jihadist Groupe Islamique Armé hijacked an Air France flight in December 1994, intending to crash it into the Eiffel Tower. It was stopped while the plane was refueling in Marseille, but three passengers were killed. In 1995, the Groupe Islamique Armé waged a four-month bombing campaign against the Paris metro system—eight people died and 200 were wounded. Scores of terrorist bombing plans were foiled, such as the attempts by the al-Qaeda-affiliated Groupe Salafiste pour la Prédication et le Combat to bomb the Strasbourg Christmas market (December 2000), the US embassy in Paris, the US consulate in Marseille, a munitions depot in Belgium (July 2001), and the US embassy in Rome (February 2002). Other foiled plots linked to the Groupe Islamique Armé included plans to bomb an Antwerp synagogue and the Kleine Brogel military base in Belgium (September 2001), the Strasbourg cathedral (November 2002), and the Russian embassy in Paris (December 2002). Attacks against Europeans abroad included the April 2002 bombing of an ancient synagogue in Tunisia with nineteen killed, the May 2002 bombing of French naval engineers in Karachi, Pakistan, with fourteen dead, and the October 2002 bombing of the French oil tanker *Limburg* off the coast of Yemen in which one person died. As European police and security services arrested jihadists in the aftermath of 9/11 they discovered extensive terrorist networks all over Europe.[202] These networks were linked to the al-Qaeda sanctuaries in Afghanistan and Pakistan.

Protecting Europe therefore meant eliminating the sanctuary in Afghanistan. This led to the objective of building a resilient Afghan state—which meant nation-building. Stabilization and reconstruction missions, like those that NATO had undertaken in the Balkans, would need to be repeated on a much larger scale in Afghanistan. While President Bush noted in his memoir that he changed his mind about nation-building after 9/11, his administration was not interested in leading these types of missions. So it supported the Afghan proposal from the Bonn Agreement for the establishment of a UN-authorized international security force led by someone else.[203] Discussions within NATO and at national political levels about a possible peace operations role started shortly after 9/11 as the Alliance grappled with its place in the new security environment. In November 2001, some Alliance members proposed that NATO provide security to peacekeepers in Afghanistan. But others, such as France, disagreed and the proposal died.[204] Turkey had indicated in fall 2001 that it was willing to lead some sort of post-conflict peace operation, but the collapse of the Taliban government occurred faster than expected and Turkey could not react quickly enough to take the lead of the newly authorized International Security Assistance Force in December 2001.[205] However, the United Kingdom could, so it volunteered to lead the first rotation.[206] ISAF's mandate was limited to assisting the newly created Afghan interim administration in establishing security in Kabul and facilitating reconstruction efforts.[207]

The United Kingdom originally volunteered to lead ISAF for only three months.[208] But it extended its command for an additional three months because the negotiations for Turkey to take over as the next lead nation were more difficult than expected. Turkey required funding and assistance with strategic airlift, logistics, and communications, which the United States eventually agreed to provide. Therefore, the change of command did not occur until June 2002.[209] Negotiations for the next lead nation began immediately, with Germany and the Netherlands agreeing to jointly lead ISAF III.[210] Turkey was required to extend its rotation by two months due to demands by German and Dutch trade unions for security guarantees for the troops, which slowed down the negotiations. The United States ultimately agreed to guarantee the safe withdrawal of German and Dutch troops in the event of an emergency evacuation.[211] Elements of the 1 (German/Netherlands) Corps deployed to Kabul and comprised the core of the ISAF III headquarters from February to August 2003.

Each of the first three ISAF rotations was multinational. The force numbered about 4,500 in ISAF I and increased to about 5,000 in ISAF II and III.[212] ISAF activities consisted primarily of patrolling, helping to train new Afghan security forces, and participating in humanitarian and reconstruction projects. The ISAF force itself had three components (see appendix 1): a headquarters element, a multinational brigade (which engaged in day-to-day patrols and civil-military efforts), and an airport task force (which initiated the rehabilitation of the Kabul International Airport).[213] Given the wide variation in national troop contributions—from a few (Austria, Iceland, and Ireland) to thousands (Canada, Germany, Poland, and the United Kingdom)—the burden-sharing was widely disproportionate. In effect, some nations did little more than grant political legitimacy by their presence.

While recognizing continuing violence, coalition members thought the conflict was largely over because the "large-scale fighting" was over.[214] A senior British commander in Afghanistan said al-Qaeda and the Taliban no longer posed a great threat in May 2002 and predicted OEF's offensive operations would end within weeks because "they're not showing a predisposition to reorganize and regroup to mount offensive operations against us."[215] The perception endured over the next year. The US defense secretary, Donald Rumsfeld, went as far as declaring that major combat operations were over during a visit to Afghanistan in May 2003, adding that "the bulk of this country today is permissive, it's secure."[216] According to one Western journalist, "For around eighteen months it was possible to travel anywhere without concern for anything other than the appalling state of the roads."[217] The light footprint of OEF and ISAF (with combined troop levels in mid-2003 at 17,000) seemed to be justified by a security environment where most of the violence occurred in the south and southeast of the country.

Even with relatively minimal violence, the existence of a security vacuum was recognized as a problem. The Karzai government, the UN secretary general, and various NGOs asked that ISAF's mandate be expanded outside Kabul and the number of peacekeepers increased. Despite repeated requests from the interim government, the contributing nations refused.[218] Turkey in particular agreed to assume leadership of ISAF II on the condition that the mandate was not expanded beyond Kabul. Its resistance was partly due to concerns about cost, but also partly because it feared a backlash if its soldiers killed fellow Muslims.[219] The United States kept the debate alive when the Bush administration announced a policy shift in September 2002 and stated it supported expanding ISAF's mandate.[220] However, the proposal was initially resisted. The EU's envoy to Afghanistan, Francesc Vendrell, asserted that expanding ISAF outside Kabul was "virtually impossible at the moment" because European governments lacked necessary resources.[221] The issue of the mandate continued to percolate for another year until fall 2003. It took time for national policy positions to converge on such a significant change.

Furthermore, despite the relatively low violence levels and the perception that the conflict was over, the international effort to identify successive lead nations for ISAF was painful. Nations were not eagerly lining up to command a rotation. Negotiations were also time consuming and took longer than expected for the Turkish and Germany-Netherlands rotations. The successive change in lead nation for ISAF I through III was also inefficient, since each new lead nation had to start from scratch: learning the nuances of a fairly complex situation and executing a difficult deployment and logistics effort to set up a completely new headquarters with new equipment.[222] According to Colonel Phil Evans, who witnessed firsthand the negotiation process from his position in NATO, "It became really, really hard. It became really messy." He added that as a consequence, key national governments and the NATO and UN secretaries general had "open discussions about how to help Afghanistan in an orderly fashion" and as such they explored NATO's potential role in bilateral and multilateral discussions.[223] Among other meetings, the United Kingdom's prime minister, Tony Blair, met with Bush administration officials to discuss expanding NATO's missions.[224] However, NATO's eventual involvement in Afghanistan was never a given. It took almost two years for incremental shifts in political will and organizational capacity to occur before NATO took over leadership of ISAF in August 2003.

A major shift in NATO's strategic culture occurred first, opening the door to its eventual involvement in Afghanistan. The German defense minister, Rudolf Scharping, indicated the shift in thinking about NATO and the out-of-area debate when he argued in early May 2002 that the Alliance had to be ready to defend its vital security interests anywhere—to include Europe "or some other corner of the world."[225] Foreign ministers at a May 14 ministerial meeting in Reykjavik, Iceland, announced the Alliance's intention to combat terrorism and deal with other strategic threats wherever they occurred in the world. To that end, they pledged to acquire the capabilities necessary to "field forces that can move quickly to wherever they are needed" and sustain them over distance and time.[226] In theory this would relieve long-standing burden-sharing complaints, but the difficult road ahead for NATO's adaptation was highlighted by the German foreign minister, Joschka Fischer, when he said his country was not prepared to increase defense spending.[227]

NATO's global perspective was codified at the Prague Summit in November 2002 and expressed in measures to strengthen the Alliance's ability to meet contemporary security challenges, regardless of where they originated. The measures included organizational changes and a modernization plan.

The major organizational change was the decision to transform the military command structure. The two strategic commands, Allied Command Europe and Allied Command Atlantic, were to be transformed into Allied Command Operations and Allied Command Transformation. This change was significant because it moved the Alliance away from its traditional regional and geographic focus, on Europe and the Atlantic, and toward a functional focus.[228] As such it institutionalized the change in NATO's mind-set about out-of-area operations and gave it the organizational capacity to manage global operations. The month before the Prague Summit, it had taken a small step toward global operations when the North Atlantic Council approved the German and Dutch request for the Alliance to help them with ISAF III. SHAPE hosted a force-generation conference in November, it facilitated information sharing among the contributing nations, it gave them access to NATO intelligence and communications networks, and it helped coordinate air transportation.[229] The Alliance did not know at the time that this activity would continue for the next twelve years.

The transformation of the strategic commands created a streamlined chain of authority and command that gave the Alliance a plug-and-play capacity that turned out to be very useful for Afghanistan. After NATO took over ISAF, the strategic and operational command chain never changed (the North Atlantic Council for political direction, Allied Command Operations at SHAPE for strategic direction, Joint Force Command at Brunssum, Netherlands, for operational direction, and ISAF headquarters in Kabul for operational execution), while the six-month rotations of ISAF headquarters elements continued. Even though the Prague Summit had also created the NATO Response Force, it was not the only deployable headquarters and the Alliance continued a practice it had established with the Stabilization Force and Kosovo Force. Between August 2003 and the end of the ISAF mission, the Alliance deployed the various NATO component commands, as well as affiliated European commands, such as the Allied Rapid Reaction

Corps, NATO Rapid Deployable Corps–Italy, NATO Response Force, Eurocorps, and allied land component commands, through Kabul.

Another significant measure announced at Prague was the capabilities initiative, a result of what then NATO secretary general Lord Robertson called "Europe's military incapability."[230] The Prague Capabilities Commitment improved on the 1999 Defense Capabilities Initiative by focusing on acquiring the most urgently needed capabilities and attempting to get firm promises from national governments that they would deliver.[231] In some areas the capability shortfalls were not just a gap, but a chasm: in spring 2003, the United States had 250 long-range transport aircraft, the United Kingdom had four, and the remaining allied nations had none.[232] This capabilities gap fed European concerns about US unilateralism.[233] While many of the capabilities were critical for subsequent operations in Afghanistan, the initiative was only partially successful. Progress was made in the purchasing and leasing of sea lift, for example, but serious shortfalls in airlift and aerial refueling remained for years after Prague.[234] Structural organizational capacity continued to lag due to domestic restraints on defense spending in many NATO members and only intensified after the global financial crisis. As such, this was a fraying force that never dissipated and that contributed to enduring Alliance tensions over burden-sharing.

NATO experienced a watershed moment in April 2003 on the order of its decision to become involved in the Balkans in the 1990s.[235] The North Atlantic Council agreed to take over responsibility for ISAF. This open-ended, out-of-area decision was unprecedented in the organization's history. It was especially surprising considering it was made during a contentious time: the lead-up to and invasion of Iraq. The Iraq issue could have been a hugely damaging fraying force. Paradoxically, it was not. The Iraq War was deeply divisive, both among European nations and between Europe and the United States. While there was general agreement something needed to be done about the Saddam Hussein regime, there was disagreement on timing and processes: continue to use the United Nations and diplomacy or use force to remove the regime? It was not a case of all European nations opposing the

United States. Eighteen European nations expressed their support for Bush administration policy in two joint declarations of solidarity that were published in European newspapers in January and February 2003.[236] Germany, France, Belgium, and Luxembourg, however, vocally and vociferously opposed American policy and the movement toward military intervention. Statements by political leaders increased the rancor. For example, Rumsfeld referred to France and Germany as "problems" in the Iraq crisis and dismissed them as "old Europe" in January.[237] France's Chirac exacerbated the tensions after an EU summit on February 18 when, according to the *New York Times*, he "derided those Central and East European countries that have signed letters expressing their support for the United States as 'childish,' 'dangerous,' and missing 'an opportunity to shut up.'"[238]

The actual Iraq intervention on March 20, 2003, was multinational: forty countries provided ground, air, or naval forces, or logistical or other support. The ground force totaled 183,000 soldiers and Marines, the vast proportion of whom were American, but also including 41,000 British, 4,000 Australian, 1,300 Spanish, and a contingent of Polish special forces.[239] At the same time, seven NATO aspirants were moving toward Alliance accession. They attended a signing ceremony for the protocols of accession in Brussels on March 26.[240] Some of the countries felt they were put in a position where they had to choose between the United States and Europe, and this they wanted to avoid.[241] In the meantime, the allies were searching for the successor to the German / Netherlands Corps as the lead for ISAF. By early April, there were no volunteers. The ISAF commander admitted "there's a little bit of panic" about it.[242]

By April, Alliance members wanted to restore harmony and get past all the acrimony.[243] Serious international challenges still needed to be addressed, including additional terrorist attacks and the rebuilding of Afghanistan, not to mention NATO efforts at transformation and enlargement. According to Colonel Evans, civilian and military leaders at NATO perceived that the mission in Afghanistan "seemed to be done . . . the kinetics were done . . . all you've got to do is help [the

Afghans] help themselves." Taking over ISAF would be "honorable . . . and you've got all the people on the ground anyway." The fact that there were few combat operations "made the mission easier for everyone to undertake."[244] National political leaders saw moral and ethical reasons and also practical reasons for NATO to get involved. As a consequence, France "dropped its opposition to NATO taking the lead in Afghanistan's military operations."[245] This enabled the North Atlantic Council's decision to take over command of ISAF on April 16 at the formal request of Germany, the Netherlands, and Canada.[246] Essentially, this was a way to bring the allies back into harmony and give them an area where they could work together cooperatively. In a way, the decision was easy because NATO had already become formally involved during the ISAF III rotation. There was also continuing consensus that Afghanistan would need international assistance over the long term. The stabilization mission was essential, it was considered legitimate, and it was welcomed by the Afghans. The NATO commitment was also a way for the allies to signal to the Afghan people that the international community would not abandon them this time, as it had done before. The decision was also based on the flawed assessment that the conflict was largely over and that stabilization and peace-building would be the primary security mission going forward. The allies were confident in their ability to execute such a peace operation, given their experience in the Balkans. In the end, Iraq contributed to the convergence of political will with regards to Afghanistan, due to a shared desire to get past the acrimony. This, combined with the shift in strategic culture (global focus) and the perceptions of the conflict, led to the decision to take over ISAF.

The allies agreed to execute the ISAF mission under the prevailing UN mandate. As military planners began developing the operational plans for NATO's assumption of the ISAF mission, they estimated they would be ready to assume the ISAF lead as the German/Netherlands Corps rotation ended in August 2003.[247]

An effort was made to clearly distinguish between OEF and ISAF, one NATO official calling them "wholly distinct in nature and purpose."[248] An attempt was made to articulate the difference in ISAF's Military Technical Agreement with the Afghan interim authorities.[249] But the lines separating their activities quickly blurred. For example, even though the Office of Military Cooperation–Afghanistan had the lead for army training, British forces in ISAF began training a battalion of Afghan troops in February 2002, several months before the OEF training effort started. Similarly, the first battalions trained by Combined Joint Task Force Phoenix were assigned in Kabul to the first Afghan corps activated for the Afghan National Army. As the units arrived in the capital, ISAF forces gave them specialized training, such as checkpoint training by the Italians.[250] In some cases, OEF and ISAF were directly linked. For example, between October 2002 and April 2003 a tri-national detachment of eighteen Danish, Dutch, and Norwegian F-16 fighters and one Dutch KDC-10 tanker aircraft provided day and night air support to both OEF and ISAF.[251]

Despite the emphasis of the contributing nations on maintaining a light footprint, the OEF and ISAF coalitions came together quickly to a remarkable degree. They were able to seamlessly execute operations in very short order in austere and remote locations. Besides the multinational ground operations mentioned earlier (such as Operation Anaconda), by spring 2002 eight nations were working closely together at the Manas air base. Six American and six French bombers were supported by tanker aircraft from Australia and France and by transport aircraft from Denmark, the Netherlands, Norway, and Spain, while South Korea provided medical support to the entire base. One journalist credited American commanders with being able to "quickly [master] the tricky art of integrating forces from a number of nations."[252] The mastery was likely a result of solid organizational capacity and cultural familiarity developed among the allies and partners through the experiences of operating together in the Balkans and decades of training and planning activities at NATO.

Operational cooperation and interdependence did not mean contributing nations were in unison. Chirac epitomized the point in an interview in March 2002. While insisting that French-American solidarity was an enduring trait of the bilateral relationship, he added that France is not "an aligned ally, but it is a faithful ally . . . When something important is at stake, France is always there."[253] The allies and partners had joined the civil and military multinational coalitions, volunteered to be lead nations, and in some cases made contributions that were historic, such as the British government's deployment of 1,700 marines and army artillery in March 2002, the country's largest combat deployment since the 1991 Gulf War.[254] However, this did not mean they agreed totally with US policy on Afghanistan or the wider war on terrorism. Early on, the European Union warned against a disproportionate military response and the potential for civilian casualties.[255] The French president emphasized that military action was insufficient to fight international terrorism and that the long-term solution for Afghanistan was political, not military.[256] There was also consistent concern about US unilateralism. However, throughout this period allies and partners stayed engaged and cohesion endured within the OEF and ISAF coalitions. This was somewhat surprising given there was no vital security threat, so the stakes were low. In addition, the coalitions became larger over time and nations did not drop out as free riders even though the burden-sharing was widely disproportionate.

The operations in Afghanistan were not something for which NATO had been created. But the organization slowly adapted to the changed security environment when members agreed it needed to change. More important, members also achieved consensus that the Alliance needed to be global. For the major decisions related to ISAF, individual members triggered the decision-making processes when they requested the organization provide support to ISAF and then take over the mission. Interestingly, it was not the most powerful members of the Alliance who initiated these decisions.

National reasons for contributing forces for both OEF and ISAF were varied and political will was derived from both Alliance and domestic influences. Besides the direct experience of terrorist attacks and plots by Western European nations, the new NATO members and

the aspirants shared concerns about the threat of international terrorism. More important, they wanted to fulfill the obligations of Alliance
membership or they hoped to increase their chances of joining the
Alliance as full members sooner rather than later by participating in the
coalition.[257] This political will was the initial impetus for coalition cohesion. As the conflict changed and a variety of fraying forces surfaced,
the allies would need operational adaptation to sustain it over time.

By summer 2003, as NATO prepared to take over the next rotation of ISAF, positive and negative developments could be seen in the
country over the previous two years. The political transition road map
was being executed largely on time. A *loya jirga* (grand tribal council)
to select the transitional government had met in June 2002. A constitutional commission wrote a new constitution and presented it to
the Karzai government in March 2003 and planning for a constitutional *loya jirga* (scheduled for October 2003) and voter registration
(for the 2004 national election) was on track. On the development
side, girls returned to school in spring 2002 for the first time since the
Taliban came to power and three million children were enrolled in
school.[258] Economically, the newly introduced national currency, the
afghani, was accepted and stable and the International Monetary Fund
estimated GDP growth in 2002 had been 28 percent.[259] Mobile phone
systems had been built in several cities, major infrastructure projects
had started, and Afghanistan, Pakistan, and Turkmenistan signed a deal
to build a gas pipeline through Afghanistan.[260] Finally, more than two
million refugees returned home.[261]

But there were also significant problems. Many of the returning
refugees had no homes or jobs. Mortality and disease rates remained
high.[262] Opium poppy production exploded, which funded not only
the provincial governors who resisted the authority of the central government but also criminal elements and the emerging insurgent coalition.[263] Training of army and police forces was too slow, leading to
a security vacuum where violence increased, particularly in the south
and southeast. By summer 2003, aid agencies and the United Nations

suspended their activities in the south due to the danger. Donors were also slow to honor their aid pledges. Although $4.5 billion had been pledged at the 2002 international conference in Tokyo, only $1 billion had shown up.[264] Perhaps the most significant problem was the rogue provincial governors, or "warlords." Even though former war heroes like Ismail Khan made Herat one of the safest cities in Afghanistan, the fact they maintained independent militias, engaged in local rivalries, and resisted and undermined the authority of the Karzai government (for example, Khan kept customs duties) made them a challenge that had to be addressed.[265] Many of them were also brutal, corrupt, and unpopular with local citizens.[266] Worst of all, the fact that the OEF coalition continued to support some of the warlords and relied on some local militias and armed groups to hunt down remnants of al-Qaeda and the Taliban undermined the purpose of the DDR program and the building of a legitimate government with effective army and police forces.

Against this backdrop, the OEF and ISAF coalitions (numbering 11,000 and 6,100, respectively, by August 2003) can be credited with some achievements by summer 2003. Most, if not all, terrorist training camps were destroyed. ISAF helped produce a safe and booming Kabul.[267] Combined Joint Task Force Phoenix had trained 7,000 Afghan soldiers, although due to high attrition rates (which would be an enduring problem), only 4,000 turned up to serve in units.[268] Afghan National Army troops were, however, operating in various locations, such as Bamiyan, where villagers said they felt safer due to the army's presence and the activity of the PRT.[269] The PRTs were contributing to governance and economic development requirements in four regions. However, the PRTs were a drop in the ocean compared to the massive requirements, training efforts were insufficient, and strategically the enemy remained unvanquished. The coalitions underestimated how long and difficult the training efforts would be, the difficulty of the governance and economic development lines of effort, the danger posed by the sanctuaries in Pakistan, and the immense security gap in the provinces. The inaccurate assessment by the coalitions that combat operations were tailing off and their lack of appreciation for the resilience of the Taliban and al-Qaeda movements, exacerbated by the institutional weakness and corruption of the Afghan government, helped create the conditions for the emergence of the insurgent coalition. The NATO decision to take over ISAF was made with little appreciation of what the Alliance was getting itself into because it did not understand that the character of the conflict was changing.

CHAPTER 3

August 2003–September 2008: NATO Gets into the Game

As NATO prepared to take over ISAF, an overwhelming majority of Afghans supported the international mission and were more worried that foreign troops would leave the country prematurely than stay too long.[270] The Alliance's strategic-level adaptations after 9/11 (expanded strategic culture, new missions, transformed organizational command structures) had laid the foundation for NATO-led ISAF operations. Both NATO and the ISAF coalition had a sense of confidence about the mission based on prior experiences (rotating commands, conducting stability operations) and an expectation that ISAF would be operating in a relatively benign environment in Kabul.[271] From 2003 through 2005, the members of the coalition also had the sense the war was largely over since violence levels were relatively low and combat activity seemed to be concentrated in limited areas in the south and east.[272] In fact, in 2005 US commanders assessed that the cumulative effect of four years of combat, combined with political and economic developments, "had weakened the insurgency to the point of virtual irrelevance."[273] Condoleezza Rice expressed the Bush administration's optimism after her visit to the country as secretary of state in March 2005: "In 2005 we thought that the Afghan project was in relatively good shape."[274]

These assessments turned out to be inaccurate. After a period of reconstitution, insurgent activity and violence gradually increased and expanded geographically. By 2006 the insurgent coalition was able to launch large, organized attacks. Because the insurgency progressively worsened to the point where Taliban forces actually held terrain, there was a widespread perception that ISAF was failing by 2007–08.[275] Despite the negative perception, members of the coalition stayed engaged. This was due to the two drivers identified in the analytical framework. The ISAF commander, General David Richards, starkly articulated the collective strategic political reason for the enduring commitment even as the conflict escalated in 2006: "We can't afford to lose this. And we will dig deeper if we have to. If NATO doesn't succeed in the south, it might as well pack up as an international military alliance."[276] Thanks to existing organizational capacities, the coalition was able to learn and subsequently adapt operationally. In effect, ISAF continually evolved as it created, or assumed control of, new command and control structures and undertook new missions as the coalition recognized it was in the middle of a complex conflict. The combination of the two drivers sustained cohesion. In the end, ISAF settled down to fight back as well as rebuild.

The adaptation was not smooth or problem free. One could argue this period (August 2003–September 2008) was characterized for the ISAF coalition by a posture of continuously playing catch-up because it seemed to be constantly reacting to a situation that progressively worsened. The overall goal remained unchanged: prevent Afghanistan from reverting back to becoming a safe haven for terrorists by assisting in the creation of a stable, secure nation.[277] The strategy remained what came to be called "the comprehensive approach" at the Riga Summit in November 2006.[278] That is, civilian and military efforts continued in the domains of security, development, and governance, but ISAF's operational approach shifted to encompass counterinsurgency operations (as did OEF's). However, even though combined OEF and ISAF troop numbers gradually increased from about 17,000 in August 2003 to over 60,000 in February 2008 (see appendix 3), none of the contributing nations committed adequate resources to pull off the strategy and succeed along the three lines of effort, let alone succeed at counterinsurgency.

NATO Deploys and Expands

NATO's assumption of ISAF followed a deliberate institutional process that began with decisions by political authorities. As mentioned in the previous chapter, the North Atlantic Council announced in April 2003 that the Alliance would take over the ISAF mission. The Council would exercise overall political direction, in close consultation with non-NATO partners, and SHAPE would exercise strategic planning and control of ISAF. Procedurally this would entail the deployment of successive "composite headquarters" with personnel augmentation, as necessary, from within NATO and from contributing nations, as well as communications and logistic support. Furthermore, the SACEUR would choose who the ISAF commander would be from among the contributing nations. After the formal announcement, the Council subsequently tasked its military bodies to execute the ISAF IV rotation, as well as the subsequent rotations (see appendix 2).[279] While NATO's assumption of lead for ISAF provided long-term coherence and stability to the overall command situation, the frequent headquarters rotations meant the problem of "learning from scratch" endured for each unit, even for those that deployed more than once. However, this was mitigated somewhat because many of the staff personnel were rotated in and out of Kabul in a staggered way. This was considered a positive because it made the basic structure more permanent. But it also meant some of the staff members were always on a steep learning curve.

In recognition of the inherently civilian-military nature of NATO's engagement in Afghanistan, the North Atlantic Council created the position of senior civilian representative in October 2003. The senior civilian representative acted as the civilian counterpart of the ISAF commander and colocated with him in the headquarters. As such, the senior civilian representatives spoke for the Alliance's political leadership. The NATO secretary general appointed the successive senior civilian representatives, all of whom were experienced European diplomats, parliamentarians, or senior government ministers. Their key roles included communicating NATO policy and its political-military objectives to local and international media and coordinating with the Afghan government and civil society, the UN Assistance Mission in Afghanistan, the European Union, other representatives of the international community and international organizations, and representatives of neighboring nations to facilitate development and reconstruction efforts and support the political process.[280] This did not mean things progressed smoothly. According to Italian diplomat Fernando Gentilini, the senior civilian representative between 2008 and 2010, "The truth is that when it comes down to coordination, everyone wants to coordinate and nobody wants to be coordinated."[281] To an extent, the senior civilian representatives were just another voice in the cacophony of actors pursuing what were frequently independent agendas. However, they also served as a direct communication channel between ISAF, NATO headquarters in Brussels, and the North Atlantic Council. This meant they could provide critical advice from a political and diplomatic perspective to Alliance leaders as they grappled with how to ensure coherence among the security, economic development, and governance efforts.

The unit designated to form the core nucleus of ISAF IV, the Joint Command Center in Heidelberg, Germany (one of the Alliance's two land component commands), received its alert order in June. Since it could only deploy about half its staff, due to ongoing operational and exercise commitments in other theaters, SHAPE convened a force-generation conference that merged the 120 deploying members of the command with staff officers and specialized elements that were already in Afghanistan and other new national contributions. The new headquarters rotation, about 240 personnel, occurred in parallel with a new multinational brigade rotation led by Canada. The combined ISAF force included 6,100 troops from thirty-one nations.[282]

The Alliance's assumption of ISAF was almost a routine action. It had a highly developed organizational capacity to take over this limited mission. It had extensive experience from the Stabilization Force and Kosovo Force rotations, both in the actual deployment of a succession of commands and in the types of missions performed. It had a command structure that readily provided units for deployment as well as training and operational direction since the organizational transformation of the military command structure announced at the 2002 Prague Summit was complete.[283] In addition, the Alliance's consultation and decision bodies met routinely, with Afghanistan at the top of their agendas. The military planning bodies were in constant action.[284] Senior military leaders from SHAPE and Joint Force Command Brunssum travelled to Afghanistan almost every month.[285] The NATO ambassadors visited the country annually. The contact was not only one way. Besides formal written reports from the ISAF commander and the senior civilian representative, ISAF hosted a weekly video teleconference with Joint Force Command Brunssum. The ISAF commander travelled to Belgium periodically to brief civil and military leaders on what was happening in the country, the status of progress or problems, and the coalition's operational plans.[286]

When NATO assumed command of ISAF on August 11, 2003, its stated mission was no different from the previous rotations: conducting operations in Kabul and its environs "in order to support and assist the Afghan Transitional Authority in developing a safe and stable environment." In practice, ISAF performed political and military functions and the German commander, Lieutenant General Götz Gliemeroth, developed a campaign plan with five lines of operation. These included enhancing security through patrolling activities, supporting the security sector reform activities where possible (such as assisting the DDR program and sending the command's legal adviser out to help the Italian judicial reform efforts), supporting the development activities of NGOs, actively maintaining positive public perception and public support, and establishing long-term ISAF operating capability (by building a permanent headquarters building) since the mission was seen as no-fail for NATO. ISAF also considered liaison a key task. It established constant communications with the Afghan government, the United Nations, the command headquarters of OEF (Combined Forces Command–Afghanistan, or CFC-A), the coalition contingent commanders, and international development agencies. ISAF also worked with visiting groups of national representatives. International interest in participating in Afghanistan was high. According to Evans, visiting delegations asked ISAF, "Where might we go? Where [can we] do the most good?"[287] The headquarters therefore had to quickly develop the capacity to integrate new contributions into the areas and missions they best suited. The ISAF staff elements created to do this coordination ultimately linked back into NATO's force-generation processes.

In the meantime, the interim Karzai government, with UN and US support, had continued to ask that ISAF's mandate be expanded. So on September 18, after national political positions converged, the North Atlantic Council tasked its military planners to develop options for expanding ISAF outside Kabul.[288] The shift in political will was influenced by the fact that the environment was peaceful in large parts of Afghanistan. The expansion was not contentious since ISAF would only be continuing the stability operations it had begun in the capital. The expansion decision was also influenced by Alliance and domestic politics. According to a former political adviser to the US mission in NATO, the "allies realized it was in their interest as well as ours that we come back together" after the damaging split caused by Iraq. The allies' perception of Afghanistan was that "all the fighting, the hot and heavy stuff, it's over here in the east. OEF is there . . . we won't have to worry about that" because the Americans are taking care of it. Domestically, it was easier for the allies "to do something in Afghanistan," particularly those which had opposed the Iraq intervention. According to the political adviser, politicians in France and Germany could not go back to their people and say, "All right, well, you've already invaded Iraq so we'll go in there and help you out." They wanted to heal the Alliance damage "as long as it wasn't Iraq."[289] On October 6, NATO's secretary general informed the United Nations that NATO was ready to expand. Later that month, the UN Security Council extended the ISAF mandate to cover all of Afghanistan in Resolution 1510.[290] In December, the North Atlantic Council authorized the SACEUR to start the expansion. ISAF's first action was to assume responsibility for the PRT in Kunduz, which Germany had taken over from the United States.[291]

The initial ISAF expansion plan entailed little more than the assumption of responsibility for existing PRTs and the creation of new ones. It was very short on details. It was also a very slow, deliberate process that played out over three years (and as it was happening OEF was busy establishing PRTs—by 2005 it had thirteen in the south and east).

Each phase of the four-stage expansion began with an announcement by senior NATO officials, followed by ISAF operational action. In June 2004, at the Istanbul Summit, Alliance officials announced ISAF would take over the British PRT in Mazar-e-Sharif and establish three additional PRTs in the north, in Meymaneh, Feyzabad, and Pol-e-Khomri. Once they were stood up in October 2004, stage 1, into the north, was considered complete. In February 2005, NATO announced ISAF would expand into the west. It took over the PRTs in Herat and Farah in May and established two new ones in Chaghcharan and Qala-i-Naw in September. This completed stage 2.[292]

The actual ISAF presence on the ground, after these stages, was nine PRTs and two forward support bases in Mazar-e-Sharif and Herat which provided logistical support to the PRTs.[293] Their presence was overlapped by OEF forces because by 2004 the commander of Combined Forces Command–Afghanistan had realized he needed to establish a permanent presence across the country. He could not rely on basing the bulk of his forces in Kabul, its environs, and a few forward operating bases and sending troops out for operations for discrete periods of time, particularly since he had introduced a new approach—counterinsurgency—in fall 2003. Therefore, in 2004 and 2005, various task forces were assigned geographic operational areas. As a result, they established new commands that became known as Regional Command (RC)-South, RC-East, RC-West, and RC-North.[294] In practice this meant OEF's multiple combat and stabilization operations and ISAF's stabilization operations were executed in parallel with little cross-coordination. It was an inefficient way to propagate the security-governance-development strategy.

Since the period from 2003 to 2005 was relatively (if deceptively) quiet, the geographic and operational overlapping of OEF and ISAF was not considered a critical issue. Typically, the low level of organized violence in the majority of the country and the sense the conflict was over would be expected to lead to an unraveling of the ISAF coalition. After all, there was no significant security threat that could serve as a bonding agent. But such an unraveling didn't happen. Instead, step by step the coalition grew larger, in terms of both the number of troops deployed and the number of contributing nations. It assumed a larger geographic footprint and it expanded its missions and activities. Coalition members recognized the massive need for development activities in the regions and they wanted to help the Afghan government establish its legitimacy with the population. In the absence of faster, more comprehensive civilian development efforts, they needed to kick-start activities. Their experience in the Balkans gave them confidence they could undertake this mission. They also assumed the areas would remain "permissive," or calm and stable, particularly in the north and west, so the reconstruction and governance activities would be relatively simple to coordinate and oversee. Thus, it did not matter very much that the expansion plan was thin on details, especially since the participants did not think they would be deployed in the country for very long.

The allied perceptions and assumptions reinforced national decisions—the political will—to contribute to NATO's ISAF. The decisions were based on a variety of national interests that derived from domestic and Alliance politics. Some nations, such as Canada and New Zealand, were involved for humanitarian reasons to assist a stricken nation.[295] For the United States, according to the defense secretary, Robert Gates, it was the right thing to do since Afghanistan had been abandoned after the Soviet-Afghan war.[296] Sweden decided it could not remain neutral in a security environment threatened by international terrorism, but because it would not involve itself in combat activity it volunteered to lead the multinational PRT in Mazar-e-Sharif.[297] Canada contributed one of the largest contingents and volunteered to lead the ISAF V rotation because it did not want to become involved in Iraq.[298] (Thus nations could have multiple reasons for contributing.) Norway contributed and stayed due to loyalty to the United States and to NATO.[299] Spain contributed initially because it wanted to be taken seriously as a top-tier member of the international community. Later it wanted to continue to be seen as a reliable ally despite Iraq. That is, Spain withdrew from Iraq after the Madrid bombing but the new

Socialist government of José Zapatero wanted to show it still valued NATO, so it increased its troop contribution to Afghanistan.[300] Other countries wanted to demonstrate their value in a complex global security environment as new or aspiring Alliance members. Small nations like Lithuania and Croatia wanted to be members of a security organization that shared their values and interests and also felt that joining was a form of protection against external threats.[301] For Albania it was about more than just earning an invitation to join NATO. According to Albanian officers who served in Afghanistan, their country harbors a fierce loyalty toward the United States. They credit their current existence as a nation to US support after World War II and as such "they will always be our allies . . . they will follow America anywhere, anytime, to do anything."[302] In addition, there was a desire to repair the frayed relationships caused by the Iraq intervention. Afghanistan seemed a good vehicle to bring the allies back into harmony.[303] The allies reiterated at the 2004 Istanbul Summit that they wanted to ensure the country did not slide back into being a sanctuary for international jihadism, especially since al-Qaeda and its affiliates continued attacks in Europe and around the world.[304] These included the November 2003 Istanbul bombings (fifty-seven killed and 700 wounded); March 2004 Madrid bombings (191 killed, 1,500 wounded); and July 2005 London suicide bombings (fifty-six killed, over 700 wounded). Numerous plots were also discovered and prevented in the United Kingdom, Belgium, Spain, Germany, France, and the Netherlands.[305] The international jihadist threat therefore remained real for the allies. This combination of confidence (from organizational capacity) and commitment (political will) led to a level of cohesion within ISAF.

This cohesion did not prevent ISAF from having an ad hoc character. During the first two expansion stages, the political- and strategic-level authorities issued very little concrete guidance to the ISAF commanders. According to General Rick Hillier, who commanded ISAF V between February and August 2004, Joint Force Command Brunssum did not provide a military strategy for the expansion and did not articulate what NATO was trying to achieve or how it would do it.[306] While this left a lot of room for the commanders on the ground to figure out how to execute the mission in general, they were hampered by the fact that national governments retained control of the overall organizational structure of the PRTs and their aid and development activities since their foreign ministries and aid agencies provided the funding. Moreover, while the PRTs were adapted to the needs and conditions of the regions in which they were located, each lead nation had a different agenda. This meant there was wide variation in the level and type (civilian vs. military) of manning and operational focus. The PRTs were also required to report through national lines and in the early years they often did not share information or coordinate with ISAF or Afghan authorities. General Hillier's criticism indicated he was uncomfortable with the light touch of the strategic civilian and military leaders in NATO. However, this attitude gave him and the later ISAF commanders a lot of autonomy, which proved useful as the conflict changed. They had the latitude and the authority to adapt operations when they felt they needed to do so. In the case of the PRTs, the learning and adaptation included ISAF assuming some oversight and control as PRT activity expanded into training, governance, and security activities. The coalition otherwise had to figure out ways to coordinate PRT activities without stepping on the toes of lead nation governments.

NATO supported ISAF operations as best it could, but it was often less than perfect. For example, it had some difficulties initially in fielding necessary resources. NATO leaders had trouble convincing members to contribute sufficient aviation assets (tactical airlift and close air support) and quick reaction forces to support the PRTs.[307] The fact that NATO leaders such as the secretary general and the SACEUR followed the expansion announcements with pleas for nations to volunteer to establish, lead, or contribute to new PRTs and to provide resources probably exacerbated the situation.[308] It created the impression that NATO was constantly catching up with itself as it undertook and expanded ISAF.

The general idea in the expansion plan was to help the Afghan government establish its presence in the provinces by assisting local authorities with reconstruction and security. The ISAF PRTs were intended to support and coordinate the work of humanitarian aid and development agencies, rather than doing the bulk of the reconstruction work themselves.[309] According to General Jean-Louis Py, who commanded the ISAF VI rotation, it did not work out that way, since development money was slow to manifest and major projects took time to culminate. Since expectations were very high—on the part of the international community and the Afghans—that development and reconstruction results would appear quickly, the PRTs got involved in quick impact projects and progressively became more directly involved in reconstruction and development activities, especially as the security situation worsened in 2006 and aid agencies withdrew from some rural areas.[310] The increase in insurgent violence affected the next two stages of the ISAF expansion.

In December 2005, NATO announced ISAF would expand into the south.[311] Not long afterward, in February 2006, the Norwegian PRT in Meymaneh, in Faryab Province, a region that had hitherto been peaceful, was attacked. Given the way ISAF was structured in this northern region, there were no combat forces available to come to its aid and the national caveats of nearby coalition nations prohibited them from participating in combat operations. Eventually British forces deployed to the area and saved the PRT.[312] Clearly, an insurgency was rising and the current form of the NATO footprint was woefully insufficient. This led to the implementation of a proposal that had been percolating at NATO since fall 2005 for ISAF to officially assume the lead role in all regions.[313]

As a result, Germany officially assumed command of RC-North on June 1, 2006.[314] The stage 3 ISAF expansion into the south on July 31 meant taking over command of RC-South, all the battle groups in the region, and four PRTs.[315] Contributing nations also deployed additional forces into the region, bringing ISAF totals up to 15,000 troops from thirty-seven nations.[316] Most notably, the nations deployed in the south imposed virtually no caveats on how their forces could operate.[317] The stage 4 expansion into the east was similar. ISAF assumed command of

RC-East and all forces in the region on October 5, 2006.[318] Italy also assumed command of RC-West and ISAF created RC-Capital during the year.[319]

During the first few years after NATO took over ISAF and the command expanded throughout the country (2003–05) there were few forces fraying coalition cohesion. Violence levels were low and insurgent activity scattered. This reinforced the allied perception that the conflict was over and the environment would remain benign, contributing to a sense of confidence about the mission. Conducting stability operations through patrols and ANSF training and overseeing governance, reconstruction, and development activities were not totally new, due to the Balkans experience. However, despite their beliefs in the legitimacy of the mission and multiple national reasons for joining, contributing nations were reluctant to commit substantial forces. The rationale for maintaining a light footprint was one useful excuse, but many nations were also involved in other multinational operations worldwide. The pool of available military resources had many competing demands. This reluctance ultimately allowed a security vacuum to develop. The nature of the ISAF expansion also allowed the development of a complicated relationship with OEF and US forces.

OEF Evolves and Expands

While ISAF was expanding, OEF was also adapting and changing, with new organizational structures and new missions. OEF's expansion into reconstruction and training activities, along with security operations, meant it needed to coordinate closely with the Afghan government, the United Nations, coalition partners and ISAF, and governmental and nongovernmental development organizations. This was too much for the Combined Joint Task Force-180 commander to handle. Therefore, CENTCOM decided to create Combined Forces Command–Afghanistan, which stood up in October 2003. This was a theater strategic headquarters that concentrated on political-military affairs (it essentially mirrored the ISAF headquarters). In particular, the new commander, Lieutenant General David Barno, concentrated on building a strong relationship with the Afghan government and harmonizing civilian and military efforts through close coordination with the American embassy and ISAF.[320] The existing commands of Combined Joint Task Force-180 and the Office of Military Cooperation–Afghanistan were subordinated to it (see appendix 1). With the creation of the new headquarters, OEF was no longer temporary or short term. Barno transitioned the command and mission to a long-term posture and built permanent basing infrastructure.

Barno concluded that previous OEF efforts had been too focused on enemy forces. His longer-term view, based on an overall objective similar to the ISAF goal, concluded that OEF needed to shift its focus to "rebuilding the physical and social infrastructure" of Afghanistan so that the people would support the nascent Afghan government and reject the Taliban and the associated groups. He therefore implemented a campaign plan, which his successor continued, that involved five lines of operation. The "defeat terrorism and deny sanctuary" line involved special forces counterterrorism activities against al-Qaeda and traditional counterinsurgency operations that involved combat operations against insurgents, negotiations with rival groups, and reconstruction. The "enable Afghan security structure" line involved rebuilding and training the Afghan security forces (both army and police). The "sustain area ownership" line involved creating regional commands and permanently deploying forces in them. The "enable reconstruction and good governance" line was undertaken by the PRTs and the "engage regional states" line involved coordination with bordering nations. This very ambitious campaign plan suffered from serious resource shortfalls. Combined Forces Command–Afghanistan never received enough combat forces to "hold" territory and secure the population in the provinces in the absence of sufficient Afghan security forces. It even had difficulty fully manning the headquarters. Coalition partners were slow to contribute officers to the multinational staff and the United States was reluctant to provide additional forces because it had shifted its attention to Iraq.[321]

The Office of Military Cooperation–Afghanistan also experienced major changes as its mission expanded. As noted earlier, Combined Joint Task Force Phoenix was created in June 2003 to build the Afghan National Army, a hugely ambitious multinational undertaking that involved the creation of a new Afghan army from the ground up. The program was developed in consultation with Afghan leadership and involved basic training for enlisted soldiers (US lead), officer training (French lead), and noncommissioned officer training (British lead) at the Kabul Military Training Center.[322] The troops were then equipped and formed into units. The army development plan approved by the Karzai government in 2002 called for the activation of five regional Afghan corps: 201st Corps in Kabul, 203rd Corps in Gardez, 205th Corps in Kandahar, 207th Corps in Herat, and 209th Corps in Mazar-e-Sharif. The 201st Corps was activated first (in fall 2003) and received a full complement of battalions and brigades (10,000 troops) by mid-2004. In the latter half of 2004, the Ministry of Defense activated the four other corps and Combined Joint Task Force Phoenix started training their forces. By 2005, all of the Afghan corps had sufficient troop strength to support the parliamentary election. To the extent possible, the Afghan corps headquarters were located near OEF's regional commands. After Afghan battalions, called *kandaks*, were formed in Kabul, they were posted to the Afghan corps and Combined Joint Task Force Phoenix continued their training through ETTs. Rather than conducting individual training, these training/mentoring teams engaged in collective training of squads, platoons, and companies. They also mentored leaders at the battalion, company, and platoon level, as well as staff officers. In addition, they accompanied *kandaks* on operational missions as advisers.[323] ISAF got involved in the collective training effort in 2005 when the PRTs began training Afghan army forces too.[324] It called the teams operational mentoring and liaison teams (OMLTs), not ETTs, and they were eventually embedded into Afghan units.

This building of the Afghan corps process shared the ad hoc, or catching-up, character of ISAF. For example, the first *kandaks* for the 209th Corps began arriving at Mazar-e-Sharif in RC-North in

February 2005, but they had no billets. Their permanent base was still in the process of being built, so the training/mentoring team had to find temporary billets at a satellite camp while also coordinating the contract to build and open their base.[325]

Besides training, the Office of Military Cooperation–Afghanistan (OMC-A) had overall responsibility for coordinating security sector reform activities, an area that overlapped ISAF.[326] One activity in particular was critical for long-term security: the collection and cantonment (guarded storage) of heavy weapons and the demobilization of the militias. It was only through a successful DDR program and the building up of the Afghan National Army that the United States could stop the corrosive policy of relying on Afghan militias. OMC-A also had to reform the Ministry of Defense and create the general staff, primarily through a mentoring program that initially relied on US soldiers and contractors. However, allies were also asked to assist with the defense mentoring program.[327] Ministry mentoring was mirrored by ISAF when Hillier agreed to Karzai's request to help the Afghans build "a functioning government structure." Hillier established a strategic advisory team that worked for Karzai and the Afghan government between 2004 and 2008. The Canadian military officers and civil servants who comprised the team were assigned within a variety of Afghan ministries, where they advised various ministers on how to do strategic planning, explained budgetary processes, and educated Afghans on intergovernmental coordination processes.[328] These initial mentoring efforts were eventually expanded into a formal ministerial mentoring program and subsumed into the NATO Training Mission–Afghanistan.

OEF forces expanded into police training in 2005. The German-led Afghan National Police development program, oriented toward training traditional law enforcement methods, was slow to produce sufficient trained police officers.[329] The German efforts were hampered by funding and personnel shortages.[330] By December 2004, 33,000 police were on duty to support a population of twenty-seven million Afghans in a country the size of France (the Afghan army numbered 18,000 at the time).[331] As the insurgency heated up and violence levels increased, the country needed significantly more police forces with an expanded set of skills so they could assist the army in protecting the population, but the German program was constrained by national caveats and could not meet this demand.[332] The coalition had unintentionally allowed a serious security gap to open. It needed to quickly catch up the Afghan security forces to meet the challenge.

In late 2004, the Office of Military Cooperation–Afghanistan was tasked to study the program. The army training program was considered both comprehensive and successful and Barno wanted the OMC-A to see if it could replicate the program for the Afghan National Police. After developing a detailed plan to restructure the police training program and gaining the approval of the Germans, NATO, the United Nations, and the Afghan government, the OMC-A was officially assigned the mission in July 2005. It was intended to support the German effort. As a result, the Office of Military Cooperation–Afghanistan was renamed the Office of Security Cooperation–Afghanistan and it stood up Combined Joint Task Force Police, which paralleled Combined Joint Task Force Phoenix. The next year, the Office of Security Cooperation–Afghanistan was renamed the Combined Security Transition Command–Afghanistan.[333] With the increased American involvement came massive resources: between 2005 and 2008 the United States provided $5.9 billion for the Afghan National Police program.[334] For all intents and purposes, the United States became the lead nation for police training. It was also an embarrassing demonstration of the lack of allied will to commit sufficient resources to the effort and the unacknowledged need for US leadership.

The reformed police training program was just as ambitious as the army program. It involved training the Afghan Uniformed Police, the regular, local uniformed police; the Afghan National Civil Order Police, a gendarmerie-like elite force; and the Afghan Border Police. It also assisted the Ministry of Interior through mentoring. The program emphasized quality over quantity (since attrition and corruption were major problems) and included providing equipment, reforming recruitment methods, making pay improvements, and building infrastructure such as the Wardak Police Academy and regional training centers.[335] Smaller police elements also received training: counternarcotics police, a criminal investigation department, and counterterrorism police. Other forces were added later, such as the Afghan Public Protection Force. The international community paid the salaries of these police forces through a funding pool called the Law and Order Trust Fund for Afghanistan.[336]

Like the army program, training continued after police officers were posted to their duty stations. Combined Joint Task Force Police created police mentoring teams, which mirrored the army's ETTs.[337] ISAF also got involved, but it called the teams police operational mentoring and liaison teams (POMLT).[338] The pressure to produce sufficient numbers of policemen and the problem of demand outpacing training capacity induced the Combined Security Transition Command to continue a practice begun by the German program of allowing untrained policemen into the force during the early years of the Afghan National Police program. This interim measure meant Afghans who never should have been inducted into the force were let in. The allies inadvertently created the conditions for corruption. ISAF later had to try to weed them out.

The police training program adapted over time in response to changing conditions and other emerging challenges. As the insurgency heated up, the Taliban and associated groups increasingly targeted police officers and assaulted police facilities to undermine morale and recruitment efforts. By 2008, Afghan police deaths were triple Afghan army deaths. Furthermore, many local police were implicated in criminal activity and were perceived as corrupt by the public. To improve the capabilities of the Afghan Uniformed Police and overcome cultural conditions that encouraged corruption, Combined Security Transition Command–Afghanistan implemented the Focused District Development program in 2007.[339] This ambitious program aimed to reform police at the district level by pulling out the entire district police force for reconstitution (which included weeding out corrupt and criminal officers), equipping them, and providing a special eight-week training program at the regional training centers. The police officers were backfilled by Afghan National Civil Order Police forces while they were absent. When they returned, they were assigned police mentoring teams to continue their development.[340] In addition, judges and prosecutors in the districts were given special training and police infrastructure was repaired.[341] By August 2008, thirty-one police districts had gone through Focused District Development.[342] Where it was implemented, the program was largely successful. But due to shortfalls in resources (money and trainers) it was not possible to implement it in all 365 districts. To maximize impact, Combined Security Transition Command concentrated on districts that had particular police problems or were located in strategic geographic locations that included key cities or key roads.[343]

The countries and entities involved in police training also changed over time. Given the enduring challenges to the German training efforts, ISAF's senior civilian representative urged the European Union to step in and help both police and judiciary efforts in November 2006.[344] NATO's secretary general followed up the request in early 2007.[345] After consultation and consideration, the European Union took over from Germany in mid-2007. The EU mission, the European Police Mission in Afghanistan, attempted to tie together the non-US efforts and coordinate activities with the United Nations and Combined Security Transition Command, but it was seriously understaffed (only 184 people were assigned to the mission by the end of 2008) and suffered logistical and funding problems. Furthermore, its personnel were dispersed into PRTs and the ISAF regional commands.[346] In the end, the police training and reform efforts were a complex, and in some cases disappointing, example of interlocking international institutions. Combined Security Transition Command–Afghanistan, ISAF, the European Union, and the United Nations were involved and a number of countries also had bilateral efforts, including the United Kingdom, United States, Italy, Germany, the Netherlands, and Canada. The various efforts were poorly coordinated and the establishment of the International Policing Coordination Board, chaired by the Afghan minister of interior, did not solve the problem. Despite the EU contributions to police development and reform, the American and Combined Security Transition Command efforts dwarfed everything else. Furthermore, Combined Security Transition Command's involvement raised concerns that the Afghan police force would become too militarized, particularly since it was increasingly used to help the Afghan army fight insurgent forces.[347] This was later addressed by ISAF when NTM-A was established.

The final OEF changes involved command and control. The US combat forces and PRTs in RC-South and RC-East transferred under ISAF, and thus foreign, command in 2006 in stages 3 and 4 of the expansion. This was a first (since World War II) for the United States and the issue was discussed well in advance of the expansion.[348] Coordination for the remaining US forces in OEF was also discussed in advance since the proposal to merge OEF and ISAF had stalled. The final arrangement was rather unorthodox. According to General David Richards, who commanded the ISAF IX rotation, May 2006–February 2007, coordination with OEF forces was made through his deputy commander for security, a US two-star general. Richards maintained he had no problems with the arrangement and that all US forces, both those within ISAF and the remaining OEF elements, operated in line with his intent.[349] However, this was really just an informal arrangement based on good personal relations between American and British senior leaders. With the consequent operational reduction in OEF command responsibility, CENTCOM made the decision to deactivate the Combined Forces Command–Afghanistan headquarters shortly after Lieutenant General Karl Eikenberry relinquished command in January 2007.[350] This left major military elements in Afghanistan which did not come under formal ISAF control. They officially belonged, and reported separately, to CENTCOM: Combined Security Transition Command–Afghanistan with its expanding training mission; Combined Joint Special Operations Task Force–Afghanistan, with its special forces operations; and a task force that conducted detainee operations. Even after an American became the ISAF commander in 2007, the deputy commander for security continued to be the coordination point between ISAF and OEF forces until late 2008.[351] These command and control changes further blended the original OEF and ISAF missions but they also partially disconnected the security and reconstruction activities from the training efforts for almost three years.

The disjointed nature of military operations, combined with the continuing problem of insufficient forces, contributed to both multinational coalitions' failure to secure the population and achieve, in a durable manner, the security objectives. On the other hand, the foundations laid by Combined Security Transition Command, particularly the building of basing and training infrastructure and the creation of the nascent ANSF forces, later proved useful to ISAF. When the training mission was subsumed into ISAF in 2009, it had a foundation to build upon. In the meantime, ISAF was about to face its toughest test.

Fighting Heats Up

The other reason OEF and ISAF missions increasingly blurred together was because ISAF could not avoid combat operations as the insurgency heated up. In particular, contrary to the expectations reflected in the strategic guidance document—Operation Plan 10302 (which NATO issued in December 2005 for the next stages of the expansion)—the Canadian, British, and other coalition forces in RC-South could not just conduct reconstruction and development activities because they found themselves in the middle of serious combat operations by summer 2006.[352] That year was a major test for the Alliance and ISAF because the organized nature of insurgent operations shattered the assumptions of the allies. By the end of that year, the ISAF coalition could no longer maintain it was only there to do stabilization and peace operations. The pressure of intense combat operations could have been a destructive fraying force. But rather than falling apart, the forces in RC-South knuckled under and fought, and ISAF shifted its operational approach, even as forces remained thin.

Meanwhile, the insurgent coalition had a strategy that it began to implement in 2002. The core Taliban leaders who had escaped in 2001 did not consider themselves defeated and did not accept the new Afghan government. They believed it was their religious duty to continue fighting. They primarily spent 2002 reorganizing, resuscitating networks, recruiting, and establishing training camps and bases in Pakistan. By 2003, phase I had begun: infiltration into the east, southeast, and southern areas of Afghanistan. Small teams began recruiting local fighters and assessing which villages were receptive to the insurgents. If necessary, they used hostile methods to gain influence over local communities: threats, night letters, or assassination of anyone who cooperated with the government (police, doctors, teachers, judges, clerics, government officials, and NGOs).[353] Sporadic attacks, primarily rockets and mortar fire, targeted coalition forces in the south and east.[354]

By 2004, phase II had begun. This included consolidation of base areas in Afghanistan, the creation of authority structures in safe areas, and small-scale attacks.[355] Insurgent consolidation efforts were aided by the light footprint of coalition and Afghan security forces—there was no one to stop them. They were also aided by the institutional weakness of the Karzai government, which had a minimal presence outside Kabul (and some Taliban recruitment was the result of the predations of government officials); the autonomy of the provincial governors (some of whom sided with the insurgents in the context of local power struggles); and the complex networks of criminal activity and corruption (for example, some Afghans joined the Taliban as a response to poppy eradication because they had no livelihood alternatives).[356] The Taliban and their associates were experts at capitalizing on the cultural, economic, and political conditions in the provinces which helped facilitate their return.[357] However, they were more successful in some areas than others in consolidating their presence. In the east, the insurgents operated freely in Kunar, Nuristan, and the north of Laghman. In the southeast, they established a presence in Ghazni and parts of Paktika and Paktia. They were most successful in the south. Most of Zabul came under insurgent control by 2004. Much of the countryside in Helmand was under de facto Taliban control by 2006 and insurgents penetrated into Kandahar in 2006 and Uruzgan in 2007.[358]

With the consolidations, insurgent tactics changed. In 2004, attacks against coalition forward operating bases increased to almost daily. They involved not only rockets, mortar fire, and snipers, but also assaults and ambushes by small groups of insurgents. Attacks against Afghan security forces, Afghan officials, and aid workers were not confined to the eastern-southern border region. The insurgents also began kidnappings and they used suicide bombers and IEDs more frequently. They also attacked reconstruction projects. By 2005, coalition and Afghan security forces as well as infrastructure experienced approximately fifty attacks a month.[359]

By late 2005, the insurgent coalition included ideologically motivated hard-core jihadists, local recruits who joined for a wide variety of reasons (such as local power struggles, resentment at coalition heavy-handedness and collateral damage, and need for money), a small number of mercenaries, and the Haqqani and Hekmatyar groups. The coalition was so confident of its strength in the south by 2006 that it moved into phase III, large coordinated offensives.[360] The attacks were given religious justification by Mullah Omar's Taliban, which issued a fatwa in 2005 that ordered the death of all infidels and others who supported the Afghan government.[361]

Between March and July, the insurgents launched a series of attacks against the Canadians in Kandahar and then massed in Pashmul, about twelve miles from Kandahar City, for what appeared to be an imminent major attack in August.[362] The British also found themselves in serious, constant combat operations as soon as they deployed into northern Helmand Province in the summer.[363] The attacks had multiple objectives. Author Antonio Giustozzi concluded that the insurgents were so confident of their strength that they actually thought they could launch a final set of offensives and win the war. This did not turn out to be the case because, unexpectedly for the insurgents, ISAF fought back and inflicted hundreds of casualties.[364] However, the insurgents were also well aware of the ISAF expansion phases and some evidence indicates the insurgent attacks were meant to test ISAF resolve. Taliban propagandists explicitly stated they wanted to discourage ISAF members from deploying troops in the south.[365] Failing that, they hoped to force the European troops to withdraw because the insurgents believed Europeans were weak and would run away if they were struck hard.[366] In fact, ISAF intelligence sources intercepted message traffic in December 2005 in which Taliban leaders talked "about targeting the Dutch and other NATO countries to try to get them to retreat, as the Spaniards did out of Iraq."[367] Initially, the insurgents were supremely confident of their abilities. One Taliban spokesman declared, "We are here to destroy the British."[368]

It was clear for ISAF, as soon as it expanded into the south in 2006, that its original plan to conduct reconstruction, development, and governance activities, primarily with PRTs, was insufficient.[369] It had a full-blown, well-established insurgency on its hands and its military footprint was too light. The previous concerns about creating dependency and being perceived as an occupation force were irrelevant, especially since the Afghan government and security forces could not fill the gap. In addition, Pakistan's efforts to clear its tribal areas of militants failed in the years before 2008. Initially, Pakistan relied on the poorly trained and equipped Frontier Corps, a locally raised paramilitary force in the Federally Administered Tribal Areas. But even after it began sending large numbers of army troops into the autonomous provinces in 2005, it suffered embarrassing defeats and heavy casualties at the hands of the insurgents. This led to a series of peace agreements that ultimately failed in 2007 when Pakistani insurgent groups launched a widespread rebellion. Pakistan allegedly responded quickly to US demands to seal the border after 9/11. It established a thousand border posts along its 1,559-mile border with Afghanistan, but this was an impossible task given the extreme nature of the terrain—high mountains and deep ravines that could not be visually policed. The Pakistani military forces were seriously hampered by their lack of four-wheel drive vehicles and helicopters.[370] The insurgent coalition's sanctuary in Pakistan was therefore secure for years after 2001, guaranteeing the next phase of the conflict.

The massing of insurgent forces in Pashmul was the precipitating agent for NATO's first conventional land battle in its history.[371] According to General Richards, Operation Medusa was "a Second World War-style battle for Kandahar."[372] Over the course of two weeks, September 1–14, 2006, Canadian, US, and Afghan combat forces—assisted by British, Danish, Dutch, and French close air, artillery, and other support—assaulted Taliban forces who had established themselves in fortified defensive positions.[373] The operation was tactically successful. Hundreds of insurgents were killed and the Taliban did not launch any further major operations that year.[374] However, it was not a glittering example of coalition warfare because requests before the operation by the RC-South commander, Brigadier General David Fraser, for combat troops from the European allies were refused. He said in frustration, "We found out what NATO could not do. We simply couldn't get everyone we needed . . . the Germans wouldn't come down here; the French company weren't allowed to come down here; and I couldn't get the Italians . . ." He added that many of the enablers he requested, such as intelligence and aviation support, came with restrictions due to national caveats.[375] Strategically, the operation was a draw because even though ISAF did not have sufficient forces to consolidate security and ensure the Taliban did not come back to the area later, the battle itself was a significant psychological victory for the coalition. It demonstrated to the Afghans that they could trust ISAF's capabilities and it made the Taliban take ISAF seriously.[376] However, it also demonstrated the operational impact of political decisions. National governments had decided where to deploy French, German, and Italian troops. For domestic political reasons they wanted their forces to operate in the quiet regions. For ISAF this was an operational limitation imposed by political will. The decisions put stress on cohesion when the conflict intensified. In hindsight, the coalition seems to have missed an opportunity in 2006. Despite its ability to launch coordinated operations, the Taliban were still fairly weak and it is possible the insurgents could have been definitively defeated if the allied forces in the north and west had been allowed to augment RC-South. That said, the allies recognized that the character of the conflict had changed. They were forced to acknowledge the war wasn't over, nor was it winding down. As a consequence, ISAF adapted. It instituted counterinsurgency operations under Richards during ISAF IX. ISAF was again playing catch-up as it was essentially forced into combat operations by the large, coordinated insurgent attacks. Operational adaptation was complicated by the fact that conditions varied widely across the provinces. As a result, contributing nations implemented different versions of counterinsurgency.

For example, US forces in RC-East applied a "clear, hold, build, and engage" approach in the Korengal Valley in spring 2006. The approach relied on constructing combat outposts and inserting Afghan army and police forces into them. Afghan security forces, with US support, were expected to underpin subsequent development and governance activities. The approach was repeated in several other operations later in the year.[377] The Dutch deployed into Uruzgan in August 2006 expecting the same kind of "welcome" the Canadians had received in Kandahar. However, they entered and operated in the province in a very different way. They were much more cautious. They did not build fortified combat outposts; instead they built "multifunctional *qalas*"— Pashtun-inspired traditional houses with a guest room for visitors. They also emphasized talking and negotiation—with local residents, with local government, and with the Taliban. They literally tried to come in and operate without fighting. By the time the first rotation of Dutch troops departed the region, they had coordinated the building of roads, bridges, schools, and clinics and they had engaged in no combat actions. Over the course of four months, they encountered only eighteen roadside bombs and seven ambushes. No soldiers were killed in action.[378] In contrast, the British and Canadians each suffered thirty-six soldier fatalities that year—significant increases over the previous years.[379] Subsequent Dutch task force rotations were not as peaceful since Taliban forces infiltrated the province. Over the course of 2007,

Dutch troops adopted a more force-based counterinsurgency posture as they began to take casualties and were forced to fight.[380]

Counterinsurgency is not a simple approach. Some coalition actions that made sense from a governance perspective actually created more conflict. For example, the British took seriously the problem of corrupt provincial leaders and the corrosive effect they had on the population. They successfully pressured the Afghan government to remove a powerful warlord, Sher Mohammed, from the Helmand provincial governorship in December 2005 because he was deeply involved in narcotics trafficking. However, this had serious negative consequences over the next year. Sher Mohammed resented being removed from a lucrative power position. Even though he became a senator in Kabul, he had lost face at the hands of foreigners.[381] He therefore played both sides in 2006. He claimed allegiance to Karzai but also ordered his militia to fight with the Taliban coalition against the British.[382] Thus a political action directly contributed to the increase in violence in Helmand as the British arrived.

Richards understood that military operations were insufficient in the long run. Short term tactical military successes had to be followed up by governance, reconstruction, and development activities.[383] He had wide latitude to adjust ISAF's operational approach and he experimented with various mechanisms to ensure a more effective comprehensive approach. Under his command ISAF seemed to demonstrate it was a multinational operational force trying to learn and adapt. He created an international civilian think tank on his staff to encourage broad and creative thinking. He made an overt effort to include civilian advisers in planning and decision efforts to ensure ISAF did not default into a "military solution" mode. More important, his command recognized that one of its most serious challenges was the mismatch between the development aspirations stated in the Afghanistan National Development Strategy and local capacity. There was no process to align intent and action or to ensure "the right project happens in the right place and without unnecessary delay."[384] To correct this deficiency, ISAF, with Karzai's support, created the Policy Action Group, which included the president, key Afghan ministers (security, foreign affairs, finance, rural development, and education), and all the key international players (European Union, NATO/ISAF, OEF, United Nations, World Bank, relevant ambassadors, and development agencies). This executive group made decisions on where to focus efforts and spending. The decisions were translated into actions in Afghan Development Zones. This was essentially an "ink-spot" approach that concentrated reconstruction, development, and governance efforts in secure but strategically important areas that were small to begin with but could be expanded.[385] The initiative ran out of steam when Richards rotated out of command, but a version of his initiative was resuscitated under General Stanley McChrystal when he assumed command of ISAF in 2009. This was an inherent deficiency of the constant ISAF command rotations. Learning could be lost and initiatives could die since each new commander had different priorities.

The unexpected combat challenges of 2006 presented an operational crisis to ISAF and a test of political will to national governments. It was a critical time when cohesion could have been strained beyond the breaking point, causing the coalition to unravel. Multiple factors contributed to the stress. Richards commanded an ISAF that was under-resourced; he complained the coalition had only 80 percent of the troops it needed.[386] The United States could not provide the required forces because it was faced with a seriously degenerating situation in Iraq and was poised to surge forces there. The shift in the character of the conflict meant the allies and partners were faced with a longer, harder, and more costly fight than they had expected. The fact that only a small number of the thirty-seven contributing nations were carrying the burden of "kinetic operations"—active warfare—led to frustration and bitter recriminations. For example, while British and Canadian political officials were careful not to specifically and publicly criticize France, Germany, Italy, and Spain, their statements made clear who they meant when they pressed for more troops and fewer restrictions. The Canadian defense minister, Gordon O'Connor, stated in October 2006, "We would like more support from those who are deployed in the west and the north."[387] Retired Canadian Major General Lewis MacKenzie echoed his demand, stating that nations contributing to a multinational coalition "are not supposed to provide troops with asterisks and caveats after them." He insisted Canada had the right to talk tough about the issue because the country had paid for it "with the blood of our soldiers and the gold of our taxpayers."[388] A Canadian Senate report concluded, "Some of our allies are doing a lot of saluting, but not much marching. So what does this say about the future of NATO?"[389] British sentiment was equally harsh. A senior Foreign Office minister told Parliament that "some European countries' helicopters might as well be parked up in leading European airports for the amount of good they are doing in Afghanistan."[390] There were also bitter debates within countries. Romano Prodi's coalition government in Italy was repeatedly challenged by radical leftists who demanded the country pull its troops out of Afghanistan. It maintained its commitment only by initiating and surviving a vote of confidence.[391] The criticism led to defensive rebuttals. Chancellor Angela Merkel declared the 2,900 German soldiers in RC-North were "fulfilling an important and dangerous mission." Her ambassador to the United Kingdom, Wolfgang Ischinger, argued that deploying the troops to the south would "be a mistake because it would create a vacuum" into which the Taliban would move. He claimed, "We are not in the north because the north is quiet, the north is quiet because we have been there since 2001."[392] French diplomats refuted Canadian charges of shirking by pointing out that fifty-one French trainers were deployed in the south and east to train the Afghan army and 1,100 ground troops secured the "fragile" capital. Furthermore, France provided air support to operations in RC-South via combat aircraft and transport helicopters.[393] In the face of such bitter words, cohesion surprisingly endured.

The primary strategic driver holding the coalition together was fear of the consequences of failure. NATO leaders acknowledged that the Alliance's credibility was on the line in Afghanistan and they stated so explicitly at the Riga Summit in November.[394] ISAF could not afford to be defeated by the insurgent coalition because of the repercussions such a major operational failure would have on the Alliance as a whole. Concurrently, the secretary general, Jaap de Hoop Scheffer, warned he was absolutely convinced a NATO failure would open up the possibility for Taliban rule to return, for Afghanistan to become a failed state again, and for the country to become "a black hole for terrorism training" which would put world security at risk.[395] This was the glue that sustained political will and held the coalition together in 2006. As such, it generated repeated requests for more combat troops by NATO's leaders and the ISAF commander.[396] These requests were based on optimistic operational assessments. O'Connor claimed operations in RC-South had "broken the back of the insurgency."[397] De Hoop Scheffer went further, claiming the conflict "is winnable, it is being won, but not yet won."[398] Some countries refused to commit more combat forces, such as Turkey.[399] But others responded quickly and agreed to send more troops: Bulgaria, Canada, Croatia, Czech Republic, Denmark, Macedonia, Poland, Romania, and Spain.[400] Latvia epitomized the attitude of the aspirants and new members. It agreed to increase its contributions to ISAF because it took its collective security responsibilities seriously. It did not want to be a "passive consumer of security" and so this small Baltic state stretched itself to participate in the Balkans, Afghanistan, and Iraq.[401] In recognition of the changed character of the conflict, Alliance members gave their formal permission for ISAF to conduct combat operations.[402] After repeated complaints about restrictive national caveats, the members agreed to loosen them. France, Germany, and Italy agreed at Riga to send troops to other regions in emergencies.[403] These political decisions reduced strategic and operational pressures and ensured that cohesion endured. The coalition did not unravel. All twenty-six NATO members remained in ISAF, along with eleven partners. Perhaps fortunately for the coalition, the new political resolve was never tested, for the Taliban never again launched large offensive operations.

The Alliance's organizational capacity to adapt to the changed conditions in Afghanistan at the strategic and operational levels continued, although it was painful and major disagreements still endured. At a NATO Defense Ministerial meeting in September 2005, the United States proposed that NATO take overall command of the Afghan

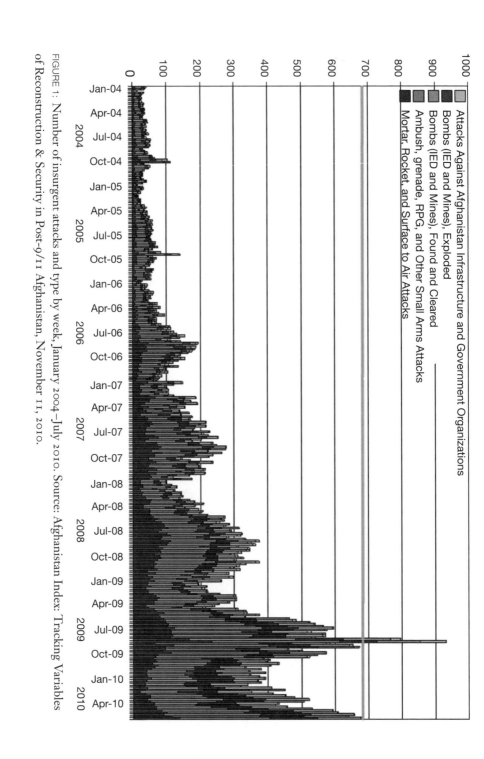

FIGURE 1: Number of insurgent attacks and type by week, January 2004–July 2010. Source: Afghanistan Index: Tracking Variables of Reconstruction & Security in Post-9/11 Afghanistan, November 11, 2010.

Legend:
- Attacks Against Afghanistan Infrastructure and Government Organizations
- Bombs (IED and Mines), Exploded
- Bombs (IED and Mines), Found and Cleared
- Ambush, grenade, RPG, and Other Small Arms Attacks
- Mortar, Rocket, and Surface to Air Attacks

mission; the OEF and ISAF operations could merge into a command structure that would keep counterinsurgency and peace operations separate.[404] French, German, and Spanish leaders rejected the idea outright because they wanted to retain the distinction between ISAF (peacekeeping) and OEF (offensive combat). But the idea did not die. De Hoop Scheffer asserted in October that "the situation, at the end of the day, of course it will be one operation in one country led by NATO . . . but we are not at that stage yet." He added NATO planners were exploring a "dual-hatted" command structure that would accommodate the naysayers.[405] The German defense minister hinted his government might accept some compromise on a "one-roof, two pillar" command arrangement but no further progress was made on the issue of merging for the next three years.[406] Political will lagged far behind the operational necessities. For a number of European leaders, the precedent that would be set by NATO assuming command of such a complex and violent mission was too much for them to accept. They held on to the belief that NATO could stick to peace and stabilization operations until they were slowly forced to acknowledge the operational realities. Once again, political decisions had an operational effect as the main lines of effort—security operations, training, and peace/stabilization operations—became disjointed and uncoordinated. Over time, the distinction between OEF and ISAF lost its meaning as both coalitions expanded their activities. This eventually paved the way for full operational merging in 2009 and 2010.

The maintenance of cohesion and willingness to fight (by some) meant the Taliban's large-scale attacks were defeated in 2006 by relatively small NATO forces using *a lot* of direct and indirect firepower. To maintain the gains, Richards recommended troop levels be increased going into 2007 so that the coalition would be ready for further Taliban attacks.[407] However, the insurgent coalition shifted tactics in 2007–08. It no longer engaged in large, organized attacks by armed groups, so the much-anticipated spring offensives never happened. Instead it greatly increased the use of IEDs, suicide bombings, ambushes, and assassinations (see fig. 1).[408] While most of the violence still occurred in the south and east, there were more frequent attacks in Kabul and in the north and west.[409] The Taliban coalition also focused more on soft targets such as pro-government civilians and construction projects throughout the country. There were reportedly more attacks against ISAF and the ANSF. This, however, was attributed to the fact that NATO and Afghan forces were increasingly operating in contested areas across the country as troop levels increased.[410] The increasing violence in 2007–08 was reflected in the number of fatalities, with Afghan civilians bearing the brunt: more than 3,000 killed, with the vast majority caused by the Taliban.[411] Among the military forces, the Afghan security forces bore the brunt: the international coalition lost 464 troops, the Afghan army lost 505, and the Afghan police lost 1,215.[412] ISAF's resolve, therefore, continued to be tested.

As violence in Afghanistan increased, terrorist attacks around the world continued, including the April 2007 suicide bombings in Algeria (thirty-three killed, 222 wounded) and the June 2007 attempted suicide bombings in Glasgow (airport damage but no fatalities).[413] In a twist of fate, the response of the Pakistani government to increasing Islamist militancy actually created more conflict in Pakistan which affected the war in Afghanistan. Militants started using the Red Mosque (Lal Masjid) in Islamabad as a base to launch attacks against local infidel activities in January 2007. After failing to negotiate a peaceful surrender, the government ordered the Pakistani army to assault it in July. This led to a wave of outrage and the formation of the Pakistani Taliban, the Tehrik-i-Taliban-i-Pakistan, which allied with the Afghan Taliban and al-Qaeda. They, along with an additional affiliated group, the Tehriq-e-Nifaz-e-Shariat-e-Mohammedi, revolted in the autonomous provinces of the Federally Administered Tribal Areas and North West Frontier Province.[414] All previous peace agreements with the insurgents became null and void. As a consequence, the Pakistani army launched a counteroffensive in November. Given the extensive reach of the insurgent groups and their threat to the Pakistani state, the army shifted to counterinsurgency operations in 2008 and progressively ramped up the scale of its operations.[415]

Pakistani military actions were coordinated with the coalitions in Afghanistan. Both the OEF and ISAF coalitions understood a regional approach was necessary and they created new organizational elements and new procedures to develop new relationships and coordinate activities on the two sides of the Afghan-Pakistan border. When Barno assumed command of Combined Forces Command–Afghanistan in October 2003, he established the Tripartite Commission. It was originally a standing committee for senior leaders from OEF and the Afghan and Pakistani militaries to meet every two months. Meetings rotated between the two countries. While primarily a strategic-level forum to build relationships, trust, and confidence, particularly between the Afghans and Pakistanis, it was also a means for Pakistan and OEF/Afghanistan to brief upcoming operations and otherwise to coordinate military activities. The commission included three standing subcommittees for counter-IED, border security, and intelligence sharing, which met monthly.[416] As ISAF prepared to expand into the south and east, it was accorded observer status at the sixteenth meeting of the Tripartite Commission in April 2006.[417] It became a full member of the commission in June.[418] Then it stepped into the lead international coalition role when Combined Forces Command–Afghanistan deactivated in early 2007.[419] Regional communication and coordination became more critical as the insurgencies became more virulent on both sides of the border. Trilateral cooperation became even closer when ISAF, Afghan, and Pakistani forces established a joint intelligence and operations cell in Kabul in 2007.[420] They then opened jointly manned border coordination centers at seven strategic locations, including the Torkham Gate, an important crossing point through the Khyber Pass, in 2008.[421] At the operational level, commanders understood they had to work together if they were to defeat the insurgencies. At one point during Eikenberry's leadership of Combined Forces Command–Afghanistan, he implicitly acknowledged the importance of the sanctuaries when he stated Pakistan was the key "because the war will be won or lost there."[422] The Taliban coalition was never definitively defeated during this period, violence increased, and counterinsurgency as an operational approach, as well as the comprehensive approach, could not succeed due to insufficient resources. Therefore, it can be argued the conflict reached a stalemate by 2008. Neither side was winning.

The period of 2007–08 can also be considered a time when the grind of conflict and violence could have been a pressure that frayed cohesion beyond the breaking point. This was a difficult period, particularly for allies who had joined believing they would only be doing reconstruction and stability operations. Several of them found they had to fight, even if their domestic populations, as in Canada, Germany, Italy, and the Netherlands, were not supportive of the mission in Afghanistan.[423] The constant requests for additional forces, the inter-ally tensions created by perceptions that some allies were not willing to fight or take casualties, and the escalating costs required to maintain deployed forces affected domestic politics, which in turn put pressure on the coalition. For example, in October 2007 there was furious public debate in the Netherlands as the Dutch Parliament weighed whether to extend the mandate of the forces deployed in Uruzgan beyond August 2008. For the country, there were countervailing pressures. Militating against an extension was the enormous cost of the military mission; it was estimated the two-year (2006–08) deployment of 1,800 troops, fighter aircraft, and helicopters would cost $1.4 billion. Militating for an extension was a desire to expunge the ghost of Srebrenica, when Dutch soldiers stood by as thousands of Muslim men were massacred in July 1995. Added to this moral position was stark recognition of the dangers posed by radical Islam after a recent terrorist attack in the country.[424] The domestic political debate was watched closely by allies and partners, particularly those who were integrated into, operated with, or depended on the Dutch. The previous year, Australia had deployed a battle group devoted to reconstruction activities. But its ability to maintain it in Uruzgan was hinged on a Dutch extension since the battle group was embedded with the Dutch forces and also depended on them for protection.[425] The Dutch Parliament ultimately decided to extend the mandate an additional two years. This was fortunate for the coalition because a Dutch "no" decision could have started a spiral of unraveling. In the end—despite the challenges and difficulty of the fighting between 2006 and 2008—the ISAF coalition did not fracture and no contributing nation pulled out. In fact, the coalition increased to forty nations by early 2008.

Cohesion endured for political reasons related to Alliance and domestic politics. Too much had been invested for NATO to allow failure or for ISAF to withdraw in the near term. While British leaders like Des Browne, the defense secretary, and General Richards called it a noble cause and said that Afghans deserved the international community's help after all they had been through since the 1980s, one of the officers interviewed articulated in more concrete terms the reasons for Britain's continuing involvement and its increase in forces from about 3,000 in 2006 to 9,500 by early 2010.[426] He said for Britain, "NATO must be seen to have delivered success" in Afghanistan because the Alliance's viability is a "vital national interest" for the United Kingdom. NATO is "really critical for the future because it offers you a credible force package and headquarters . . . a deployable capability that can do stuff on behalf of the UN . . . and it's important." He added, "Britain wishes to be a global player . . . [but] we don't have the resources" to do it alone. A viable multinational organization is therefore critical. He further described a very particular reason for trying to achieve a British success in Afghanistan. He said, "We are adamant to demonstrate to the Americans that we are worth . . . we can be trusted . . . We lost a little bit of credibility in Iraq" and so the government had "a very strong desire to change that [negative American] perception." Essentially, the United Kingdom wanted to regain US respect in order to maintain the "special relationship."[427]

The collective belief in the legitimacy and importance of the mission, which underlay the political will of contributing nations even in the face of low public support, resulted in public statements of enduring commitment by a variety of national and Alliance leaders. The German foreign minister said in mid-2006 that Germany's "engagement in Afghanistan is long-lasting."[428] The Canadian government stated it would "finish the mission" and "get the job done" in fall 2006.[429]

Canada then reiterated its commitment in early 2007.[430] The New Zealand defense minister pledged his country's commitment to the Alliance's mission shortly after New Zealand troops came under ISAF command.[431] The US ambassador to Afghanistan, Ronald Neumann, and President Bush repeatedly stated that the United States would stay committed in Afghanistan.[432] This cross-national solidarity was reinforced by improved relations between the United States and European allies. The anti-American hostility generated by the Iraq War was receding by 2007 and relations were "on an upswing," according to Gates.[433] De Hoop Scheffer stated after an informal defense ministers meeting in February 2008 that the allies "were of the opinion that we are there having entered a long-term commitment."[434] The Alliance's long-term commitment was formally reiterated at the Bucharest Summit in April 2008.[435] This enduring political will was supported by cautious optimism that ISAF could succeed in the end, but there were challenges that needed to be surmounted.[436] ISAF repeatedly demonstrated its operational competence because it defeated the Taliban whenever they attacked, and so political leaders developed a level of confidence in the deployed forces. This generated a sort of top-down cohesion.

More important, cohesion was reinforced and sustained from the bottom up for organizational reasons. The coalition was deeply multinational. Most units and regional forces (battle groups, PRTs, and OMLT/ POMLTs) and all major headquarters (from the regional commands to ISAF and even Combined Forces Command–Afghanistan) included multiple contributing nations. In RC-North, eighteen nations operated together and some of the smaller nations received German logistical support (Albania, Croatia, Macedonia).[437] In RC-West, a Spanish helicopter squadron provided transport, attack, and maneuver support to all the multinational forces in the region.[438] In RC-South, Danish and Canadian armor units, with an Estonian maneuver company and medical element, were embedded with the British in Helmand.[439] In Uruzgan, the Dutch task force included combat engineers, a combined arms battle group, and special forces from Australia, a Slovenian platoon, and a Singapore medical element.[440] Even the predominantly

US region of RC-East was multinational. For example, the Polish battalion and brigade battle groups deployed after 2006 were embedded in American units in the volatile regions of Paktika and Ghazni.[441] A US battalion task force commander in Kunar and Wardak Provinces stated he operated with a Lithuanian OMLT, which was embedded in one of his partnered Afghan army battalions, and Hungarian special forces, who trained one of his partnered Afghan police units.[442] The battle space for another US brigade covered five provinces. The unit operated and coordinated with the New Zealand and Turkish PRTs, Norwegian special forces, and the French regimental battle group and OMLT in its area.[443] When Jordan decided to join ISAF it insisted it be embedded with US units, so its 800-man combat battalion deployed to RC-East.[444] The nature of national contributions also produced multi-nationality. For example, by 2008 the Australian contributions included a special operations group operating across the country, a battle group conducting training and reconstruction that was embedded in the Dutch task force in Uruzgan, an engineer task force embedded in the Dutch PRT in Tarin Kowt, a detachment of CH-47 transport helicopters embedded with the combat aviation battalion in Kandahar, an air force radar detachment in Kandahar, an artillery detachment embedded with a British artillery battery in Helmand, and individuals assigned to various OMLTs and the RC-South and ISAF headquarters.[445]

Major operations were multinational. A former Dutch commander of RC-South, Lieutenant General Mart de Kruif, described the situation well:

Now, when [a young Dutch commander] leaves the base, he's accompanied by Afghan national army and Afghan national police. They are mentored by Australians and by French. The camp is guarded by Slovakians. His top cover comes from Belgian F-16s and Mirages from France and US fighters from Bagram. If he gets in a fight in troops-in-contact, and one of his soldiers is wounded, we call in the MEDEVAC helicopter from the United States, which is accompanied by Apaches from the Dutch Air Force. We bring him back to the field dressing station where a surgical team from Singapore saves his life, probably with blood from the British blood bank from Helmand. Then we call in a Canadian C-130; we fly him back to Kandahar where nurses from Romania will take him to the operating room where a surgeon from the United States will stabilize him. We fly him back with a British plane to the United Kingdom and we pick him up there. This is reality . . . on a day-to-day basis.[446]

The interweaving of units and specialist capabilities, particularly combat air support, intelligence, medical, and transport, forced the allies to rely on each other. This generated constant training efforts once forces arrived in the country. To ensure interoperability, units ironed out communication and coordination procedures through exercises before crisis situations or combat operations because, as Colonel Horst Busch of the German army noted, there was "constant concern" about the need to minimize "misunderstandings."[447] Training and operating together generated trust and the norms and practices that partners do not abandon each other, especially in adversity. In fact, "the heat of battle" acted as a sort of incubator of cohesion. According to the officers interviewed, as units fought together, their feeling of mutual trust and confidence tended to increase over time. The bonding was so extensive that, according to a Croatian officer, Colonel Denis Tretinjak, "From the first moment when you got to Afghanistan, actually you forget your nationality. You just need to bond with . . . any other level who actually brings you some support, help, whatever . . ."[448] A Polish officer, Colonel Piotr Bieniek, echoed this sentiment: "There isn't nationality, there's just the team."[449] A Hungarian officer, Colonel Romulusz Ruszin, called the deployed military forces "a big family . . . and on the ground nobody cares which nation, what kind of uniform you have, even the Afghans . . . if you are under attack or kinetic contact, you just do your job."[450] A Spanish officer who commanded a helicopter squadron in RC-West, Lieutenant Colonel Javier Marcos, stated, "The flags don't matter when you are fighting . . . the most important thing is that you are helping the Afghans and you are fighting with other soldiers, regardless if he is Italian or American . . . there is no difference in the fight. Cohesion was something real, above all in difficult situations."[451] An American officer, Lieutenant Colonel Timothy Davis, attributed the high levels of trust to the common values shared by soldiers from contributing nations, long-standing relationships from the stationing of American and other allied forces in Europe (and decades of training and operating together), and the shared ethos of professional soldiering: "I'm a soldier, he's a soldier. We're there to protect the people and accomplish a mission."[452] Busch observed that the standing multinational formations in Europe, such as the Eurocorps, German-French Brigade, and 1 (German/Netherlands) Corps, generated cohorts of officers, NCOs, and soldiers who were "used to working with other nations, on a day-to-day basis." This was advantageous in Afghanistan, especially at the tactical level, because the troops "would know how others would react . . . [they would] know their way of thinking about things,"[453] which was critical in high-stress combat situations when split-second decisions needed to be made. A Danish officer, Lieutenant Colonel Ken Knudsen, further noted that the familiarity gained from working together in various multinational operations also meant "we know the differences between our allies."[454] That is, troops with multinational experience gained an awareness of the cultural and operational differences among the allies and partners and this knowledge helped facilitate practical actions. The knowledge and familiarity aided the seamless integration of coalition forces and produced both interoperability and cohesion.

The trust and commitment of military forces on the ground also seem to have influenced national political leaders, and thus sustained national policy and political will through the senior military commanders. For example, the Spanish officer, Marcos, claimed Spanish senior military leaders and the minister of defense convinced their prime minister to increase troop levels in Afghanistan in 2004 even though he had come into office promising "no more troops."[455] The political commitment was strong enough for the Spanish defense minister, Jose Bono, to promise Spain would "remain in Afghanistan for at least eight [more] years in order to guarantee stability and facilitate reconstruction efforts" during a visit to Herat in August 2005.[456] According to another officer:

> One of the histories of the British presence in Helmand Province is military officers, who've been blooded or have . . . leading their men, saying we've got to do more here, we've got to do more . . . and that becomes a voice. We've got to support our troops. We've got to get this right. We've got to get the strategy right, therefore politicians deliver this . . . deliver us the right equipment. Deliver us the right manpower levels. You have got to own this now, because we're fighting for you and we're fighting with these allies . . . and they are critical to us.[457]

The fighting forces, therefore, generated and sustained cohesion from the bottom up. Over this period, the various ISAF commanders repeatedly asked for more forces. While the coalition forces managed to successfully defeat insurgent attacks where they occurred, many times they were barely sufficient.[458] Given the hard-won gains, commanders did not want to lose them, and they could not do this without more forces, either Afghan or coalition, to hold territory, especially since the reliance on overwhelming firepower could produce unacceptable levels of civilian casualties which undermined Afghan support. To assuage Afghan government concerns, maintain public support, and counter Taliban propaganda, the coalition needed to shift its approach, but it took years for this to happen. Force levels were eventually substantially increased, the ISAF commanders imposed more restrictive rules of engagement to reduce civilian casualties, and the coalition changed its operational approach by implementing a coordinated civilian-military campaign plan.

As the forces on the ground operated together, NATO's strategic-level organizational capacities incrementally changed in ways that supported ISAF. The changes were adaptations based on learning. Just as ISAF learned and adapted operationally, so did NATO learn and adapt. The creation of Allied Command Transformation meant the Alliance had the structural capacity to prepare units and specialist teams for deployment. In 2004, the NATO Joint Warfare Center in Stavanger, Norway, began providing mission rehearsal training and exercises for the ISAF headquarters commanders and staffs before their deployment to Kabul.[459] In 2007, the new NATO Joint Force Training Center in Bydgoszcz, Poland, began providing mission rehearsal training and exercises for the regional command headquarters elements as they prepared to deploy. In 2008, it began training brigade-, corps-, and garrison-level OMLT teams (*kandak* OMLTs were trained at the US Joint Readiness Training Center in Hohenfels, Germany) and in 2010 it began training POMLTs.[460] Due to the difficulties NATO headquarters had in filling shortfalls in national force contributions and operational enablers (such as transport helicopters), SHAPE instituted annual force-generation conferences in November 2004. The conferences identified all of the Alliance's operational needs (ISAF, Kosovo Force, etc.) for the next twelve months. Thus, it tried to minimize issuing reactive, short-notice requests for forces. The conferences also provided a venue for allies to see how equitable the burden-sharing was.[461] In November 2005, NATO convened a workshop in Brussels for all the countries and organizations involved in PRTs. Discussions involved the roles, tasks, and practices of the diverse array of PRTs in order to share lessons learned, disseminate best practices, and harmonize PRT activities.[462]

Some of the incremental changes and adaptations were only partial. For example, the US Army and Marine Corps jointly published a new counterinsurgency doctrine in 2006.[463] However, during the period under examination here, NATO did not have a counterinsurgency doctrine.[464] There were no uniform standards for certifying battle groups or for training the PRTs or the army and police training/mentoring teams. Nations were not required to send their forces to the Allied Command Transformation facilities in Norway or Poland. The larger contributing nations, such as the United States, United Kingdom, France, Italy, Canada, and Germany, developed their own national training programs; the smaller contributing nations relied on the NATO training infrastructure because they lacked sufficient national training capabilities. The SACEUR announced a standardized system for tracking progress in Afghanistan using sixty-three metrics in December 2005.[465] But national capitals, as well as ISAF and NATO headquarters, had voracious appetites for reports and there was no single standard for calculating successes and failures.[466] Finally, command structures and relationships were incrementally adjusted as force levels increased, missions changed or expanded, and the conflict intensified. However, by and large, during this period they were disjointed. Additional learning and adaptation were clearly needed to ensure more effective operations and to break the stalemate.

Fraying forces at the operational level included collective action problems as NATO got involved in Afghanistan and then expanded ISAF. For example, the German forces did not fly at night, so they could not provide MEDEVAC (medical evacuation) support during night operations; they also did not fly in bad weather.[467] These conditions were imposed on the German military by its political authorities, who were casualty averse and concerned about low public support.[468] According to an Italian officer, Colonel Alberto Vezzoli, Italian reluctance to loosen caveats and its refusal to send troops to the south in 2006 to conduct combat operations were related to its constitution, which outlaws war.[469] In fact, this constitutional view was used by the prime minister in 2006 and 2007 as he fought a political battle against the Italian hard Left. He argued the 1,900 Italian forces deployed in Kabul and Herat were not engaged in an "undertaking of war" and that the post–World War II constitution which "rejects war as a way of solving international conflicts" nonetheless legitimized Italy's "duty to take part in military missions aimed at peace and stability."[470] The coalition had to figure out how to operate within myriad national constraints. Sometimes partners shifted their positions: France, Germany, Italy, and Spain would not permanently send troops to the south but agreed at the Riga Summit to deploy them to the region in emergencies.[471] This was essentially an ad hoc solution that only partially resolved an important operational problem.

It can be argued that many countries constrained what they did due to the attributes of their national militaries—their national strategic cultures, size, and competencies—rather than a desire to free ride. Just as there is a collective strategic culture at NATO, so there is national-level strategic culture which prescribes when, how, where, and against whom military force can be used. The shift in the Alliance's strategic culture after the end of the Cold War was mirrored at the national level and has resulted in a wide variation in strategic behavior and military activity among the European allies and partners. The variation is quite noticeable among the smaller countries. Since 1990, both Denmark and the Netherlands have shifted from a nationally focused defensive posture to an internationally focused one which views war-fighting operations as legitimate ways for the nations to advance their interests in achieving a more peaceful world. Norway and Sweden did not experience such a shift. While retaining a belief that the use of force is legitimate for national defense, they insisted that conflicts should be solved peacefully and the international use of force should be a last resort.[472] For them, deployment of military forces outside their countries should be for humanitarian or peace operations. The consequences of these differing views in Afghanistan were the Dutch and Danish willingness to deploy battle groups and fight in the more volatile south, while the Swedes and Norwegians opted to take up the PRT mission in the quieter north. Interestingly, the Norwegians experienced a further shift in strategic culture after their PRT was attacked in 2006: it chose to embrace war-fighting as a means of defense and protection. As a consequence, the Norwegian PRT underwent a substantial organizational change as combat equipment and combat forces were deployed to RC-North. The PRT developed into a hybrid structure, with 600 personnel, which merged the stabilization activities of the original element with a battle group task force.[473] In general, strategic culture wields significant influence over the size and structure of national armed forces and their range of operational competence.

For Afghanistan and other multinational operations, European countries had much smaller pools of available forces to draw from than the United States. The American military was massive compared to its allies and partners. In 2005, the US Army numbered 490,000 (also known as the active component). This pool of manpower was augmented by Army Reserve and National Guard forces, of which 150,000 were activated and deployed with active component forces that year.[474] Thus, the US Army was more than three times larger than the largest European army, Germany's (table 1). Those European countries with conscript armies were further constrained by national laws which banned conscripts from being involuntarily deployed on foreign missions. They relied on volunteers, which necessitated the creation of ad hoc units for deployment. Interestingly, as the interviewed officers from countries with conscript armies talked about the rotations of battle groups, PRTs, training/mentoring teams, and special operation forces, they never mentioned having difficulty finding volunteers. Rather, many of them explained they had selection processes to pick the best since they had more volunteers than they needed. While eleven of the countries listed below phased out conscription between 2003 and 2011 (Czech Republic, Germany, Hungary, Italy, Latvia, Lithuania, Poland, Portugal, Slovakia, Slovenia, and Sweden), the pool of available forces for most countries decreased as governments cut defense budgets. The largest allies made the deepest cuts. By 2010, the British armed forces had been reduced to 180,000, the French armed forces to 211,000, and German armed forces to 252,000.[475] Moreover, the gap between Europe and the United States widened during this time because the United States increased its forces. The US Army, active component, topped out at 570,000 in 2012.[476] These distinct differences in the sizes of allied and partner armed forces exacerbated the tensions over burden-sharing.

Many allies and partners with smaller armies were not organized or equipped to conduct high-intensity combat operations, much less complex counterinsurgency operations.[477] Their abilities were more limited so they volunteered to do the missions where they could be useful. For example, Bulgarian, Macedonian, and Slovakian, as well as Mongolian, forces guarded bases. Other countries provided trainers: Albania, Croatia, and Slovenia. Singapore and Malaysia provided medical units. Operational competence could change, however, as national armies

TABLE 1. European armed forces (2002/2003). Source: Jolyon Howorth, "A European Union with Teeth?" in Jabko and Parsons, eds., *The State of the European Union*, Vol. 7, 50.

Country	Prof/Consc	Army	Navy	Air Force	Total
Austria	Conscript	34,600	0	6,850	34,600
Belgium	Professional	24,800	2,450	10,250	39,200
Czech Rep.	Conscript	39,850	0	13,100	49,400
Denmark	Conscript	14,700	4,000	3,500	22,700
Estonia	Conscript	2,550	440	220	5,000
Finland	Conscript	19,200	5,000	2,800	31,800
France	Professional	137,000	44,250	64,000	260,000
Germany	Conscript	191,350	25,650	67,500	296,000
Greece	Conscript	114,000	19,000	33,000	177,000
Hungary	Conscript	23,600	0	7,700	33,000
Ireland	Professional	8,500	1,100	860	10,500
Italy	Conscript	116,000	36,000	48,000	216,000
Latvia	Conscript	4,000	620	250	5,500
Lithuania	Conscript	7,950	650	1,150	13,500
Luxembourg	Professional	900	0	0	900
Netherlands	Professional	23,150	12,130	11,050	49,600
Norway	Conscript	14,700	6,100	5,000	26,600
Poland	Conscript	104,050	14,300	36,450	163,000
Portugal	Conscript	26,700	10,950	7,250	43,600
Slovakia	Conscript	13,700	0	7,000	26,000
Slovenia	Conscript	6,500	0	530	9,000
Spain	Professional	95,600	22,900	22,750	177,900
Sweden	Conscript	13,800	7,900	5,900	33,000
Turkey	Conscript	402,000	52,750	60,100	514,850
UK	Professional	116,670	42,370	53,620	210,400

underwent learning and adaptation over the course of ISAF's existence. For example, the battle groups Romania contributed to RC-South incrementally changed. Initially, the country deployed a battalion battle group to Kandahar, but according to Colonel William Butler, in 2005, "their national caveats and limitations and constraints" were such that "they couldn't leave the wire at Kandahar airfield so they were perimeter security." As a new member of NATO, the country wanted to do more so it built a national training facility in Cincu to assist the reform of its army. Butler noted the results, which included shifts in caveats, in 2006. He said, "They had gotten to a point where they could do very short distance patrols in and around Kandahar airfield, so it was kind of a work in progress, if you will, and that started the evolution of them being able to gain greater capacity and then given greater responsibility." By 2008, the Romanian battle group had moved to Zabul and undertaken security responsibilities within the province. By 2011, the battle group had grown to a brigade-size element and was responsible for the entire province.[478] The myriad of capabilities and competencies of the contributing nations required an ISAF staff skilled at knitting the multitude of smaller contributions into the overall coalition. This included the ability to shift forces around as they changed in operational competence and as national caveats shifted. The complexity and constant change were persistent pressures on coalition cohesion.

The plethora of ongoing multinational missions worldwide put further pressure on the coalition because national governments did not have an unlimited pool of military resources. In effect, political will was strained by other multinational deployments which constrained ISAF. As mentioned above, the coalition never had sufficient resources during this period to achieve its campaign objectives. The competing multinational missions included the ongoing stabilization missions in Bosnia and Kosovo. By 2004, the United Nations had legitimized the stabilization mission in Iraq and thirty-nine countries joined a multinational effort comprised of 163,930 military forces. Poland and the United Kingdom had also volunteered to be lead nations for two of the five regional commands, Multinational Division Center–South and Multinational Division South-East.[479] The British contribution to Iraq was large in relative terms (more than 8,000 in 2004, reduced to about 4,500 in 2007). However, the war degenerated badly, forcing the United Kingdom to stay longer than originally intended, which had consequences for Afghanistan. Between 2006 and 2008, Britain found itself fighting "two campaigns without being able to resource either of them properly" and consequently it found itself "mowing the grass" in Helmand—repeating tactical operations in the same areas over and over because it did not have sufficient forces to hold what it cleared.[480] In the United States, Gates realized he had a similar resource problem in 2007. President Bush announced the surge in Iraq the same month that US commanders in Afghanistan requested more forces. Gates realized he could not "deliver in both places at once." While he was able to provide some of the requested forces to Afghanistan, the Iraq surge meant US "ground forces were stretched very thin."[481] France also felt the pressure. In 2007, it had 16,000 forces deployed in multiple locations (Chad, Côte d'Ivoire, Lebanon, Balkans, and Afghanistan), so as with other nations it was spread thinly and did not have a lot of excess to deploy to Afghanistan.[482] In addition to active deployments, allies and partners were further constrained by their commitments to the NATO Response Force and EU battle groups. National units serving six-month rotations on standby for NATO or the European Union could not be deployed for other missions. The wide variation in abilities was a weakness for the coalition. ISAF could not plug-and-play contributions. That is, it could not move forces around to the places they were most needed without taking into consideration the attributes and caveats of individual contributions.

The diverse nature of national military capabilities and the wide range of ISAF's missions required headquarters staffs that would knit the various contributed elements together in the most effective manner possible. This was a time-consuming, often difficult, continuous process, since most contributing nations maintained short troop rotation periods—six months was common. Their efforts were complicated by overlapping OEF and ISAF mandates. OEF forces operated independently in the north and west in 2004–05 during the ISAF expansion. NATO's assumption of all the regional commands did not centralize command and control. Largely autonomous OEF forces (the training command and special operations forces) were still operating throughout the country. Furthermore, there was no unity of effort within ISAF.

Even though the ISAF headquarters created campaign plans that were sent to Joint Force Command Brunssum for formal approval, the ISAF commander left it to the regional commanders to carry out operations independently and individually. Not only did each of the regional commands essentially "fight their own war,"[483] but, according to Colonel Johannes Hoogstraten of the Netherlands, who served in the regional headquarters, RC-South itself had three different conflicts ongoing in Helmand, Kandahar, and Uruzgan and there was no cooperation between the provinces.[484] This decentralized execution of military activities produced major problems. Some of the officers interviewed commented that the Taliban coalition recognized the lack of coordination and cooperation within ISAF and subsequently exploited the seams between the regional commands. The conflict developed a kind of "whack-a-mole" character as a result, which produced frustration among the coalition partners. For example, two of the interviewed PRT commanders were in the country at the same time. Colonel Ruszin commanded the Hungarian PRT in Baghlan in RC-North and Lieutenant Colonel Hugh McAslan commanded the New Zealand PRT in Bamiyan in RC-East. They both commented on the problem of insurgents crossing the operational boundary from Baghlan into Bamiyan to conduct attacks. In one attack, several New Zealand soldiers died. The New Zealand commander blamed the Hungarians for the casualties and criticized their inability, as the battle space owners, to secure the area on their side of the operational border. While acknowledging the rugged terrain, McAslan said, "They didn't come down to that area . . . very infrequently . . . so you had a real sort of hole in that area." The Hungarian commander tried to smooth over the tensions by visiting the PRT in Bamiyan and inviting McAslan to visit Baghlan so they could improve mutual understanding.[485] The Norwegian PRT commander and battle space owner, Colonel Ivar Omsted, commented on a similar problem between RC-North and RC-West. He said, "My biggest problem was the border issue with RC-West. I was not allowed to cross the border. So all the bad guys, when we pushed them too hard, they just disappeared . . . either into Turkmenistan or further west into Badghis" in RC-West.[486] Colonel Tretinjak described a similar situation. His OMLT accompanied his *kandak* on an Afghan-Norwegian task force operation that ended up pushing Taliban forces from Meymaneh in Faryab Province (RC-North) into Ghormach in Badghis Province (RC-West). A week later, an RC-West operation did the opposite; it pushed the Taliban forces back into RC-North. Tretinjak indicated his frustration with the situation by saying, "That was a really shocking experience for me . . . that we cannot achieve any coordination between big guys [RC-North and RC-West regional leadership] in the area. It was just a wasting of time, I guess."[487] Overall, the command and control structures and processes were unwieldy during this period and they created an additional vulnerability for the coalition. Personal relationships became critical. In fact, all of the officers interviewed remarked on the importance of personal relationships among the troops of the contributing nations. They agreed good relationships were sometimes the only thing that ensured coherence.

The overlapping of ISAF and OEF was more than geographic. For a time, both coalitions were engaged in combat operations as well as stabilization and reconstruction. In other words, both of them conducted counterinsurgency operations, supported security sector reform activities, mentored and operationally partnered with the Afghan army, trained the ANSF, and conducted PRT activities. Redundancy and overlap among the three areas of military activity occurred. Battle groups conducted security operations as well as governance—which included key leader engagements, *shuras* (consultative assemblies), and coordination with province and district leaders—and other training and stabilization activities. PRTs conducted governance, development, reconstruction, and humanitarian activities as well as security operations and training-partnering-mentoring. OMLTs conducted training-partnering-mentoring activities and accompanied Afghan units on security operations while coordinating air, fire, and medical support.[488] The three areas of military activity were frequently uncoordinated, despite the overlap. However, at times they blended completely. For example, Colonel Tretinjak, team leader for an OMLT in RC-North, described a joint Afghan-coalition operation in 2008 that encompassed a battle group, PRT, and OMLT. His OMLT deployed with its *kandak* to Meymaneh in Faryab Province for an Afghan-led security operation. The Norwegian task force in the region was a combined battle group and PRT. It operated with his Afghan partners while his OMLT coordinated emergency combat and medical support.[489]

The OEF and ISAF coalitions slowly realized that their most crucial long-term activity was training and equipping the Afghan security forces. Just how difficult the process would be also slowly became evident. For example, there was an unprecedented need to institute literacy education and basic skills training, like drivers' training, for both the army and police.[490] Leaders perceived that a capable ANSF would be the agent that would allow the multinational forces to eventually withdraw, but the increasing violence over time meant they progressively increased the end-strength goals for the Afghan National Army and Afghan National Police. In December 2002, the coalitions and Afghan government initially set the goals of building a 70,000-man Afghan army and 62,000-man Afghan National Police force by 2006.[491] In February 2008, they revised the goals to 80,000 army and 82,000 national police by 2010.[492] In September 2008, they revised the army goal again to 134,000 by 2013. By the end of 2008, 79,000 army members and 75,954 national police officers were on duty.[493] The constant revisions upward meant the coalitions were constantly playing catch-up in the training missions. Commanders repeatedly highlighted their shortages in trainers. By 2008 both Combined Security Transition Command–Afghanistan and ISAF could articulate in hard numbers what their requirements and shortfalls were. For example, at the end of the year, American ETTs required 2,225 trainers, but only 1,138 were assigned (50 percent fill); 2,375 trainers were required for the US police mentoring teams, but only 886 were assigned (37 percent fill); and NATO had filled only forty-two of the 103 OMLT teams it had promised.[494] These shortfalls were one reason the PRTs and battle groups took up training and mentoring too. As Afghan National Army forces increased over time and were stationed across the country in the various army corps, they needed assistance in order to increasingly be involved in operations.

As soon as Afghan security forces were available, they were employed in partnership with coalition forces. The Afghan army began joint patrols in Kabul in 2003 with ISAF's multinational brigade.[495] The Afghan army and police supported the elections in 2004 and 2005.[496] Afghan army *kandaks* began assisting special operations forces in the south in 2004.[497] By 2006, almost all ISAF operations against the Taliban involved Afghan army participation.[498] The standing up and employment of Afghan security forces occurred while the militias were dismantled under the DDR program, which was formally declared complete in July 2005.[499]

Overall, there was tremendous pressure on the ISAF coalition during the hard time of 2006–08. The multiple potentially destructive fraying forces could have strained cohesion beyond the breaking point. First there was the shock of tough combat in 2006 which shattered the initial assumptions about the character of the conflict. Then there was the grind of escalating violence through 2008. The ISAF coalition came to realize it could not just engage in stabilization and reconstruction but had to be ready to engage in complex counterinsurgency opera-tions. Its effectiveness was undermined by political decisions regard-ing national caveats and where governments were willing to deploy their forces. In addition, reluctance to commit significant forces to Afghanistan, in combination with competing international operational demands, meant ISAF never had sufficient resources. This increased the risk for the coalition, which in turn translated into casualties. The shortfalls in troops and enabling capabilities forced commanders to rely extensively on overwhelming direct and indirect fire support. This in turn resulted in collateral damage that eroded Afghan support. The political and operational stresses produced intense intra-alliance acri-mony about burden-sharing as the conflict turned out to be longer, harder, and costlier than expected. Disagreements on the role and pur-pose of OEF and ISAF and the disjointed nature of their command and control relationships, despite their functional and geographic overlap-ping, hindered the coherent execution of the comprehensive approach. Furthermore, the decentralized execution of operations within the regions led to short-term tactical gains. This produced frustrations among the forces on the ground and a widespread perception that the international effort was a failure.

Taken together—and based on the historical experiences of alliances and coalitions—the pressures militating against cohesion (centrifugal forces) should have fractured the coalition. However, they did not, for they were outweighed by the pressures militating for cohesion (centripetal forces). The coalition held together due to the interaction of the two drivers. Political will endured, derived from multiple Alliance and domestic political influences. These included humanitarian and moral aspirations, solidarity in the face of a shared terrorist threat, and the overriding belief that ISAF's defeat by the Taliban would be fatal for NATO as a security institution. As such, national governments incrementally made critical decisions which reduced strategic and operational pressures. Political will was sustained by cautious optimism that ISAF could prevail over the Taliban because the incremental adaptations seemed to make the coalition more effective. This top-down cohesion was supported by the bottom-up cohesion produced by bonding at the operational and tactical levels through shared adversity. Together, the drivers produced continuing cohesion even as the differences in national strategic culture, availability of military resources, and variation in operational competence made knitting together the coalition extremely complex. This was an enduring weakness for the coalition especially as it grew from thirty-one to forty nations and included new countries such as Azerbaijan, Georgia, Jordan, and Ukraine.

Surprisingly, the hard time of 2006–08 led to further commitments by many allies and partners. Between spring 2006 and November 2008, coalition forces significantly increased from 9,000 to 51,100 (see appendix 3). ISAF seemed to demonstrate it was a learning organization as it fought back (Operation Medusa was a significant psychological success), shifted its operational approach, and undertook new missions in training, mentoring, and counterinsurgency. In short, both ISAF and NATO learned and adapted to the changed character of the conflict as NATO got into the game. After a limited beginning in Kabul in

2003, by 2008 the ISAF footprint encompassed the whole country and was comprised of five regional commands along with the ISAF headquarters, twenty-six PRTs, a multitude of training/mentoring teams, and a wide variety of battle groups. However, the major shortfall in ISAF's coalition operations was the continued national unwillingness to commit sufficient resources to ensure success. This contributed to the "catching-up" nature of coalition activities during this period.

Between 2003 and 2008, major positive developments in Afghanistan included the completion of the Bonn Agreement by the holding of presidential and parliamentary elections and the initiation of the Afghanistan Compact. The economy more than doubled in six years, more than five million children were enrolled in school, and more than 2,400 miles of roads were paved.[500] But despite this progress, there was a perception of failure since the conflict was at a stalemate. By 2007–08, the Bush administration realized something needed to change and it took the initial, tentative steps toward assuming a leading role. American concerns about the conflict were paralleled at NATO headquarters. After consultation, plans were made to increase troop numbers and adjust the command and control configuration.[501] President Bush decided to increase US forces over the course of 2007 and 2008 in what he called a "silent surge." Troop numbers rose from 21,000 to over 35,000. He doubled reconstruction funding, increased PRTs, ordered more civilian experts to Afghanistan to help the ministries in Kabul become more effective and less corrupt, and encouraged the allies and partners to do more.[502] The president also decided to establish better unity of command for US forces and to improve coordination between ISAF and OEF. General David McKiernan took command of ISAF in June 2008 and later took command of the OEF forces (Combined Security Transition Command–Afghanistan and Combined Joint Special Operations Task Force–Afghanistan) in October 2008. Furthermore, allied assessments of the situation resulted in significant decisions that changed entirely the scope of the coalition's activities.

CHAPTER 4

October 2008–December 2014: NATO Surges

By fall 2008, the international coalition recognized it was in an untenable position as insurgent violence continued to rise. The allies and partners knew something needed to change if ISAF was to break the Taliban momentum. As a consequence, national governments, NATO headquarters, and the ISAF headquarters initiated a variety of strategic reviews. At the same time, multilateral and bilateral forums which included key Afghan representatives held intensive discussions about Afghanistan. De Hoop Scheffer articulated the common view in February 2009: NATO allies and partners, through the ISAF coalition, needed to do more.[503] The question was what and how.

The answers—developed through a series of discussions and consultations at formal and informal defense and foreign minister meetings in 2008 and 2009—ultimately reflected substantial changes in the two drivers of the analytical framework. The United States, under its new president, Barack Obama, decided to substantially increase its contributions in both personnel and material resources and take a leading role in the coalition. The surge in US commitment, particularly the tripling of forces deployed from 35,000 to over 100,000, sustained the collective political will of the allies and partners and led to further contributions from them. It also facilitated a significant change in ISAF's organizational structure, multiple adaptations in its operating procedures, and an expansion in its activities as OEF and ISAF fully merged. Although the ISAF coalition knew it still had a long, hard road ahead of it, the massive increase in resources finally gave it the means to prosecute a more effective counterinsurgency campaign and implement a

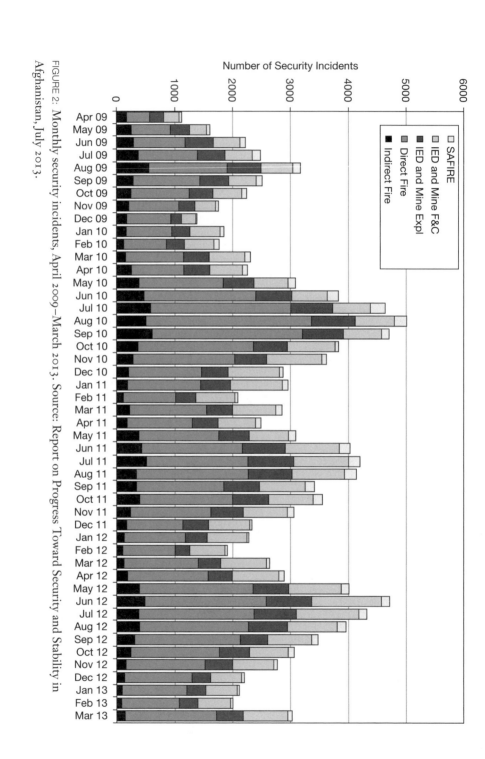

FIGURE 2: Monthly security incidents, April 2009–March 2013. Source: Report on Progress Toward Security and Stability in Afghanistan, July 2013.

more robust comprehensive approach: civilian and military efforts in the domains of security, economic development, and governance.

The changes in the coalition's organizational capacity produced more effective operational action, which in turn reinforced political commitment. In fact, the conflict shifted in 2010 when coalition and Afghan forces started to gain the upper hand due to erosions in Taliban capabilities. While national governments were openly starting to think about the timeline for withdrawal that year, the progressive improvements in Afghan army and police capabilities enabled the coalition to sustain its gains as it transitioned responsibility for security to Afghan forces between 2011 and 2013 and then conducted its withdrawal. In the end, the combination of the two drivers sustained cohesion throughout the period examined in this chapter: October 2008 through the end of the ISAF mission in December 2014.

The Conflict Escalates and NATO Changes Direction

Insurgent violence—IED attacks, suicide bombings, small arms, mortar, and rocket attacks, and small-scale ambushes—was on a greatly escalating trend between 2008 and 2010 as the Taliban coalition regained some territory and fought hard against a strengthening ISAF. During this period, the conflict spiraled into more intense fighting because the ISAF coalition increasingly operated and remained, in partnership with ANSF forces, in areas that had previously been uncontested as their troop levels increased. The coalition was also increasingly successful in deactivating and clearing IEDs before they exploded, based on information provided by local Afghans (see fig. 1, page 92, and fig. 2).

As the conflict escalated, coalition nations, NATO, and ISAF conducted major strategic assessments as they consulted together. The result was a succession of decisions in 2008 and 2009 that dramatically increased resources. Between November 2008 and November 2010, coalition forces almost doubled from 70,100 to 130,930.[504] The coalition also agreed to undertake major organizational changes that enabled activities that were substantial orders of magnitude larger than previous combat and noncombat operations.

The Bush administration's review and planning effort in the latter half of 2008 started the process. It was a coordinated effort among the president's National Security Council, the new commander of CENTCOM, General David Petraeus, NATO, ISAF, and the UN Assistance Mission in Afghanistan.[505] The first major change for the multinational coalition was the president's decision to appoint McKiernan as the commander of OEF forces in October 2008. This was meant to improve coordination between the OEF and ISAF coalitions.[506] The dual-hatting of McKiernan improved the US operational unity of effort but it did not establish unity of command for the rest of the multinational forces. While Combined Security Transition Command–Afghanistan and Combined Joint Special Operations Task Force–Afghanistan came under McKiernan's command, they were still formally separate from the ISAF mission, so the ANSF training and mentoring mission, as well as special operations, remained de-linked from the security and stability operations of ISAF. The new command arrangements put McKiernan in a position where he reported to two different command chains: to NATO for ISAF operations and to CENTCOM for OEF operations. This meant military operations remained disjointed, with neither unity of command nor unity of effort for all the multinational forces.

In fact, the whole coalition suffered from very complex command and control structures. McKiernan's position was not unique in that he was required to serve multiple masters. Each contributing nation designated a national contingent commander. These senior officers in Afghanistan held a wide variety of positions. Some held "just" the job of contingent commander, which allowed them to focus on supporting their national forces. But others were dual hatted with another responsibility such as serving as a PRT commander, a battle group commander, or as a commander or staff member in a regional command or in the ISAF headquarters. They were required to report back to, and were ultimately answerable to, their national governments, as well as to serve the ISAF/NATO chain of command.[507] This complexity was unavoidable because it was an enduring aspect of NATO. Even when operating in multinational formations, sustainment and logistical support remain the responsibility of the contributing nations.

The United States further complicated the situation when it created US Forces–Afghanistan in October 2008 when McKiernan took over Combined Security Transition Command–Afghanistan and Combined Joint Special Operations Task Force–Afghanistan (see appendix 1). This new command filled the gap CENTCOM created when it deactivated Combined Forces Command–Afghanistan in 2007. It brought all American forces under one commander. The command had the institutional capacity to provide the administrative and logistical support that the RC-East headquarters had been incapable of providing to the increasing US footprint. (Headquarters RC-East had become the default national support element for all US forces when Combined Forces Command–Afghanistan deactivated.) However, US Forces–Afghanistan was also partially merged with the ISAF headquarters. For example, a US officer was dual hatted to serve as the personnel officer for both ISAF headquarters and US Forces–Afghanistan. But if a senior staff position in ISAF headquarters was filled by an allied nation, the United States created a mirror position in US Forces–Afghanistan. For example, in 2010 the deputy commander of ISAF was a British officer and the ISAF chief of staff was a German officer, so US Forces–Afghanistan created mirrored positions filled by Americans for its headquarters staff.[508] Staff officers within the various departments also worked for both elements. This created a confusing situation which was never rectified. Overall, the command and control structures remained too unwieldy. They needed further change, particularly as violence continued to increase.

While the Bush administration was conducting its review, McKiernan requested additional forces—three combat brigades and an aviation brigade—totaling about 20,000 troops. The president supported the increase in forces, but since the troop deployments would not occur until 2009, the administration decided to quietly pass its support for the review's recommendations and the troop increase to the incoming

Obama administration. The ISAF staff was aware of the proposed surge and began preparing for the reception of additional forces in fall 2008, for it is a complex undertaking to deploy large numbers of troops into an already mature theater. Colonel George Woods, who was involved in the planning, said in an interview that the staff discussed in depth where to put the troops because the command would have to ensure new infrastructure was built to house and support the forces as they flowed in. He said they decided on a "troop infusion in the south to try to stem the tide of the Taliban sort of rebirth . . . regrowth if you will . . . they were really starting to make some significant damages to the coalition efforts there. I mean the Canadians and the Brits were notoriously the hardest hit forces anywhere in Afghanistan, in terms of casualty rates, so it was becoming intolerable." He added the US Marines, who "were campaigning pretty hard to be the force selected" for the first wave of US troop increases, were ultimately deployed into Helmand. He also acknowledged that the staff was looking into the future and that it was aware of national-level political discussions in Canada and the Netherlands. He said, "We were looking at trying to be able to use Kandahar airfield as the next hub, if you will, of US activities" because the command expected the Canadian combat forces "to be reduced in 2011, we knew that, as was the Dutch effort in 2010. So some additional US forces would have to be put into theater to, I think, eventually transition [RC-South] into a US headquarters."[509] Decisions that helped relieve the strain on allies who were carrying a significant part of the combat burden contributed to the maintenance of coalition cohesion.

In February and March 2009, President Obama approved an increase of over 21,000 troops as he simultaneously announced his strategy for Afghanistan after an initial strategic review.[510] The new administration's assessments and reviews continued the rest of the year. Senior officials—the vice president, secretary of state, and defense secretary—consulted with NATO allies and partners and kept them informed throughout the year.[511] Gates and the NATO secretary general, Anders Fogh Rasmussen, also tasked McChrystal to conduct a comprehensive review when he assumed command of ISAF in June 2009.[512] McChrystal concluded that the security situation was serious and deteriorating but success was achievable if significant changes were undertaken.[513] He requested another large force increase: 40,000 troops. After extensive and contentious deliberation, the president announced in December 2009 that the United States would send an additional 30,000 troops the next year.[514] The surges in US forces meant the American commitment to ISAF increased from about 15,000 troops before Bush's silent surge to 90,000 by October 2010. (The combined American OEF and ISAF force levels increased from about 21,000 to 101,000 during this time.[515]) The United States therefore clearly communicated its concern about the seriousness of the security situation and increased its commitment to Afghanistan to try to make ISAF operations more effective. These political decisions also relieved a great deal of pressure on the coalition.

While Obama's surge announcement in December 2009 reflected a significant change in direction, which was welcomed by the allies, it also created some uncertainty. It meant the United States would assume a leadership role as ISAF transformed its command and control configuration and modified its operational approach once again. The president's remark that the US commitment was not open ended, that forces would begin withdrawing in July 2011, and that combat operations would end by 2014, opened the door for the allies and partners to start overtly planning for the ISAF transition and withdrawal. However, the July 2011 date was widely misinterpreted by many Afghans who feared international abandonment once again. To create some damage control, Gates bluntly stated at the June 2010 NATO Defense Ministerial meeting that the July 2011 date was the start of a process. Any transition to ANSF and coalition withdrawal would depend on the recommendations of the ISAF commander, the senior civilian representative, and the Afghan government based on security conditions on the ground. He also repeatedly reassured the Afghans that the drawdown would be gradual.[516] In the end, the United States did not withdraw surge forces until 2012. The secretary of state, Hillary Clinton, also assured the

Karzai government that the US commitment would endure "long after the combat troops have left."[517]

As the US administration increased troop levels it pressed the allies and partners to do the same. Rasmussen echoed the requests.[518] SHAPE formalized the process by adding the need for additional troops to its statement of requirements for ISAF.[519] With the significant increases in military forces, better coordination and implementation of operations and training became more important. The existing command and control configuration was wholly inadequate. In fact, it actually worked against the synchronization of activities. Woods was involved in the command restructuring and then served as the adviser for Afghanistan's minister of defense at the time, Abdul Rahim Wardak. Woods said, "There was an awful lot of confusion and lack of coordination that were going on because of separate mandates and chains of command."[520] Furthermore, as ISAF's activities and span of control increased, the ISAF commander was forced to balance strategic, diplomatic, and political responsibilities with the operational responsibilities of a fighting commander. This did not work well. He and the ISAF staff should have been focusing on the big picture and coordinating at the national level with the Karzai government, the UN Assistance Mission in Afghanistan, allied and partner ambassadors, and the multitude of international organizations engaged in the country. Instead, he was constantly pulled down to focus on the operational and tactical levels, especially as the conflict escalated.[521] The surge in resources put further pressure on the command.

Leaders at the national, strategic (NATO), and coalition levels knew the command and control configuration needed to change. At the same time, consensus was emerging within NATO and the coalition partners that they needed to step up support for the ANSF in training, equipping, and mentoring because this would ultimately be the vehicle for the security transition and the coalition's withdrawal.[522] After a series of discussions, political authorities agreed on a major organizational change: the coalition would establish two intermediate commands between the ISAF headquarters and the regional commands. The decision allowed a significant adaptation that improved the coalition's operational effectiveness. It also finally ended the years-long debate about the merging of OEF and ISAF.

The genesis for the first of the commands, the NATO Training Mission–Afghanistan, included discussions at the informal defense ministerial meeting in Krakow, Poland, in February 2009 and the subsequent foreign ministerial meeting in Brussels in March. The allies formally announced their decision to create NTM-A at the April 2009 NATO Summit at Strasbourg, France-Kehl, Germany.[523] The command would concentrate on the higher-level training and mentoring of the Afghan National Army and Afghan National Police. The Combined Security Transition Command–Afghanistan with its ongoing activities would merge into it, bringing all ANSF training and mentoring activities and ministerial development and mentoring programs into one unified command.[524] The merger was not inconsequential. By 2009, the Combined Security Transition Command was a huge organization with 15,000 civilian and military personnel spread around the country in the headquarters staff and the regional support elements, in the basic training institutions in Kabul, in the army and police regional training facilities, in the hundreds of army and police training and mentoring teams, and in the ministries as mentors. Combined Security Transition Command–Afghanistan was also not deactivated as NTM-A stood up due to US national caveats. The United States provided the vast preponderance of funding for the Afghan security forces, which was used to generate and integrate the Afghan forces; train, develop, equip, and sustain the forces; build and maintain infrastructure; and build ministerial capacity. By 2012, this cost $12 billion a year. Therefore, annual funding laws authorized by Congress required that US commanders maintain control and fiduciary responsibility.[525] As such, NTM-A and Combined Security Transition Command had to merge and its commander had to be a US officer. This US law and national caveat also meant the ISAF command structures remained complex.

The genesis of the ISAF Joint Command (IJC) followed a similar sequential process. Gates stated in his memoir that leaders in the

Defense Department began considering the idea of creating a deputy ISAF commander with some sort of operational headquarters that would be in charge of the day-to-day fight in spring 2009.[526] The idea was discussed in Alliance forums and the defense ministers agreed in principle to create a new headquarters during a ministerial meeting in Brussels on June 12, 2009.[527] McChrystal fleshed out the concept for the major change to the ISAF command structure in his comprehensive review. The new IJC would give the coalition an operational planning, command, and management capability it had previously lacked. Its focus on coordinating day-to-day combat operations and the civil-military activities of the PRTs would enable a more effective implementation of the comprehensive approach. The North Atlantic Council approved the proposal on August 4, 2009.[528] With the command restructuring, OEF and ISAF operations merged almost completely (special operations were still partially separate).

However, while a deliberate effort had been made to rationalize the command and control relationships and structures and make them more efficient, some complexity still remained. For example, IJC and NTM-A/Combined Security Transition Command overlapped in a number of ways. Officers involved in the planning and restructuring process acknowledged that the command structure was not ideal. Nor could it be. Lieutenant Colonel Jeffrey Dickerson was one of the planners who assisted in the creation of IJC. He said, "I got to become very intimately aware of the command structures in Afghanistan . . . and it was very, very unique and there were a lot of different nuances that you had to take into account. The lines just weren't clear and you couldn't make them clear in some instances."[529] Another officer who experienced the restructuring, Lieutenant Colonel Christopher Moretti, observed that "if you want to keep this coalition together" you have to compromise.[530] Inefficient and complex command structures and relationships were therefore enduring weaknesses for the coalition. For the troops deployed to Afghanistan, it was the cost of multi-nationality.

Once overarching decisions were announced in NATO forums, the coalition staff had to figure out the nuts and bolts of implementation.

These would include identifying the functions and compositions of the new commands and building infrastructure to support and house them and then moving people and equipment. The organizational changes required some reshuffling of billets. That is, some ISAF headquarters billets were moved to IJC as the command stood up. Overall, the organizational changes required a methodical planning and execution process by the coalition staff which lasted six months.[531] It was also a complex, time-consuming process because—as with other NATO multinational headquarters—a bidding and negotiation process occurred at SHAPE planning conferences to determine which nations would fill which positions.[532] IJC was activated on November 12, 2009, and NTM-A/ Combined Security Transition Command–Afghanistan was activated on November 21, 2009. The creation of the two intermediate commands marked the conclusion of a significant transformation in ISAF's operational-level command and control structures. From the humble beginnings of a 240-man ISAF headquarters in August 2003, the command and control structure had become enormous. By 2009, the ISAF headquarters staff had expanded to 2,200 billets.[533] IJC had 873 billets and NTM-A had 1,028 billets.[534]

The IJC and NTM-A activations included the implementation of one further change. Once the new commands were established, command and control of the army and police training and mentoring teams moved from Combined Security Transition Command into IJC.[535] With this change, all forces deployed within the battle space of the regional commands came under the same chain of command. As a consequence, the combat operations, stability and reconstruction, and training and mentoring activities could be better coordinated and executed. Previously the battle groups, PRTs, and army and police training teams had operated under separate chains of command. It was up to the individual leaders of the elements in the districts and provinces to coordinate activities among themselves. Sometimes they worked well together, but often they did not because their commanders were focused on different objectives.[536] There were cases when the battle groups were not even aware they had PRTs or training/mentoring teams operating in their areas.[537] This had degraded the coalition's ability to achieve its security, development, and governance goals and it meant personalities were extremely important. More seriously, the realignment resulted from learning the hard way. Dickerson witnessed the frustration of the ISAF and IJC commanders in mid-2009 after an ETT was ambushed with its *kandak* in RC-East and suffered casualties. The event was not unprecedented as the violence increased. The coalition's battle space owner had not been aware of the Afghan operation and, according to Dickerson, "Everyone was like 'How the heck does this happen? How do we have these people moving around on the battlefield and the landowner doesn't know?'" The generals decided, "We've got to get everyone nested. We've got to have some unity of command here so if you live and work and operate in this battle space, you answer to that battle space owner, you work for him." Once the control of ANSF mentoring teams moved, Combined Joint Task Force Phoenix and Combined Joint Task Force Police deactivated.[538] As OEF and ISAF more fully merged in November 2009, there was little drama because, despite assertions for years that the missions were separate and distinct, they had been slowly converging since 2003. At this point, there was more complete unity of command and much better unity of effort.

The major organizational changes and the command realignment were accompanied by four complementary surges. The surges came in waves. US forces substantially increased (2009–10) and forty of the allies and partners committed to increase their forces by 9,700 (the increases arrived 2009–12).[539] The Pakistani government substantially increased military operations in the North West Frontier Province and Federally Administered Tribal Areas, putting pressure on the insurgent sanctuaries (2009–14); and ISAF greatly increased the scale and scope of ANSF development (2010–13). Furthermore, ISAF's main effort shifted from combat and counterinsurgency operations (which were the focus through 2010) to NTM-A's training, mentoring, and advising mission, which became ISAF's main effort in 2011. The four surges were mutually dependent and built on each other. In effect, the massive increases in coalition military forces were only temporary and were meant to beat back the Taliban momentum and reduce the insurgency as much as possible in order to create time and space for the surge in ANSF training and development. As the surge forces started drawing down, between 2012 and 2013, ANSF was supposed to step into the gap and take over security responsibility. As the ANSF increasingly took over security, ISAF could gradually withdraw.

Obama had called for a "dramatic increase in the US civilian effort" in his Afghan strategy speech in March 2009, but this civilian surge never materialized. According to Gates, even though commanders in the field pleaded for more civilian expertise, the State Department and other federal agencies were incapable of fielding more than a trickle of civilian experts. While the administration examined every military move under a microscope, Gates said, "no comparable attention was paid to the civilian side," which allowed the nondefense agencies to shirk their responsibilities in the governance and economic areas.[540] By November 2010, the number of non-Defense Department civilians deployed in Afghanistan topped out at about 1,100, equating to 1 percent of the US military commitment.[541] This also ensured continued military involvement in the nonmilitary lines of effort.

McChrystal's comments on the dire situation were not understatements. ISAF recognized that there was a new insurgent strategy by 2009–10. Based on the loose structure of the Quetta Shura Taliban and its regional *shuras*, plus the autonomy given to the various insurgent elements, the Taliban coalition initiated a loosely coordinated, two-pronged approach. Forces comprised primarily of the Taliban pushed from the south toward Kandahar while primarily Haqqani and Hekmatyar forces pushed from the east toward Kabul. Both groups concentrated on attacking coalition and ANSF forces. Their goal (according to writers Max Boot, Frederick W. Kagan, and Kimberly Kagan) was "to inflict enough pain on the coalition to force public opinion in Europe and North America to demand a withdrawal. Once the coalition [was] gone, they figure[d] the government of Afghanistan [would] fall like rotten fruit."[542] ISAF faced a determined opponent.

Due to McChrystal's assessment of the deteriorating situation, he modified ISAF's operational approach. The organizational changes and command realignment improved the coalition's operational capabilities and gave it, for the first time, the organizational capacity to develop and implement a truly coordinated and adequately resourced comprehensive approach. The newly established IJC developed an overarching national civilian-military campaign plan called Operation Omid (Dari for "hope"). It was developed and executed in partnership with the relevant security, governance, and development ministries in the Afghan government. It was approved by Joint Force Command Brunssum and updated annually.[543] While the RC commanders still prepared and executed operations within their regions, they had to be approved by IJC and be in accordance with the overall campaign plan. Thus the regional commands no longer operated independently. Consequently, the entire ISAF coalition could finally prosecute more effective counterinsurgency operations in partnership with the ANSF and the Afghan government. In reality, ISAF implemented the clear-hold-build approach, modified in each region to account for local conditions, that had been attempted in previous years. But this time it finally had sufficient forces, both coalition and ANSF, to clear and hold terrain and thus secure the population, which established a more stable foundation for governance and economic development activities. It also minimized the Taliban coalition's ability to exploit the seams between the regional commands.

The coalition also implemented across the regional commands an operating procedure that had been pioneered in 2007 in RC-East. That year, the battle group commander in Khowst had dispersed his troops in small outposts, called force protection facilities, throughout the province and in each of the district centers where they lived among the people. This enabled them to directly mentor and protect local officials and the Afghan police, operate with the Afghan army, and coordinate PRT activities. The approach was very effective. Their enduring presence created a sense of security among the population. Districts that were pro-government increased that year from twenty-two to fifty-eight (out of a total of eighty-six).[544] McChrystal called it "embedded partnering." Not only were ISAF forces dispersed among the population in key areas, but coalition and ANSF forces were also colocated and operated in partnership. According to McChrystal, the intent was they "would train, eat, bunk, plan, patrol, fight, celebrate, and mourn together."[545] This approach produced a new sense of security among communities.

McChrystal also resuscitated the ink-spot approach that Richards had pioneered in 2006. The IJC identified eighty "key terrain" districts which were focal points for concentrated security, development, and governance activities. They included all the major population centers, major transit areas, and key roads. Security operations in the districts were followed by a new initiative, the District Delivery Program. Coalition forces coordinated with the district leaders, provincial governors, and relevant government ministers to establish government services and launch development projects.[546]

Coalition operations were supported by more strategic enablers. The increased material resources improved operational capability. During the height of the conflict in Iraq, the United States had moved strategic assets, such as intelligence capabilities and helicopters, out of Afghanistan to support Operation Iraqi Freedom.[547] With the success of the US surge in Iraq in 2007 and the subsequent withdrawal of forces from Iraq under Bush and Obama, the United States not only had more military forces available for its troop surges in Afghanistan, it also moved strategic assets back, in particular intelligence, surveillance, and reconnaissance (ISR) assets and rotary aircraft.[548] Gates had become concerned about the situation in Afghanistan in 2007. He not only directed the Department of Defense and Combatant Commands to shift critical ISR assets, particularly drones, to CENTCOM, but he also succeeded in acquiring new funding ($2.6 billion) to increase desperately needed additional capabilities, such as information processing hardware, linguists and analysts, ground sensors, and reconnaissance aircraft.[549] The additional capabilities started arriving by 2008. They gave the coalition the intelligence enablers it needed to implement more effective counterinsurgency operations and reduce civilian casualties.

In 2009, the most volatile regions continued to be the south and east. Even though insurgent attacks generally increased across the country, particularly in the run-up to the August presidential election, the north, center, and west remained relatively more secure.[550] The forces in RC-East had also produced some counterinsurgency successes in 2007 and 2008, making the region relatively more stable than the south. For example, by 2009, Jalalabad, in Nangarhar Province, was booming economically and violence levels were low enough for the ANSF to assume responsibility for security.[551] Due to this "permissive environment," the PRT surged its development activities and by 2010 it was managing $60 million in projects.[552] Khowst Province had also seen improvement. Ambassador Neumann observed when he visited Khowst in 2005 that it was regularly attacked with rockets.[553] Gates noted improvements when he visited the area in December 2007, calling the civilian-military efforts a model of genuinely comprehensive counterinsurgency.[554] By the end of 2008, Khowst was so secure and had made such economic and civil progress that conditions were better than the neighboring Federally Administered Tribal Areas and refugees were leaving Pakistan to take advantage of the new opportunities in Afghanistan.[555] Moretti described in overall terms the difference between RC-South and RC-East in 2009: "For us, RC-South as it was named was much more kinetic than any of the RCs. RC-East was second, but there was a significant difference in the level."[556]

McChrystal and his successor, Petraeus, therefore concentrated ISAF's main effort toward operations in the south—first in Helmand, then in Kandahar. This meant RC-South was the priority for theater-level resources, including intelligence, ISR, and lethal and non-lethal fire support.[557] As US surge forces arrived in 2009, British and Canadian-led forces conducted a series of operations in Helmand and Kandahar to prepare the ground.[558] However, the new coordinated civilian-military campaign approach was not initiated until RC-South launched Operation Moshtarak (Dari for "together") which focused on the region around Marjah and Nad Ali in Helmand.[559] The operation was much larger than previous ISAF efforts, including 15,000 forces, with the Afghan army and police integrated as full partners, as well as British, Canadian, Danish, Estonian, and American troops.[560] Innovations in operating procedures included an initial "shaping" phase (late 2009 to February 2010) when *shuras* were held to inform the population and local leaders about the upcoming operation and assure them the coalition would stay in the area to consolidate security. When combat operations, the "clearing" phase, began in February 2010, supporting fire was strictly controlled to avoid killing civilians and damaging civilian infrastructure.[561] Once the major population centers were largely secured, in the spring, the District Delivery Program was launched.[562] ISAF understood consolidating successes would take time, and its increased resources meant it was ready for the Taliban resistance it encountered. Over the rest of the year, and through a series of complex engagements, it slowly achieved substantial results.[563] For example, clearing Marjah meant it could no longer serve as a Taliban sanctuary.[564] By December, Marjah was transformed.[565] Dramatic progress continued in 2011, according to the Defense Department, as counterinsurgency operations expanded gains in central and southern Helmand Province.[566] In March, Petraeus observed in testimony to the US Senate Armed Services Committee that Marjah no longer served as a hub for either the Taliban or the illegal narcotics industry. He said the markets "which once sold weapons, explosives, and illegal narcotics, now feature over 1,500 shops selling food, clothes, and household goods."[567] Max Boot observed during his visit in October that "Marjah, once the epicenter of violence in Afghanistan, had turned remarkably peaceful."[568] Lashkar Gah and Nad Ali underwent a similar transformation. A British officer, Colonel Robbie Boyd, who deployed there in 2009–10, noted the dramatic improvements in security and economic activity in Lashkar Gah. He stated when his unit first arrived "the streets were empty" but by the time it left, eighteen months later in November 2010, "The market was 4,000 to 5,000 people every day . . . the police wanted to be in Lashkar Gah because they had everything they needed. You could buy anything you want . . . It's an urban area and it's growing and it was secure."[569] As a consequence, Karzai announced in November 2011 that the area would transition to Afghan security responsibility during the second transition phase which occurred in 2012 as the US Marine surge forces withdrew.[570]

The surge in forces and material resources meant the coalition could turn to Kandahar, even as Operation Moshtarak continued, which was a vast improvement in the coalition's organizational capacity. However, the huge scale and complexity of operations also generated an additional organizational change. The span of control for the RC-South commander had become huge by early June 2010; he commanded 65,000 troops, whereas RC-East had 32,000 troops, RC-North had 8,000, RC-West had 6,000, and RC-Capital had 5,000.[571] Therefore, after receiving North Atlantic Council approval on May 21, 2010, ISAF created RC-Southwest in June.[572] It split Helmand Province and Nimroz Province from RC-South to create the new RC and it also incorporated three districts from RC-West's Farah Province.[573] The new regional command took over Moshtarak operations, allowing RC-South to concentrate on Operation Hamkari (Dari for "cooperation"), which it had initiated in April 2010.

The new operation was in effect an application of the ink-spot concept. It focused on securing Kandahar City and its environs and was intended to connect the key districts and major population centers of Helmand to Kandahar, which lay along the ring road, Highway 1.[574] The "shaping" phase of the operation, April to August 2010, was a little longer than Moshtarak had been because RC-South applied a number of lessons learned from the earlier operation.[575] It also invested more time in building support for the operation among local leaders and the population.[576] The "clearing" phase of Operation Hamkari began in September, involving 7,000 troops. More significantly, for the first time Afghan forces outnumbered ISAF forces. Afghans also took the lead in some areas, which focused on Kandahar City and the districts to its west, Zhari, Panjawyi, and Arghandab.[577] By December 2010, an anonymous Taliban commander admitted, "the [Afghan] government has the upper hand now" in Kandahar and "the local people are not willingly cooperating with us."[578] A year later, the coalition continued to solidify its gains. The Taliban's campaign in 2011 to regain lost safe havens in Helmand and Kandahar and reassert dominance in Khowst, Paktika, and Paktia failed. Furthermore, RC-South noted improvements in Afghan governance capacity at district and provincial levels. As a result, popular support increased for the government across Kandahar, Uruzgan, and Zabul.[579] Through 2012, despite Taliban efforts to regain their lost territories, the security gains achieved in the Helmand and Kandahar Provinces were sustained. The security situation in the other regional commands also improved, in some cases dramatically, as they also implemented more fully coordinated civilian-military operations.[580] In fact, by mid-2012, large portions of RC-North, RC-West, and RC-Southwest had transitioned to the ANSF's security responsibility, about half of RC-East was in transition, and in RC-South the entire Uruzgan Province and portions of Zabul and Kandahar were in transition.

To complement the coordinated civilian-military campaign, ISAF increased special forces operations across the country during 2009–11. Most important, the ISAF commander was finally given control of Combined Joint Special Operations Task Force–Afghanistan in spring 2010 (up until that point, CENTCOM had retained operational control).[581] McChrystal also concurrently stood up a new organizational element, ISAF SOF (ISAF Special Operations Forces). The creation of this staff element formalized what had previously been an informal coordination link between liaison officers from NATO special operations task forces in the regions and the ISAF command group.[582] ISAF SOF was a command, control, and coordination element for the NATO and partner special operation forces which had long been operating in the country but were not part of the Combined Joint Special Operations Task Force. It was supported by the NATO Special Operations Headquarters at SHAPE.[583] This consolidation meant all military operations and missions were finally folded into ISAF control, greatly enhancing the coalition's unity of effort.

ISAF's surge in special operations included precision strikes against insurgent leadership. It was believed this would unbalance the insurgent coalition, degrade its capabilities, and undermine the enemy's confidence, particularly as the coalition got ready to launch operations Moshtarak and Hamkari. McChrystal then expanded the special operation missions by initiating village stability operations in spring 2010. This bottom-up initiative embedded twelve-man teams into remote rural villages where ANSF and ISAF presence were limited. The teams connected district and provincial leaders, as well as the PRTs, to remote areas. The initiative started with five teams and expanded quickly. By October 2011, the initiative had 6,000 troops engaged in 103 locations across the country. The initiative was considered highly effective.[584] The precision strike operations were also successful in eroding the insurgent leadership. By early 2011, Petraeus noted the "enormous losses" suffered among Taliban and Haqqani mid-level leaders which appeared to generate "unprecedented discord among members of the Quetta Shura."[585] Intelligence sources also found some Taliban commanders were afraid to keep fighting.[586] Later in the year, ISAF commanders concluded the insurgents could no longer mount coordinated or complex attacks and instead resorted to horrific, high-profile attacks, such as the September Haqqani attack in Kabul, when the group launched rockets at ISAF headquarters, the American embassy, and Afghan government buildings.[587] However, Petraeus's successor, General John Allen, noted that every one of the high-profile attacks that year was handled by an increasingly capable ANSF "which responded promptly and courageously and effectively."[588]

Finally, the operational-level organizational changes and the shift in operational approach generated organizational changes and new procedures within the regional command headquarters. According to an officer deployed in RC-North, after the IJC creation, "a complete new structure [was] established in all the regional commands . . . the staff were completely newly arranged, in order to integrate better the coordination with IJC." The reorganization included the establishment of new staff elements, the most significant of which was the Forward Planning Cell, a subdivision of the Operations Department. The staff element's primary responsibility reflected the coalition's increasing emphasis on partnership with Afghan forces with a view to eventually putting Afghans in charge of security operations. The cell acted as a bridge that linked the operational planning efforts of the RC staff with the ANSF. It coordinated directly with Afghan army corps and brigade commanders, as well as Afghan police elements and representatives from the National Directorate of Security, to ensure the development of combined operational plans that synchronized ANSF activities with coalition battle groups and PRTs.[589] This staff element facilitated combined Afghan-coalition operations and then pushed the Afghans into the lead.

Another regional command innovation was less effective. In addition to the traditional departments found in an operational headquarters—personnel, intelligence, operations, logistics, and communications—a new department was created in 2011, the Stability Department. Its mission was to coordinate with all the civil partners operating in the region: the UN Assistance Mission in Afghanistan and other UN organizations, the US Agency for International Development (USAID) and other national foreign aid organizations, the Red Cross, and other NGOs. The idea was to better synchronize the regional commands' counterinsurgency operations with the development activities of civil partners, because coalition forces realized that the center of gravity for operational success in Afghanistan was civil development.[590] Better RC coordination would also facilitate the security transition process and coalition withdrawal. However, the Stability Departments were never adequately resourced. The German officer who led this department in RC-North, Colonel Uwe Hartmann, had a staff of twenty multinational personnel, none of whom were specialists in civil affairs. In contrast, and despite this new department's importance, the Operations Department had 200 staff assigned.[591] To further complicate matters, many NGOs were extremely wary of contact with coalition forces. This meant coordination was always inconsistent and haphazard.

Sufficient security gains had been achieved by November 2010 that the allies announced at the NATO Lisbon Summit their decision to stay the course with their comprehensive approach. They also announced their intention to transition security responsibility to the ANSF and conclude the ISAF mission by December 2014.[592] In addition, they announced NATO would remain engaged in Afghanistan after 2014, and as such signed a Declaration on an Enduring Partnership with the Afghan government.[593] The allies also announced a new strategic concept for NATO which acknowledged that counterinsurgency, along with stabilization and reconstruction, were enduring missions.[594] This was a validation of the Alliance's expanded strategic culture, for it formally incorporated and institutionalized what ISAF had been doing for more than four years. Overall, it seemed the increase in resources, organizational changes, and revised operational approach had produced sufficient gains to sustain national political will and thus commitment. This in turn enabled the start of the security transition in 2011 as well as the shift in ISAF's main effort from combat operations to NTM-A's training and mentoring initiatives.

The high point of the violence occurred in summer 2010. It was not clear to the coalition at the time, but that year was also a tipping point in the conflict, when the correlation of forces began to shift to the side of ISAF. In any event, 2008–10 was a very tough period as coalition fighting and fatalities greatly increased. The pressure of the conflict could have strained cohesion and fractured the coalition. In fact, the senior civilian representative, Mark Sedwill, later remarked on the fears of the ISAF leadership. He said, "Coming into 2010, the insurgency had the momentum; people were very skeptical about whether we could really succeed in this campaign, it looked as though there was going to be a scramble for the exit, beginning in 2011, with various countries talking about withdrawing their troops."[595] Unexpectedly, the allies and partners stayed engaged, even though European defense spending fell due to the global financial crisis.[596] Spain was a prime example of the strain some of the countries experienced. The economic crisis tipped the country into a years-long recession, impelling the government to slash the defense budget. As a consequence, Spanish officer Marcos was embarrassed to admit his country could not meet the NATO requirement for nations to spend 2 percent of GDP on defense. He said the

Spanish defense budget dropped to .58 percent of GDP. However, despite the austerity conditions, the country did not reduce its commitment to Afghanistan.[597] Surprisingly, it increased its contribution from 780 troops in June 2009 to about 1,500 troops in August 2010 and sustained the commitment until 2013. More surprisingly, the ISAF coalition increased from forty members to forty-eight. The interaction of the analytical framework's two drivers continued to produce cohesion. Political will provided resources which served as the foundation for improvements in organizational capacity, which in turn generated concrete operational successes by the end of 2010.

The clearest demonstrations of the intent to stay engaged, and thus of enduring political will, were the decisions to surge military forces and material resources. Once again, political decisions had operational impacts. In particular, the American troop increases and assumption of a leadership role were the major factors that held the coalition together at a critical time. In effect, continued US engagement in Afghanistan and the massive American troop increase pulled along the other members and influenced the decisions of allies to stay and to increase their forces. Gates's recounting of the Obama administration's deliberations suggests there was no distinction between domestic and Alliance politics for the administration. The president and his advisers framed their decisions within a domestic politics context and within the context of a struggle between the military bureaucracy (which was distrusted) and the new administration. Once their decisions were made, they informed NATO and assumed the Alliance would go along with any shift in approach.[598] The allies did. Furthermore, the US position influenced the non-NATO partners, which numbered fifteen by 2010 but later increased. For example, Bosnia-Herzegovina and El Salvador joined the coalition in 2011, providing troops to guard a base in Helmand and trainers for NTM-A, respectively.

Political will among the allies and partners was still based on the belief that an ISAF failure or precipitous withdrawal from Afghanistan would be catastrophic for the Alliance. It would be taken by al-Qaeda and other jihadist groups as a strategic victory on par with the Soviet-Afghan war because it would be a defeat of not only another superpower, but of the entire international community. There was also a belief it would result in a surge of terrorist camps and training in the region, which would destabilize Afghanistan and undermine Pakistan.[599] But this was only one strategic reason for the enduring political will. For some countries, joining and staying was simple. For example, according to Colonel Ruszin, for Hungary it was all about Alliance solidarity: literally "together in and together out."[600] For other countries, over time the national reasons for staying became multiple and layered over each other. According to McAslan, New Zealand joined the coalition in 2001 out of solidarity with the United States after 9/11 and in the face of a shared jihadist threat. Its commitment then endured for humanitarian reasons: its PRT reconstruction efforts in Bamiyan helped the Afghan people. A desire to strengthen the New Zealand-US relationship became the third reason for the country's contribution, after a change in government.[601] Italian contributions were initially based on a desire to play a larger role on the world stage and as an unstated "pay-back" for allied assistance in stabilizing the Balkans.[602] However, according to Vezzoli, honoring the agreements made at NATO also mattered for Italy. Therefore, once it promised to support ISAF, the government was determined to see it through until NATO decided to end the mission.[603]

Germany initially joined coalition operations in Afghanistan due to sympathy for the United States and a desire to help.[604] The government also invoked Alliance solidarity and loyalty to allies to justify its contribution. It subsequently cited moral reasons for its involvement—it was fighting for democracy and human rights.[605] After the Iraq intervention, Germany increased its commitment to Afghanistan to repair relations with the United States and to demonstrate to its other allies it was still a reliable partner.[606] As the security situation deteriorated, Germany stayed because it could not abandon a mission that was incomplete.[607] It wanted to complete the mission successfully, particularly since it wanted NATO as a security institution to be successful. Finally, Germany remained committed to Afghanistan out of a sense of obligation to the seventeen contributing nations that depended on it as the lead nation for RC-North.[608]

Poland was another country that not only stayed engaged but increased its commitment even as the conflict escalated. According to Colonel Bieniek, the country initially joined ISAF out of a sense of Alliance solidarity after 9/11. It also wanted to be a provider of security in NATO, not just a taker. As such, from 2002 to 2007 it provided special forces and engineers to clear and then secure the airfield at Bagram. In contrast to other European countries, Poland's involvement in Afghanistan retained public support. In 2007, the government decided to significantly increase its commitment by deploying a battalion battle group (1,200 troops) to Paktika Province, where it was embedded with US forces in RC-East. The decision was partly based on a desire to maintain Poland's special relationship with the United States. In 2008, the government decided it wanted Poland to have a more visible role within the coalition, so it volunteered to shift its combat forces to Ghazni where it assumed overall responsibility, as the battle space owner, of the entire province. When violence escalated, it did not retreat. Instead it doubled its forces, transforming the battalion into a brigade with 2,500 troops called Task Force White Eagle. The country also deployed additional enablers: helicopters, artillery, infantry fighting vehicles, and mine-resistant vehicles (MRAPs). It sustained the heightened contribution until 2012.[609] National reasons for contributions, therefore, seemed to develop into a complex mosaic based on intertwined domestic and Alliance politics for many countries.

Collective political will was expressed in the Alliance's Lisbon Summit declaration, for there was continuing consensus among the allies that ISAF needed to continue to fight.[610] Non-NATO partners also continued to express their commitment. For example, Julia Gillard visited Afghanistan shortly after assuming office as Australia's prime minister and she assured President Karzai her country would continue to support the ISAF mission.[611] However, the contributing nations also started to temper their statements; they had no desire to stay indefinitely. For example, Denmark's prime minister, Lars Rasmussen, stated during a visit to his troops, "We are determined to end our mission. . . . But we must not get so carried away that all will slip between our hands."[612] Secretary General Rasmussen reflected the allied view when he stated at a NATO press conference in summer 2010 that "Allies and partners will stay committed as long as it takes to finish the job. Obviously, that does not mean forever."[613] The allies and partners were starting to think about withdrawal, but they did not want to throw away their hard-won gains. The transition plan gave them a road map for ending the mission and it ensured that cohesion endured for the final years of ISAF's existence.

National and collective political will was reinforced by organizational capacity changes within NATO, ISAF, and national militaries. The hard fighting was taken as an opportunity for learning and adjustment—in organizational structures which affected the command and control of ISAF forces, in mission execution and operating procedures, in doctrine and training, and in national force structures. For example, at the strategic level NATO finally published a counterinsurgency doctrine in February 2011.[614] It incorporated counterinsurgency operations into its training institutions and programs, such as the mission rehearsal exercises at the NATO training facilities in Stavanger, Norway, and Bydgoszcz, Poland.[615] The Alliance also refined the strategic-level forums that allowed non-NATO contributing nations to share information, be more involved in "policy-shaping," and have their voices heard in decision making.[616] ISAF commanders continually tinkered with the command structures. They never stopped trying to create a more functional command and control configuration, but the evolutions literally took months and years because major changes required NATO and national government approval. There was also a downside to the constant command and control changes: it meant constant disruption and as such was an enduring weakness of ISAF. In fact, taken together the OEF and ISAF command structures underwent major organizational changes almost every year for ten years, 2001–10.

In general, ISAF's operational expansion impelled many allies and partners to adjust their equipment and training programs, accelerating

the reform of some Cold War legacy forces into expeditionary formations.[617] For some countries, reform was slow and occurred in the face
of a difficult fiscal environment. For example, Italy developed a more
capable and professional military only by reducing its size and slowing
modernization.[618] Canada wasted no time after 2006 in gathering lessons learned from Kandahar and making adjustments in training and
operational practices. It published its own counterinsurgency manual
in 2008 and implemented a reformed counterinsurgency approach in
2009.[619] German reform efforts were slower because of the more stable conditions in RC-North. However, repeated attacks by insurgents
and a trend of increasing violence during 2007–10 across the northern
provinces induced change. A German officer described RC-North's
general operational orientation. He said the command "was very much
stabilization operation focus with a defensive character, you know,
security assistance. That was the mindset . . . and suddenly [we got]
really severely attacked" in 2007. He admitted it took some time for the
command to grasp that conditions had changed. It was not until 2009
that it concluded that "things seemed to [be getting] out of control."
They had a "real fight" on their hands, particularly the "insurgency
in Kunduz." As a result, "a lot of stuff changed." Within the German
military, he said, "We recognized that we had a lot of deficiencies in
terms of capabilities and some doctrinal elements . . . the overall question was really how to improve." As a consequence of learning the hard
way, the German army not only updated officer training but also gained
political support to deploy additional resources. German force numbers increased from 3,200 in 2008 to 5,000 in 2011 and the country
deployed armored personnel carriers and Tornado reconnaissance aircraft. As part of the increased contribution, it deployed two full battle groups to Mazar-e-Sharif and Kunduz in 2010. These units took
over the role of battle space owner from the PRTs in the areas. The
forces were no longer defensive or reactive but undertook "offensive
operations against the insurgency." They were supported by five thousand US surge forces and additional enablers (intelligence capabilities,
MEDEVAC, and combat air support).[620] German forces later expanded

their offensive operations, via additional battle groups, to Feyzabad and Baghlan.[621] It became evident the German army would fight when circumstances forced it to in the northern provinces. But for historical reasons, it was hesitant to publicly utilize the term "counterinsurgency operations," preferring the more neutral term "networked security." To accommodate political and public sensibilities it also heavily emphasized the civilian and reconstruction aspects of its operations.[622] The United Kingdom was also slow to apply and update counterinsurgency doctrine and reform training. Despite suffering difficult lessons in Basra, Iraq, and years of "mowing the grass" in Helmand, it did not open a counterinsurgency center to train units deploying to Afghanistan until June 2009.[623] National reform efforts were therefore uneven and often lagging. They produced broad variation in operational capabilities which undermined ISAF's ability to achieve its objectives. The uneven reform efforts were also a potential force fraying cohesion as it contributed to frustrations over burden-sharing.

The repeated public statements of national and NATO commitment and the significant efforts to improve organizational capacities occurred during the most violent phase of the conflict in Afghanistan. As mentioned, the fraying pressures of combat continued. America's assumption of a leadership role seems to have provided the top-down cohesion needed to sustain collective political will. By the time all its surge forces arrived in Afghanistan in 2010, the United States had more than 100,000 troops committed, which meant it carried the vast preponderance of the burden. US leadership was accompanied by unilateral behaviors, some of which the allies tolerated. Despite the SACEUR having originally been given the official role of selecting the ISAF commanders, the Obama administration repeatedly made unilateral decisions and did not consult with NATO about the command position before making official announcements. This was a change from the Bush administration. Bush had nominated Generals Dan McNeill and David McKiernan as the tenth and eleventh ISAF commanders to the NATO secretary general and SACEUR. He left it to SACEUR to make the formal selection. The succession of US leaders was not the result of a formal decision by the Alliance to henceforth have the mission led by an American. At the time it was taken by NATO as a logical proposal given the fact the United States was by far the largest contributor to ISAF and the effort in Afghanistan.[624]

However, the precedent of US leadership was taken as a given by the Obama administration and it brushed aside SACEUR's role in the process. The president relieved McKiernan in May 2009 because he was resistant to shifting to a more aggressive approach. McChrystal was relieved on June 23, 2010, after *Rolling Stone* magazine published an article that was politically damaging to the administration. The president informed his National Security Council of his decision to replace him with Petraeus before informing the Alliance.[625] According to Colonel Tucker Mansager, SACEUR's executive assistant at the time, the McKiernan relief came as a surprise to NATO officials. The SACEUR, General John Craddock, in particular was "shocked and upset" with the way the replacement was done.[626] However, Alliance officials accommodated the decision to maintain the image of allied unity and Secretary General Rasmussen publicly validated the change in procedure a year later after the McChrystal relief when he congratulated General Petraeus in July 2010 (upon his initial visit as ISAF commander to Brussels) on his appointment and unanimous US Senate confirmation.[627] The allies arguably accepted this unilateral behavior because the United States had not only solved the burden-sharing problem but also opened the door to the withdrawal process. The initiation of the transition plan meant national governments could soon end the recurring process of gaining parliamentary approval to extend the mandates for their troop deployments.

However, other unilateral behavior was not accepted. The initial CENTCOM planning in late 2008 to early 2009 for the deployment of US surge forces unilaterally changed operational boundaries in RC-South and moved some allies to different areas. According to Colonel Hoogstraten, this was an extremely sensitive issue for the contributing nations who had "put a lot of money" and expended "in some cases a lot of bloodshed" during the previous three years and they were "not willing to change responsibilities in an instant," particularly when they were not consulted. The RC-South commander, Lieutenant General Mart de Kruif, and his senior staff interjected themselves into the planning process and persuaded the CENTCOM staff to change the plan. In the end, together, they "came up with the best possible plan that accommodated all participating parties the best."[628] McChrystal's arrival at ISAF headquarters also made waves. He had long maintained a trusted circle of staff officers who travelled with him from assignment to assignment. Upon his arrival in Kabul, he tried to replace the allies who were filling senior staff positions with his team, but he officially could not because they had been negotiated at SHAPE planning conferences. Instead, he excluded them from his planning efforts, which included primarily US officers and a few British officers. The behavior set a damaging tone which was not overcome until Petraeus arrived the next summer. Some of the allies were not sorry to see McChrystal leave.[629]

Despite the disturbances created by successive ISAF commander changes, the surge in troop numbers, material resources, and operational enablers, in combination with the change in operational approach, the execution of operations that were significant orders of magnitude larger than all previous coalition operations, the command structure adjustments, and the doctrinal and training reforms had an impact on the coalition's ability to conduct both combat and noncombat operations. Canadian-led counterinsurgency operations in Kandahar were successful in securing the city in 2009 even before American surge forces arrived or ISAF initiated its reformed civilian-military approach.[630] Overall, coalition forces prevailed in every direct engagement with insurgent forces and usually inflicted devastating losses on the attackers. Even the Afghan National Army did well in major firefights.[631] The commanders on the ground were confident they could beat back the insurgency as troop numbers surged and many of the officers interviewed noted they had an increasingly capable Afghan partner to assist them. As the transition began in 2011, the coalition agreed the intensive partnering efforts were translating into a more effective

ANSF.[632] It expressed confidence in the ANSF ability to take responsibility for security in spring 2012.[633] Positive Afghan public perceptions of the ANSF and security ministries were supported by their increasing operational sophistication. By 2012, in the most contested regions of RC-South and RC-East, the ANSF was able to plan and conduct major operations that integrated military and police forces.[634] The troops on the ground, both Afghan and international, therefore, continued to generate bottom-up cohesion. The improvements in organizational capacity and operational performance sustained political will. The combat and stabilization operations of the troops on the ground were not the only activities ISAF conducted, however.

ISAF's Other Warfare

The apogee of NATO's involvement in Afghanistan was 2011 when the coalition reached fifty members and troop numbers topped out at over 132,000.[635] While the combat activity encompassed in the counterterrorism and counterinsurgency operations received the most attention, the less visible activities were the most important for the long-term security of the Afghan state and ISAF's ability to withdraw on time. By 2011, the coalition's noncombat activities were wide ranging. They included new and expanded missions and activities, with Afghan security forces development and ministerial mentoring the main effort. As such, when ISAF and NATO leaders pressed for additional troop contributions after 2010, they were not looking for more combat forces, but for more trainers and advisers.

Lieutenant General William Caldwell, the first commander of NTM-A/Combined Security Transition Command, oversaw a substantial organizational adaptation effort within his command in 2010 which was oriented on increasing and expanding NTM-A's training, advising, and mentoring activities to support the Afghan surge. This surge encompassed a push to increase both the quantity and the quality of the ANSF. This in turn required more coalition trainers and mentors. As mentioned above, the target goals for the Afghan army and police had increased between 2002 and 2008. They increased again in 2010 and 2011. Since the international community provided all of the funds for Afghan security forces, decisions on end-strength goals for the Afghan army and police had to be negotiated among the donor countries, key international organizations (NATO, United Nations, and European Union), and the Afghan government.[636] The Joint Coordination and Monitoring Board (JCMB), which included representatives from all these entities, was set up in 2006 to oversee and make decisions related to the benchmarks in the Afghanistan Compact and the Afghanistan National Development Strategy.[637] The ANSF was a key element of the security benchmarks. Due to the increasing violence in the conflict and the clear intent of the coalition to withdraw within a few years, the JCMB decided in January 2010 to increase the end-strength goal for the Afghan army to 171,600 and the goal for the police to 134,000 (by October 2011).[638] In June 2011, the JCMB increased the goals again: to 195,000 for the army and 157,000 for the police (by October 2012).[639] To accommodate the expanded Afghan army force structure, the Ministry of Defense activated a sixth Afghan corps, the 215th Corps, in 2010 as RC-Southwest stood up.[640] As a result, Caldwell determined that he needed 5,200 trainers. He attended his first force-generation conference at NATO in February 2010 with a request for the allies and partners to fill his 1,200 trainer shortfall as quickly as possible.[641] Secretary General Rasmussen encapsulated why the trainers were so important: "No trainers, no transition."[642]

NTM-A's collective focus was to help the ministries of defense and interior to build professional, self-sustaining forces. Besides increasing the through-put capacity of ANSF training at the seventy army and police training centers scattered across the country, Caldwell led an effort to reform existing training programs and initiate new ones.[643] Leader development training was improved in the basic army and police courses and NTM-A developed new courses for mid-grade and senior leaders.[644] It expanded the Afghan army's specialty schools and courses from eight to twelve, including intelligence, legal, military police, logistics, transportation, medical, finance, artillery, signal/communications, and personnel/human resources.[645] NTM-A also reformed the police training programs. It instituted internationally recognized programs that were also implemented by the European Police in Afghanistan program, the German Police Project Team, and the other bilateral police training efforts. The new Afghan Uniformed Police recruits attended an eight-week training course before assignment to their police districts. The focus of training shifted from paramilitary tasks which supported counterinsurgency operations to traditional civilian law enforcement functions. As such, they included human-rights training, rule-of-law training, and investigative techniques.[646] As the reformed programs were implemented, the Focused District Development program formally ended in February 2012.[647] ISAF and NTM-A also supported the Afghan Local Police program which had been initiated by the Afghan government and Interior Ministry. Afghan local police members served as "neighborhood watch" elements to improve local security, especially in rural areas. They were trained by the Afghan Uniformed Police and coalition forces conducting village stability operations. NTM-A provided weapons, ammunition, and communications equipment.[648]

NTM-A also undertook activities that were unexpected and unprecedented. It concluded that low literacy was an area it could not ignore. A functional level of literacy was necessary for the long-term viability of the ANSF. So NTM-A initiated an extremely ambitious literacy and numeracy education program. While the Office of Military Cooperation–Afghanistan had started literacy training years before, it had not been mandatory. In 2010, NTM-A noted that about 14 percent of incoming recruits were literate, while among current ANSF members the literacy rate for officers was about 93 percent, for NCOs 35 percent, and for enlisted men about 11 percent. Caldwell therefore decided to make literacy training (in Dari and Pashto) mandatory for all military and police and embedded educational programs in all the training courses. The goal was to ensure members of the ANSF had functional levels of literacy. This would mean all soldiers and police could perform such tasks as read a basic maintenance manual, submit a supply requisition, read their weapon's serial number, write a simple report, and verify they had received the correct pay. Increased literacy would also enable the establishment of durable accountability and logistics programs and serve as the foundation for specialist skills, all of which were critical for self-sustaining security forces.[649] To support the requirement, NTM-A hired over 3,000 Afghan teachers.[650] It also found the literacy programs were hugely popular among young Afghans.[651]

The expanded and reformed training efforts resulted in tangible improvements in recruitment and retention. The ANSF met recruiting goals in 2010 and 2011 and reduced attrition levels, even as it expanded its army and police end-strength goals. By 2011, so many young Afghans were volunteering to serve that NTM-A had to turn away more than 1,000 of them each month because the number of volunteers exceeded the recruiting requirements. As a result, the ANSF met the target of 352,000 army and police forces by October 2012.

Since the beginning of the effort to build the Afghan security forces in 2002, the coalition had been acutely conscious of the ethnic composition of the forces. In particular, it had worked hard to build an army that reflected Afghan society and the relative percentages of the main ethnic groups: Pashtun, Tajik, Hazara, and Uzbek. For years, southern Pashtuns did not volunteer. This changed in 2011, likely as a result of intensive recruiting efforts as well as the security gains achieved in the south. That year, NTM-A noted an increasing trend in southern Pashtun recruitment.[652] It had set the goal of 4 percent of new recruits from this demographic, but it exceeded it with 10.9 percent.[653]

Finally, since NTM-A ultimately wanted to work itself out of its job, it instituted a train-the-trainer program to prepare Afghans to step into the role of trainers.[654] It began to formally turn over responsibility for training to Afghans at army and police training centers in late 2011.[655] The turnover included subsequent evaluation of Afghan instructors and recommendations for improvements.[656] By the end of 2013, Afghans were conducting more than 90 percent of the training and NTM-A was reducing its trainers.[657] In 2014, it turned over the training facilities themselves to the Afghans.[658]

Competent and professional security forces needed competent ministerial oversight and leadership. While ministerial development and mentoring efforts had begun years before, NTM-A expanded the mentoring programs for the ministries of defense and interior. In particular, it significantly increased the number of full-time military advisers/mentors assigned to key personnel in both ministries. Before NTM-A's creation there were eight full-time advisers in the Defense Ministry and a handful in the Interior Ministry (a small number of contractors also worked as full-time advisers). NTM-A increased the Defense Ministry advisers to over one hundred.[659] The Interior Ministry full-time advisers increased to over 200, including bilateral contributions from the European Union, the French Gendarmerie, the Italian Carabinieri, the Dutch Marechaussee, and the German Grenz Polizei.[660] NTM-A also implemented a new training initiative to improve the quality of full-time military advisers. It created an advisers course, since the military officers assigned as advisers received no preparatory training before their deployments to Afghanistan. It identified the expertise and experiences needed for specific positions (for example, the adviser to the minister of interior had to be a military police officer) but it also took into account personalities. Final decisions for the key advisers were based on an assessment of whether they would be a personality fit with the Afghans they would be advising.[661] There was also sensitivity about calling the full-time coalition officers "mentors" since they were younger than their Afghan principals. Many of the Afghans had extensive experience as mujahedin or officers in the Afghan military in the 1980s. But while they had extensive combat experience, they frequently needed help in the institutional and bureaucratic functions of running a ministry or general staff. So the coalition officers publicly called themselves advisers and fulfilled whatever role was needed with their Afghan principals—aide, assistant, liaison, adviser, or in some cases mentors for specific competencies.[662]

In addition, many of the officers assigned to the Combined Security Transition Command–Afghanistan and NTM-A staffs were assigned as part-time advisers. They were expected to fulfill their staff duties within ISAF but also assist their counterparts in the ministries of defense and interior. This often meant they spent little time working with Afghans because their primary duties were too time consuming.[663] Finally, since NTM-A focused the advising/mentoring effort on the strategic-level institutional functions of the ministries, it initiated the Ministry of Defense Advisers program in summer 2010.[664] This program brought in senior level US Department of Defense civilians with unique skills in everything from strategic planning to budgeting. These advisers, who received six weeks of special training before they were assigned within the defense and interior ministries and the Afghan General Staff, numbered almost ninety by late 2011.[665]

The ISAF headquarters and IJC were not involved in the ministerial advising/mentoring efforts, but they did assign coalition officers as liaisons to a wide variety of Afghan ministries. They called this "ministerial outreach." The liaisons served multiple purposes. They were information conduits between ISAF and the ministries and they helped each side understand the intentions and actions of the other. They assisted the capacity-building of the ministries because they gained insights into areas where the ministries needed help. For example, liaison activities included coordinating ISAF airlift to fly ministers out to the provinces and districts and finding funds to equip ministries with computer systems and to make civil servant pay more comparable with the pay received by Afghans working for the international community.[666] Their most important role was facilitating the integration of the Afghan ministries into the ISAF governance and economic development efforts. One liaison, Lieutenant Colonel Eric Shafa, was assigned to a ministry cluster: the ministries of mines, urban development, public works, and energy and water. He stated during the interview he was explicitly given the mission of "connecting" the central government via his ministers to the provinces and districts so that they could listen to villagers, coordinate economic projects, and make the Afghan governmental processes and systems work.[667] Another liaison, Colonel Richard Lacquement, was assigned to the Independent Directorate of Local Governance, where he helped integrate it into IJC's operational planning effort as it updated Operation Omid in 2010. He also facilitated the directorate's governance role in the counterinsurgency operations in Kandahar.[668] The emphasis on ministerial development and outreach in 2009 and later was part of ISAF trying to work itself out of a job. Helping the relevant Afghan ministries to promote security, governance, and economic development on their own, or with minimal international assistance, would facilitate the transition and ISAF's withdrawal.

The overlap of IJC and NTM-A was not limited to the assignment of coalition officers to the Afghan ministries. Even though IJC took over control of the army and police training/mentoring teams, NTM-A still played a support role because it provided funding to them.[669] It also funded and ran the army and police regional training centers, funded and coordinated the building of new infrastructure (bases and barracks) to support the new Afghan units being created to support the Afghan surge, and provided logistical and training support to the Afghan formations once they were assigned to the Afghan army corps (this included such activities as fielding new equipment, paying for fuel, and providing literacy and drivers' training). This NTM-A support was provided through Regional Support Commands that it established in the five regions (north, west, south, east, and capital), mirroring ISAF's regional command structure.[670]

While training and mentoring teams had been embedded in Afghan army and police units since 2003, their roles and functions adapted over time as their assigned Afghan units became more competent. They essentially went from being trainers, coaches, and mentors to being combat advisers and partners. They also served as liaison elements to ISAF forces to coordinate the provision of coalition combat air support, artillery support, or MEDEVAC support to ANSF formations engaged in combat. The training team mission surged after 2009 to keep pace with the increase in ANSF end-strength. ISAF set the hugely ambitious goal of embedding teams throughout the army and police formations. For the Afghan army, it wanted a team in every *kandak*, brigade, and corps, as well as at garrison level. For the Afghan police it wanted teams in every district and province police station and in the Afghan National Civil Order Police and border police *kandaks*. This generated a huge need from the contributing nations. Lieutenant Colonel Dickerson, who coordinated the assignment of all army and police training teams in 2009 and 2010, said that at any one time he was tracking 13,000 coalition troops. It was a hugely complex task, since most teams deployed for only six months, they varied in size (from a dozen to forty members) and nations set caveats on the types of units—such as infantry, artillery, or logistics units—that their troops could train and where their teams could operate.[671] For example, an Albanian-US OMLT assigned in Kabul could not travel outside the city limits even if the combat support battalion it was mentoring was sent outside the city for a mission.[672] A Slovenian OMLT assigned to a combat service support unit in Herat was even more restricted by its government: it could not leave the confines of its base.[673] Despite constant calls by NATO leaders for more national contributions, there were chronic shortfalls in fielded teams.[674] ISAF never met its goals.

The teams were also trying to work themselves out of their jobs, and as such they submitted unit assessment reports to IJC every six to eight weeks.[675] The idea was to bring the units to "capability milestone 1," which meant they could plan, coordinate, and execute operations independently.[676] Once a unit reached this level, the team would be removed. However, ISAF still assigned a small liaison element at brigade level to coordinate ISAF enablers when necessary (close air support, medical support).[677] ISAF initially called these elements military advisory teams and police advisory teams in 2012.[678] But it shifted to the generic term of security force assistance teams by the end of the year.[679] While there were still shortfalls in security force assistance teams as ISAF was withdrawing, there were also a large number of ANSF units that did not need them. For example, ISAF concluded that ninety Afghan army and 356 Afghan police units (*kandaks*, police stations, or headquarters) were fully capable and were in fact operating autonomously in mid-2013.[680]

The noncombat activities of training, advising, and mentoring were complemented by the activities of the PRTs, the initiation of counternarcotics operations, and coordination with a surge in Pakistani army operations in the Federally Administered Tribal Areas and North West Frontier Province. Like the training and advising missions, the PRT mission expanded over time. By 2010, there were twenty-eight PRTs spread across the country (see appendix 4). They varied from eighty to 600 members and engaged in a wide range of activities, since they responded to the conditions within their provinces. The focus of the PRTs also shifted over time since they also wanted to work themselves out of a job.

Besides serving as the primary element in the coalition's economic development efforts, the PRTs complemented the ministerial mentoring efforts by their bottom-up mentoring and facilitation of local governance. They were initially oriented on "quick wins" and "quick impact" projects in a variety of areas: education (building and supplying schools), health (building clinics and hospitals), power generation (micro-hydro and micro-solar projects), agriculture (irrigation and canal projects, assistance to farmers), and rural development (digging wells, building roads and bridges, building police stations and other local administrative buildings). These projects were coordinated with local Afghans: provincial and district leadership and local representatives from the ministries of education, health, agriculture, rural development, public works, etc. The PRTs tried to synchronize these short-term development projects with the longer-term efforts of the UN Assistance Mission in Afghanistan, USAID, and other national and international development agencies. They supported the security operations of the battle groups in their areas by providing humanitarian relief and conducting medical and veterinary assistance activities. Many were involved in police training, some interacted and negotiated with the leaders of rival groups to reduce ethnic and tribal tensions, and some provided election assistance when necessary. Over time, especially as the coalition started to think about withdrawal, the PRTs realized they needed to spend far more time on developing Afghan capacities. They shifted from coordinating and managing development projects themselves to developing the various Afghan players' ability to do it. As such, they worked to connect the villages, districts, and provinces to the agencies of the central government. They also mentored district and provincial Afghan officials on how to create and manage a provincial development plan, build and manage a budget, identify and prioritize projects, solicit funding, and then execute projects.[681] The PRTs played a key role in developing local governance—showing Afghans how provincial and district level governance should work.

Afghanistan was essentially an agrarian society with a massive need for development assistance. PRTs included few civilian agricultural experts, so the United States deployed fifteen agribusiness development teams (ADTs) in RC-South and RC-East from 2008 to 2012. These small teams included twelve to fifteen agriculture subject matter experts who worked in partnership with the PRTs, USAID, and the US Department of Agriculture. They primarily focused on human capital development, mentoring the agriculture extension agents in the districts and the provincial director of agriculture, irrigation, and livestock.[682] The ADTs were an innovative solution to a unique problem and so were another example of learning and adapting.

As IJC stood up and developed ISAF's national civilian-military campaign plan, it also administered more oversight of the PRTs by hosting periodic conferences which included the provincial governors. The IJC commander communicated his overall vision for ISAF operations and issued specific guidance to the PRTs. By late 2010, this guidance was oriented on transition. As a consequence, the PRTs began submitting reports through the regional commands to IJC that assessed Afghan self-sustainability in security, development, and governance. The reports were needed to help make transition decisions and to identify when the PRTs could close down.[683] The goal was to phase out the PRTs as the security transition occurred.

The increased oversight did not inhibit innovation and flexibility among the regions and the PRTs, however. For example, in the west, south, and east, the battle space of the regions was "assigned" to specific battalion or brigade battle groups. The other elements operating in each space—PRTs and OMLT/POMLTs—were subordinate to these battle space owners and they coordinated and synchronized their activities with these combat forces. RC-North was different. For example, according to Ruszin, the Hungarian PRT in Baghlan Province was designated the battle space owner in 2011. Even though the multinational forces in the PRT were prohibited by national caveats from engaging in combat operations, they accompanied the German battle group and the Afghan army and police units in the province on partnered operations and the PRT commander was responsible for coordinating the activities of all the coalition and ANSF elements in counterinsurgency operations.[684] According to Colonel Omsted, Norway took innovation a step further after its PRT was attacked in 2006. It deployed a battle group to Faryab Province which combined with the PRT, creating a hybrid organization. Due to its combined security, development, and governance mission, this Task Force Faryab/PRT Faryab was also a battle space owner. It was the largest PRT in Afghanistan, with 600 members.[685] Germany also created combined battle group/PRT task forces in Kunduz and Feyzabad.[686] As with the ministerial mentors and the OMLT/POMLTs, by 2010–11 the PRTs were increasingly pushing their Afghan partners to take the lead role in local governance and development activities and they began closing down or handing over projects.[687] The first PRT closed in 2011 and the rest closed over the next three years (see appendix 4).

ISAF's involvement in counternarcotics operations, a new mission, was slow and incremental because it was initially perceived as an area where civilian agencies in the international community, with the United Kingdom acting as lead nation, would support the Afghan government. Some allies were also reluctant to get involved. For example, as the ISAF mission expanded across Afghanistan and Germany took responsibility for RC-North, the German government, while acknowledging that opium poppy cultivation was a major problem in Afghanistan, insisted it was a matter for the Afghans to deal with. It therefore limited German military support to logistical assistance.[688]

The Afghan government recognized the narcotics industry threatened the country. As early as 2002 the Afghan Interim Administration banned opium poppy cultivation and began a limited eradication campaign.[689] Karzai's government later took steps to stop the illicit narcotics industry. It ratified relevant UN conventions; criminalized opium cultivation, production, use, and smuggling; created a Ministry of Counter-Narcotics and a special division of counternarcotics police; and implemented eradication programs.[690] At its most fundamental, Afghanistan had to create from the ground up a society governed by the rule of law, with sufficient police forces, and a functioning justice system in order to eliminate the illicit opium economy. It also needed to deal with extreme poverty and give farmers a viable alternative to poppy, with an infrastructure that could support the agricultural sector, including roads, markets, storage, and distribution networks. By 2008, this was all still nascent. In the meantime, the opium economy exploded. According to the United Nations, Afghanistan produced 90 percent of the world's illegal opium by the end of 2007. It represented over half of the country's GDP. The export value of the opiates produced was estimated at $4 billion, about three-quarters of which went to the insurgent coalition, drug traffickers, and "warlords."[691] The Taliban coalition also became much more deeply involved. It not only taxed drug shipments and collaborated with traffickers to provide protection to the shipments and heroin-refining facilities in the areas it controlled, but it also began running its own refineries and created opium storage and distribution networks to support local insurgent commanders.[692] The illicit narcotics industry therefore became an incubator of insurgency, criminal activity, and corruption that affected all levels of Afghan society and its government. As such, it threatened every element of ISAF's comprehensive approach.

Essentially, ISAF could not avoid becoming involved in counternarcotics, especially since the Afghan government repeatedly asked it to do more to help. By early 2008, ISAF was providing indirect support by training and equipping the various police forces and providing intelligence and logistics assistance. ISAF also helped the government explain its counternarcotics policy to the Afghan people by, for example, explicitly stating that ISAF was not involved in eradication.[693] At the April 2008 Summit in Bucharest, the allies declared they would support Afghan-led efforts to tackle the narcotics problem.[694] According to the SACEUR, General Craddock, the summit was a pivotal moment when the Alliance "resolved to play a heightened role in the counternarcotics effort."[695] The decision legitimized counternarcotics operations as a valid military mission.

In September 2008, the North Atlantic Council discussed how NATO could maximize its efforts to support the Afghan government.[696] In October allied leaders agreed to allow ISAF to conduct interdiction operations against facilitators (insurgents and traffickers) and facilities (drug processing labs), in accordance with the law of armed conflict. SACEUR followed up the decision by encouraging all contributing nations to help.[697] ISAF wasted no time implementing this new NATO mandate and by summer 2009 it had made a dent in the illicit narcotics economy by destroying forty-three drug labs, capturing a number of drug traffickers, and seizing thirty-four tons of opium, seven tons of hashish, and fifty-eight tons of precursor chemicals.[698] As with all things ISAF, the governments of contributing nations decided the degree to which their militaries could participate in counternarcotics operations, but even Germany loosened its caveats and by 2008 the Bundeswehr was interdicting opium trade routes to the north.[699] In addition, ISAF headquarters created a new organizational element, the Combined Joint Interagency Task Force-Nexus, to support the regional commands and to facilitate coordination with the Afghan government and the international civilian agencies involved in counternarcotics operations as they worked to dismantle the networks.[700] Overall, achieving progress in combating the narcotics industry was exceedingly difficult. Despite successes in improving Afghan policing capabilities and eradicating opium production in some regions, by 2014, as ISAF was drawing down, the US Defense Department said "the narcotics trade in Afghanistan [remained] large, and insurgent penetration of that market [was] extensive and expanding."[701] This new mission was a strategic failure for the Alliance.

As ISAF surged troops and expanded operations and training, it continued to coordinate with the Pakistani military through multiple venues, such as the Tripartite Commission and its subcommittees, the border coordination centers, and senior leader visits. In December 2009, it also created a new organization, the ISAF Coordination Element in Pakistan (ICE-PAK), located in Islamabad, to enable continuous liaison and coordination at the operational level with the Pakistan army headquarters. According to the officer who created and led this office, Colonel Paul Phillips, ICE-PAK consolidated a variety of coalition liaison officers from ISAF headquarters, US Forces–Afghanistan, RC-South, and RC-East into one office. The element provided information about ISAF operations along the border and it monitored and shared information about cross-border activity in an effort to reduce ISAF-Pakistan military fratricidal incidents.[702] The continuous military coordination became more necessary as Pakistan increased operations on its side of the border after 2008.

As mentioned above, the Tehrik-i-Taliban-i-Pakistan and Tehriq-e-Nifaz-e-Shariat-e-Mohammedi revolted in 2007, causing the Pakistani army to shift to counterinsurgency operations and significantly increase the commitment of army forces into the Federally Administered Tribal Areas and North West Frontier Province. The post-Musharraf government of Prime Minister Yousaf Gilani initially tried to deal with the conflict by negotiating peace settlements with insurgent groups in spring 2008.[703] But the effort failed because the peace agreements were viewed as a display of weakness by the government.[704] The insurgents exploited the safe havens that were granted to them to step up attacks against military and civilian targets in Pakistan. By early 2014, the toll was catastrophic: over 50,000 soldiers and civilians had been killed or injured in insurgent terrorist attacks. As a result, Pakistan surged counterinsurgency operations from 2009 to 2014 and ramped up the scale of its operations. Most notably, it conducted 251 brigade-level operations and two corps-level operations and deployed and maintained 150,000 troops along the border.[705] Many of the operations complemented ISAF operations. Petraeus called ISAF operations on the Afghan side of the border the "anvil" against which Pakistani Taliban forces were driven by Pakistani military operations.[706] To assist coordination of operations on both sides of the border, the IJC hosted periodic campaign planning conferences, beginning in early 2010, that included ISAF, ANSF, and Pakistani military representatives.[707] The new organizations, new operating procedures, and new relationships facilitated operational successes. By early 2014, the Pakistani government controlled 87 percent of the territory of the Federally Administered Tribal Areas and North West Frontier Province. The final remaining insurgent sanctuary and redoubt (for Pakistani insurgent groups, al-Qaeda, and Afghan insurgent groups) was North Waziristan.[708] The army launched an offensive called Operation Zarb-e-Azb (loosely translated as "strike of the Prophet's sword") into this tribal agency on June 15, 2014. By the end of the year, the army had regained control of key towns, including the agency capital of Miranshah, and terrorist attacks across Pakistan had dropped 30 percent. It appeared the various insurgent groups had lost their sanctuary and the Tehrik-i-Taliban-i-Pakistan had fallen apart.[709] Overall, these Pakistani operations and the pressure on the insurgent sanctuaries supported the ISAF transition.

All noncombat activities were oriented on trying to work the coalition out of a job. The shift in emphasis to noncombat efforts in 2011 also manifested the recognition by ISAF that it could not achieve success through fighting. This conflict was not one that international forces could win. An honorable withdrawal in 2014 depended on generating acceptable levels of competence in the Afghan army, Afghan police, and ministries and among key local officials in the districts and provinces. The incremental shifts in the emphasis and activities of NTM-A, the PRTs, and the training and mentoring teams indicated they were constantly learning and adapting as they never gave up trying to achieve coalition objectives. Some efforts were unsuccessful. The narcotics problem was unsolvable for the allies and coordination efforts with the Pakistani army did not eliminate periodic, severely acrimonious strategic and political-level relations. But taken together, these efforts contributed to maintaining coalition cohesion during the transition and withdrawal.

The Transition

By the end of 2009, the allies were starting to think about withdrawal. The Alliance formally announced its transition plan in 2010. Some contributing nations made public statements in 2011 about their proposed timelines for drawing down forces, but ISAF's general drawdown did not start until 2012. In the meantime, the surge in combat operations between 2009 and 2010 stopped the Taliban momentum and provided the opportunity for the shift in the coalition's main effort and the subsequent transition.[710] During McChrystal's command of ISAF, he emphasized the need to fully partner with the Afghan security forces. He believed the ANSF had to start standing on its own feet and stop being dependent on the coalition if it were to assume responsibility for security in the country.[711] Building competent security forces cannot be done overnight, however. Although the decisions to increase the end-strength of the Afghan army and national police in 2010 and 2011 helped to ensure a positive correlation of forces against the insurgents during the transition, the most consequential phase of ANSF development had occurred from 2003 through 2008 when the entire training infrastructure was created and when the training, equipping, and integration of the ANSF forces that fought with the ISAF coalition in 2009–10 occurred. McChrystal and his successors were able to capitalize on their predecessors' efforts when they implemented the shift in operational approach. They had increasingly competent Afghan forces which were ready to start becoming full partners and then leading because they had been repeatedly tested and blooded for years before 2009.

The security transition plan, called Inteqal (Dari and Pashtu for "transition"), depended on these competent ANSF forces. As with all other major decisions related to Afghanistan, the various NATO bodies followed a deliberate decision and planning process for the security transition. In October 2009, the NATO defense ministers set the criteria for subsequent detailed military planning. The idea was that the transition would be gradual and conditions-based. As it occurred, ISAF would assume a supporting role and then progressively thin out its presence.[712] It was also assumed that violence would endure throughout the process; the key was whether ISAF assessed the ANSF as able to handle the violence levels.[713] During winter 2010, NATO military authorities and the ISAF senior civilian representative provided advice on what the security, governance, and economic conditions should be. In April 2010, after consultation with the Afghan government, the NATO foreign ministers, at a ministerial meeting in Tallinn, Estonia, endorsed the proposed criteria and conditions.[714]

Four general areas had to be assessed as decisions were made on which cities, districts, and provinces were ready for transition: the level of violence (can citizens conduct their routine daily activities?); the level of development of local governance (does the rule of law exist and can local officials manage public administration?); the level of socioeconomic development (is it self-sustaining?); and the level of ANSF capabilities.[715] Sources for the required data would be the UN Assistance Mission in Afghanistan, ISAF, the Afghan government, and other key civilian experts and stakeholders.[716] The information was fed to the Joint Afghan NATO Inteqal Board, which was established in July 2010. The new organization was chaired by Ashraf Ghani, the chairman of the Transition Coordination Committee, and cochaired by the ISAF commander and the senior civilian representative. It included key Afghan, NATO, and ISAF stakeholders and a UN special representative. The body was tasked to make assessments and provide recommendations to Karzai and his cabinet, who would make the final decisions and announcements.[717]

In November 2010, the allies announced they were ready to enter the security transition phase at the NATO Summit in Lisbon. The implementation of the transition would be in phases, called tranches, which would occur between 2011 and 2014.[718] In reality, the transition had already quietly begun when NATO announced the Inteqal plan, because Afghan national security forces had taken over full responsibility for Kabul City in August 2008.[719] A number of areas in the south and east were turned over to Afghan control in 2009 and 2010.[720]

ISAF was involved in assessing all of the areas. It was a complex endeavor that required gathering and compiling much data. Information and reports flowed upward from the battle groups, PRTs, and OMLT/ POMLTs to the regional commands, which incorporated relevant civil information (status of rule of law, governance, etc.) from local UN Assistance Mission and USAID representatives and NGOs, and then provided a regional assessment of which provinces, districts, and cities were ready to transition to IJC.[721] A special department in IJC, the Campaign and Transition Assessment Group, then worked with NTM-A to create three interrelated reports on a quarterly basis that it submitted to the ISAF commander: a campaign assessment, a transition and provincial outlook report, and an assessment of ANSF development.[722] In effect, a durable security transition depended on positive developments in the three areas of the reports. A successful civilian-military operational campaign, in which Afghans were increasingly in the lead and operating unilaterally, would create the security conditions needed for sustainable governance and economic development in the districts and provinces, which would be supported over the long term by security forces that were institutionally self-sustaining.

Karzai announced the first transition tranche on March 22, 2011. The actual transition process for each tranche was expected to play out over twelve to eighteen months, but it could go faster based on specific conditions. For example, Bamiyan Province and the city of Mazar-e-Sharif came entirely under Afghan responsibility in July 2011. Karzai announced the second tranche on November 27, 2011.[723] The transition plan was tested to some extent by domestic events in the contributing nations. An attack on French forces that killed four and wounded fifteen soldiers in January 2012 became a presidential election campaign issue and the French government indicated it would withdraw its combat forces before 2014. The president, Nicolas Sarkozy, also proposed that NATO withdraw in 2013.[724] The issue was addressed at the May 2012 Chicago Summit. In the end, the allies agreed they would stick with the overall transition plan and end the ISAF mission in December 2014 as originally planned, but they would also accommodate national troop withdrawal decisions and reposition the remaining forces as needed.[725] For the ISAF coalition, this generated the creation of new coordination processes to accommodate national withdrawal decisions. The withdrawal process required detailed logistical planning and intensive coordination among the ISAF headquarters, IJC, and the regional commands to ensure redeploying forces had the resources and logistical support they needed but also to ensure that ongoing operational activities were not impeded.[726]

As Inteqal got under way and individual nations began indicating their intention to withdraw their combat forces, the ISAF headquarters began to think about the coalition's overall withdrawal. Like the higher-level NATO bodies, the ISAF commander and his staff followed a deliberate process for the drawdown and withdrawal, for it is no easy task to gradually reduce and move 130,000 troops and their associated equipment out of a remote, mountainous country. The ISAF commander hosted the first of a series of political-military planning conferences in early 2012 to begin discussing what ISAF and the coalition should look like in 2014. It included the regional commanders as well as senior leaders from ISAF headquarters, IJC, and NTM-A, and political representatives from the embassies of the contributing nations.[727] Once consensus was established on the vision for 2014, deliberate planning began for an organized, systematic build-down.

The coalition's plans were submitted to Joint Force Command Brunssum for approval by the North Atlantic Council. As combat forces thinned out in the regions and the command transitioned to a training and advisory posture, the staff structures also progressively thinned out and the ISAF headquarters, NTM-A, and IJC folded in on themselves. The major restructuring in 2013 included moving command authority for the Regional Support Commands from NTM-A to the Regional Commands and splitting NTM-A and Combined Security Transition Command–Afghanistan in September, making NTM-A a subordinate command of IJC while integrating Combined Security Transition Command into the ISAF headquarters staff. In July 2014, NTM-A was reduced to a staff directorate within IJC and then in November it was moved into the ISAF headquarters as a training department. In fall 2014, Regional Command-Southwest was subsumed back into Regional Command-South and all of the regional commands were renamed "train, advise, and assist commands." This was in preparation for the follow-on NATO mission. In December 2014, IJC was deactivated shortly before the ISAF mission was formally ended.[728] The remaining elements of the ISAF headquarters were re-flagged the Resolute Support Mission Command on January 1, 2015.[729]

Throughout the security transition process and ISAF's drawdown, the coalition maintained its cohesion. The mutual trust and confidence generated among the forces during the earlier phases of fighting endured, and in some cases expanded to include the Afghan partners.[730] The forces deployed to Afghanistan were proud of their mission. A German officer who commanded troops, Lieutenant Colonel Jürgen Prandtner, went out of his way to emphasize in an interview that his German troops were proud to deploy to Afghanistan and he said the morale of his battle group was very high.[731] Almost all of the officers interviewed stated their tours in Afghanistan were the most satisfying in their careers. The troops also understood that counterinsurgency and stability operations take time. They displayed a level of patience and a sense of the long view that national governments often did not share.[732] Most of the officers interviewed stated they could also see that over time progress was being made. They could see the results of the intensive training, mentoring, and partnering efforts in the increasingly competent Afghan security forces. They believed the improvement would continue if they stuck at it.[733] Lieutenant Colonel Davis was an example of this view. His unit operated in the Spin Boldak region along the border with Pakistan in late 2012. He said the Afghan *kandaks* were "true partners" and stated their counterinsurgency operations were "really just combined operations" in which the Afghans led the operations and did all the talking at the local *shuras*.[734] At one point, Gates commented that, paradoxically, "The closer you get to the fight, the better it looks."[735]

The confidence and security gains achieved by the troops influenced the commanders and other senior leaders, such as Gates and Petraeus, who asked political leaders for time and patience.[736] This in turn influenced political will. For example, Petraeus convinced Obama to give the counterinsurgency operations a little more time to produce results and not to withdraw the US surge forces in summer 2011, as he had originally planned when he announced his surge in December 2009. As a result, the US Marine surge forces withdrew from RC-Southwest in summer 2012. More important, the evolving security situation and the transition process also influenced political will. Insurgent violence and attacks peaked in 2010. They then leveled off and slowly started to decrease. Attacks dropped substantially in 2014 (see fig. 3).

At the same time, the ANSF was increasingly integrated into ISAF operationally and then took over. Through 2008 it had participated

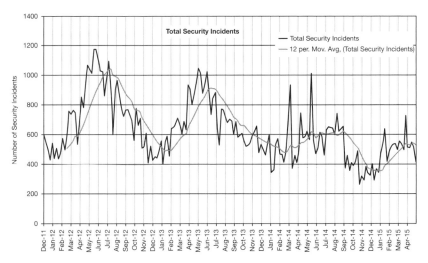

FIGURE 3: Weekly reported security incidents, December 2011–May 2015. Source: Report on Enhancing Security and Stability in Afghanistan, June 2015.

with the coalition. By 2009, it was becoming a full partner, but ISAF was still in the lead for operational planning and execution. In 2010, ANSF started leading some operations. Petraeus reported in his "review of progress" to the White House in October that the ongoing operations in Kandahar were Afghan-led and that 60 percent of the forces were ANSF.[737] By 2011, Afghans started to take responsibility for some planning, and with Inteqal the ANSF began taking full responsibility for security, operating unilaterally and independently in some areas. In 2012, the center of gravity for security shifted from ISAF to the ANSF. By the end of that year, ANSF was unilaterally conducting 80 percent of operations and was leading 85 percent of total operations.[738] As Afghan national security forces assumed security responsibility, IJC relinquished its operational planning role. Operation Omid was superseded by an Afghan campaign plan, published in January 2012, called Operation Naweed (Dari for "good news") which integrated the Afghan army, police, and intelligence services in operations in all the regional commands over the course of 2012 and into 2013.[739] Operation Naweed was further superseded by Operation Oqab (Dari for "eagle") in 2013 as the ANSF shifted to a layered security approach.[740]

The center-of-gravity shift coincided with Karzai's announcements of the third and fourth transition tranches in May and December 2012. With these two phases, twenty-three of the thirty-four provinces entered transition and 87 percent of the population was secured by the ANSF.[741] ISAF forces assumed an enabling role as Afghan forces assumed primary responsibility for security. As a result, coalition members were much less involved in fighting the insurgents and coalition casualty rates dropped precipitously in 2013 and 2014 (see figs. 4 and 5).

The Taliban coalition was aware of the transition plan and it could be argued the insurgents intentionally reduced their violent activities as they waited for ISAF to withdraw. However, this was not how ISAF assessed the situation. Throughout the transition process, the coalition continued to assess that the insurgents were resilient, although they shifted their tactics. The insurgents tried to avoid direct confron-

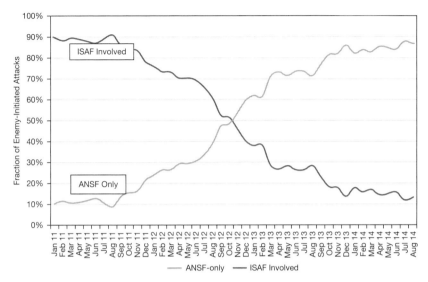

FIGURE 4: Percentage of enemy-initiated attacks involving ANSF and ISAF, January 2011–August 2014. Source: Report on Progress Toward Security and Stability in Afghanistan, October 2014.

tation with the Afghan security forces, relying instead on more IED use, high-profile attacks, and soft-target attacks, such as assassinations and kidnappings. They launched annual campaigns during 2011–13 to regain territory and influence, but they failed. ISAF attributed the declining violence and diminishing Taliban operational capabilities to ANSF capabilities and a continued high operational tempo—major operations actually increased 21 percent in 2012. As the ANSF took over security responsibility, it focused on pushing insurgents out of densely populated areas and it demonstrated the ability to plan and carry out high-level military activities. Operation Kalak Hode V in September 2012 exemplified that capability. The Afghan National Army's 205th Corps led this three-week operation comprised of 11,000 army and police forces in Zabul Province. More important, the operation was logistically supported through Afghan supply channels. The 205th Corps repeated the large-scale operation in Kalak Hode VI in

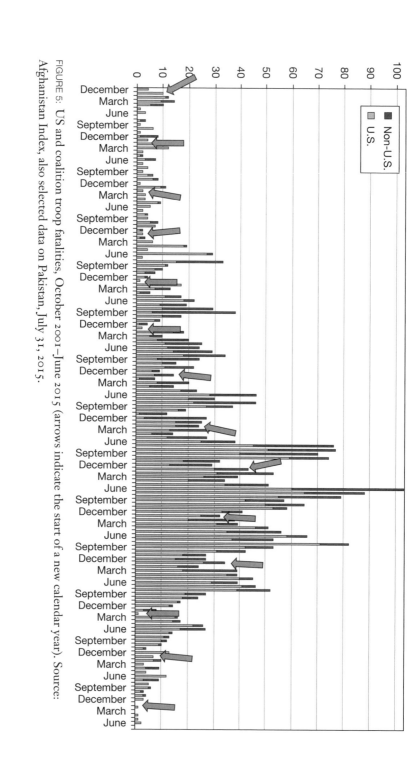

FIGURE 5: US and coalition troop fatalities, October 2001–June 2015 (arrows indicate the start of a new calendar year). Source: Afghanistan Index, also selected data on Pakistan, July 31, 2015.

2013, but in Uruzgan. Afghan-led operations in key provinces in all the regions (including Paktia, Paktika, Ghazni, Khowst, Uruzgan, Kandahar, Helmand, Badghis, Faryab, Balkh, Kunduz, and Baghlan) over the years not only ensured the ANSF maintained security in the areas that transitioned but also substantially improved the security of the large population centers. Kabul became one of the least violent areas of the country. ISAF noted that enemy attacks disproportionately occurred in rural areas.[742]

Regardless of the reason for declining insurgent violence, as ISAF involvement in operations and casualty rates decreased, nations found it politically easier to stick to the transition plan announced at Lisbon in 2010 and reiterated in Chicago in 2012 and to sustain their overall commitment into 2014. In the meantime, troop numbers decreased. In December 2012, ISAF forces numbered 102,011. In December 2013, they numbered 84,271, and by the end of 2014, they numbered 28,360.[743] Even casualty-averse nations did not have to worry about low public support because it was no longer a hot topic in the media. In many countries, Afghanistan fell out of the news headlines as coalition casualty rates dropped.[744] Singapore was the first country to completely withdraw its forces from Afghanistan in June 2013, which was the same month Karzai announced the initiation of the fifth and final transition tranche.[745] Canada was the second country to completely withdraw, leaving in March 2014. The remaining forty-eight participating nations continued to contribute some level of forces until December.[746]

National political will was sustained by the Alliance and ISAF's organizational capacities and the coalition's operational achievements. The practices of consultation and cooperation at the higher strategic and political levels—at the North Atlantic Council, SHAPE, and Joint Force Command Brunssum—provided top-down cohesion. They reflected the norm that had emerged at the tactical level on the battlefield that partners do not precipitously abandon each other. Even when coalition members decided to withdraw forces, from either a specific region or Afghanistan altogether, they announced it in advance and they engaged with NATO's consultation processes and bodies. This strategic-level activity generated subsequent operational-level activity. ISAF was able to conduct deliberate multinational planning to shift other forces to fill the new gaps when necessary. For example, the British repositioning of forces in Helmand was conducted in coordination with the deployment of US surge forces.[747] The collapse of the Dutch coalition government in February 2010 ultimately resulted in the withdrawal of Dutch forces from Uruzgan in RC-South in August that year. However, the ensuing gap was filled by American, Australian, Slovak, and Singaporean forces, including Australia taking over the PRT in Tarin Kowt.[748] The ANSF took over security responsibility for Uruzgan Province in 2012 as part of tranche 3. The Canadian defense minister announced at a security forum in November 2010 that his government was considering whether to extend the combat mission of Canadian forces in Kandahar past 2011.[749] Canada decided to end the mission in summer 2011, but US forces stepped into the combat mission and also took over the PRT in Kandahar.[750] Both the Dutch and Canadian combat forces ultimately stayed longer in Uruzgan and Kandahar than initially intended when they deployed in 2006. The original Dutch mandate was two years, but it was extended an additional two years.[751] The one-year Canadian mandate ultimately turned into five years.[752] The Dutch and Canadian combat unit withdrawals did not mean the countries left Afghanistan. They both shifted their contributions to the training/advising missions. The Dutch contribution ranged between 500 and 200 troops between 2011 and 2014. Canada's contribution ranged between 500 and 1,000.[753]

NATO continued to support ISAF in multiple ways. In June 2009, the foreign ministers agreed to deploy AWACS to Afghanistan to provide air traffic control support to the coalition. The skies of Afghanistan had become increasingly full of civilian and military aircraft and unmanned aerial vehicles (UAVs, commonly called drones) and the country did not have a network of ground-based radars to track them or coordinate their activities. The AWACS did it from the air. This helped ISAF with command and control of a critical area.[754] In addition, to keep up with the demands of the operational and training surges, SHAPE began holding force-generation conferences every six months. It also convened special Afghanistan conferences, chaired by the deputy SACEUR, to focus specifically on meeting the manning requirements for ISAF. The need for NTM-A trainers and OMLT and POMLT teams was so huge and coordinating deployment rotations was so complex that special staff elements in NTM-A and the ISAF Joint Command created matrices to literally track at the individual level what the manning requirements were, which requirements were the most important (which allowed the creation of prioritized lists), which countries were best suited to fill the requirements (which allowed informal discussions and negotiations before and on the sidelines of the conferences), which countries had committed to filling them, and whether—and when—the countries fulfilled the commitments. The staff elements worked very closely, almost on a daily basis, with SHAPE to ensure the leaders at the operational, strategic, and national levels were on the same page.[755] NATO continued to convene annual PRT conferences to harmonize activities and improve civil-military cooperation on the ground. In addition, it introduced special courses at the NATO School in Oberammergau to help prepare deploying PRT members.[756] SHAPE also published an OMLT Concept of Operations which standardized the tasks and functions of the teams and specified how they were to be organized, trained, and equipped.[757] Finally, the Alliance's training and education institutions capitalized on the knowledge gained by officers on their deployments to Afghanistan. It became a normal operating procedure for redeployed officers to prepare and teach courses at the NATO (SHAPE) School in Oberammergau or to provide training to the units undergoing mission rehearsal training at Stavanger, Norway, or Bydgoszcz, Poland.[758] Furthermore, the training centers in Norway and Poland had constant communication with the forces in Afghanistan which enabled them to provide "real world" information on the conditions in the country to deploying forces during their mission rehearsals and other training exercises.[759] Alliance institutions essentially created a continuous feedback loop to the ISAF coalition to facilitate learning, improve training and educational programs, and develop doctrine or standards.

At the operational level, the ISAF commanders continued their efforts to improve ISAF's structural configuration and streamline command and control after 2010. For years, the activities of special forces had remained outside the operational control of OEF and ISAF commanders. Allied and American special forces had what were called "tactical control" relationships with OEF and ISAF which meant CENTCOM and national governments retained overall authority over what the forces did. This was mainly due to the sensitive nature of direct-action operations (which meant high-level national government interest) but it also meant the battle space owners in the regions often did not know special forces were operating in their areas or what they were doing. The decision to give the ISAF commander operational control of the Combined Joint Special Operations Task Force–Afghanistan in 2010 improved the situation because special operations were then better coordinated with the ISAF and regional headquarters, as well as the battle space owners.[760] However, the creation of ISAF SOF meant special forces activities remained disjointed. Ultimately, the elements were incrementally merged as ISAF's combat operations wound down and the transition began. In 2011, ISAF created the deputy commanding general-special operations forces position. This one-star general coordinated and synchronized the activities of the two special operation forces elements.[761] In 2012, the elements were merged into a new element, the NATO Special Operations Component Command–Afghanistan/Special Operations Joint Task Force–Afghanistan (see appendix 1).[762] This final consolidation occurred as Afghan special forces took over the execution of such operations and the allied special forces stepped back into an advise-and-assist role.[763]

The ISAF commanders still had leeway to institute new programs. McChrystal implemented an innovative program called the Afghanistan-Pakistan Hands Program in 2009. The concept was to develop a cadre of several hundred US officers who were trained in language (Dari, Pashto, or Urdu), culture, and history and who then served in repetitive assignments in either Afghanistan or Pakistan, and in the Pentagon. It was thought they would develop and maintain personal relationships with the Afghans and Pakistanis they worked with and that their deeper understanding of the politics and the people of the two countries would improve the coalition's execution of the comprehensive approach, as well as provide insights into the region that would be useful in political and military policy making in the United States. ISAF made good use of the officers as they started arriving in 2010 by assigning them to the ISAF headquarters, ISAF Joint Command, and NTM-A (where many worked ministerial outreach), in the regional commands, in PRTs, and in special forces teams, as well as embedding them into the local governance structures of the districts and provinces. However, the US military services did not establish assignment policies that utilized the officers in follow-on tours where their skills and knowledge could be used.[764] Thus, the American military bureaucracy limited the long-term benefits of a coalition initiative.

Despite ISAF's almost continual efforts to adjust organizational structures and operating procedures, it could not solve all of its problems. One area in particular that could never be solved was intelligence. Many of the contributing nations established their own national intelligence centers in the country and they were often reluctant to share intelligence with others.[765] In addition, due to issues related to the classification levels of intelligence (confidential, secret, and top secret), and release status (that is, some intelligence was United States only, some could be released to NATO countries, and some to non-NATO countries), ISAF couldn't establish one all-encompassing intelligence system that included all the contributing nations and linked together the regional commands, ISAF Joint Command, and the ISAF headquarters. As a result, a patchwork of parallel intelligence networks emerged across the country. Intelligence officers had to develop innovative ways to ensure critical intelligence was provided to the people who needed it, such as operational forces in the field, colleagues in neighboring regional commands, and across the staffs.[766] The coalition therefore had to learn to cope with a less-than-ideal situation in a critical area.

The persistent problems from the strategic to the tactical levels, in combination with the most violent phase of the conflict, 2008–10, could have finally strained cohesion beyond the breaking point had it not been for the political decision by the United States to massively increase troops and material resources and take a leading role. While there were many reasons for national involvement in the coalition, the surge in US resources was the most critical binding agent that held the allies and partners together. This political decision facilitated the decisions of many of the other coalition partners to also increase their forces. For ISAF, the years of experience gained from operating together under difficult conditions and the ability to learn from mistakes generated a multitude of military changes and adaptations once resources started to increase. The surge gave the coalition the means to create new organizational structures, such as ISAF Joint Command, NTM-A, and RC-Southwest, which facilitated realignments in the command and control configuration. The ISAF commander could finally concentrate on strategic issues while the IJC commander concentrated on operational activities. The shift in the command and control of the OMLTs and POMLTs and special forces improved coordination among the security, development, and governance lines of effort within the regions. The surge also enabled new operating procedures, such as embedded partnering and the development of a civilian-military campaign plan coordinated with the Afghans; new training initiatives, such as NTM-A's literacy training; and new missions and programs, such as counternarcotics operations and the District Delivery Program. The wide-ranging changes also enabled a massive expansion in the scale of operations and training. Taken together, they improved the coalition's performance enough to beat back the insurgency and create the time and space necessary to develop Afghan capabilities, all of which sustained political confidence. The incremental improvements in ANSF abilities meant Afghan security forces were ready to take the lead for security responsibility as the transition unfolded and the coalition could conduct an organized drawdown.

During the last few years of ISAF's existence, 2011–14, there were few forces fraying cohesion. Canadian, Dutch, and French decisions to withdraw combat forces before 2014 could have opened the door to a general unraveling of the entire coalition, but they did not. The shift in emphasis to noncombat operations, the progressive assumption of security responsibility by the Afghans during the Inteqal transition, and ISAF's shift to a support role meant the combat pressures were removed and the coalition could conduct an organized withdrawal. In the end, the Taliban coalition did not succeed in either forcing the withdrawal of international forces or overthrowing the Afghan government. Overall, one could say NATO achieved its objective of preventing Afghanistan from regressing back to becoming a safe haven for terrorism while it was engaged in ISAF.

By the time the ISAF mission was winding down in 2013, there were some impressive achievements: five million refugees returned to Afghanistan (the largest refugee return in history), more than eight million children were in school (more than a third of them girls), one in two Afghans had a cell phone, almost all Afghans had access to health care, the Taliban had less than 10 percent support, the majority of Afghans told pollsters they thought their country was on the right track, and Kabul was described as a busy, functioning city.[767] Furthermore, in 2012 a new phenomenon emerged in the rural areas of the east and northeast: independent uprisings of local tribes against the Taliban. This "Andar Awakening" spread to the south, to include Kandahar, in 2013.[768] Political, economic, and security conditions seemed to be on a positive trend.

But will this situation continue over the long term? It was an open question whether ISAF had built enough ANSF capacity for them to hold off the Taliban coalition while the Afghan government worked toward a political settlement. As ANSF assumed responsibility for security during the transition, it could be argued that it was able to hold its own against the insurgents only because it still received assistance from ISAF via the coalition's strategic enablers—particularly intelligence, close air support, transportation, and medical support. However, by 2014, the Afghan air force demonstrated a capacity to plan and execute "air operations including emergency extraction, emergency casualty evacuation, air reconnaissance and troop transport airlift with limited

ISAF support."[769] The ANSF was on its way to developing some of its own enabler capabilities and it was striving to wean itself off ISAF dependence

By the end of 2014, Afghanistan still had major problems and challenges to overcome. They included institutional corruption and a lack of human capital, which weakened administrative capacity from the district to province and capital levels. Endemic criminal activity (such as the narcotics trade) supported by robust illicit networks continued, along with enduring tribal conflicts and tensions. Economic development needs were still massive. Government authority outside Kabul was still weak and regional warlords still too strong. But the peaceful transition of political power in 2014 with the election of President Ashraf Ghani was a positive development, even though the election process was a long, drawn-out affair.[770] By 2014 and into 2015, there were still problems with attrition rates in the Afghan army and police but they showed resilience and generally fought well against the insurgents, so the ANSF seemed to have become a stable national institution.[771] Furthermore, NATO members and partners recognized that the Afghan security forces remained dependent on international assistance and so the Alliance agreed to continue its support after 2014. At the Wales Summit in September 2014, the allies pledged three interrelated lines of engagement: the NATO-led Resolute Support mission to train, advise, and assist the ANSF; the provision of financial assistance to the Afghan security forces through the ANA (Afghan National Army) Trust Fund; and continuing consultation and cooperation through the NATO–Afghanistan Enduring Partnership.[772] The Alliance's involvement in Afghanistan would therefore continue after the completion of the ISAF mission.

CHAPTER 5

Why Cohesion Endured
under Adversity

In March 2014, NATO secretary general Rasmussen stated to a forum at the Brookings Institution that the Alliance's ISAF mission in Afghanistan was "the biggest and most effective coalition in recent history." Bringing together a quarter of the world's countries in the fifty-member coalition, it was "a coalition that only NATO could have gathered and commanded."[773] However, building such a large coalition was not the Alliance's original intention and its ultimate activities were dramatically more ambitious and wide ranging than the initial limited efforts to secure Kabul and assist the transitional Afghan government. Explaining how this happened brings us back to the central question: NATO was not initially involved in military operations in Afghanistan, but this slowly changed. First, the Alliance decided to take over the ISAF mission in Kabul and expanded the mission geographically and operationally. ISAF then surged, followed by an organized withdrawal. Why did this happen and how did ISAF maintain coalition cohesion throughout the campaign in Afghanistan?

While NATO's involvement in Afghanistan was ultimately precipitated by the September 11 terrorist attacks, it was not preordained or guaranteed. The Alliance had to deal with a new and complicated situation in 2001 and it took time to adjust to the new strategic environment. In fact, the initial default position for the allies was not to turn to the Alliance for operations in Afghanistan. A number of factors militated against action. Neither the Taliban government nor the al-Qaeda terrorist organization presented a survival threat to the Alliance and its members. NATO's strategic culture at the time did not envision action so far from NATO territory, as its out-of-area remit was peripheral to Alliance territory, or the execution of such an ambitious regime-change mission. The conception of NATO's security role as expressed in its strategic culture meant the Alliance's organizational capacities were limited. There had been no prior contingency planning to deal with a problem like transnational terrorism and the organization lacked the collective military resources to deploy and sustain combat forces far from allied territory. These organizational capacity limitations influenced national policy positions. The Alliance members lacked the collective political will to generate a decision to undertake combined action by NATO in fall 2001.

However, the dramatic shift in the strategic environment induced the allies to reconsider NATO's role and purpose. As such, the Alliance gradually began to change as it incrementally involved itself in the multinational ISAF coalition. This book argues that the drivers of political will and organizational capacity can be utilized to explain NATO's initial lack of involvement in Afghanistan, its decision to take over command of ISAF, and the coalition's dramatic transformation over time. They can also provide an explanation for the coalition's ability to generate and sustain cohesion in the midst of a conflict that escalated in violence and in the face of multiple forces that frayed cohesion.

In effect, NATO's involvement in Afghanistan and ISAF's transformation was a case of multinational military adaptation. However, developments were not as straightforward as this statement seems to suggest. As Theo Farrell has argued, "There is nothing natural or easy about military adaptation." War is a complex phenomenon and history has shown it is well nigh impossible for the combatants "to anticipate all of the problems they will face in the war." It is not unusual for them to misunderstand the challenges they face or underestimate the amount of resources needed. They can also learn the wrong lessons. Furthermore, since strategic culture frames how a military organization sees itself and sees the world and as such prescribes its range of legitimate actions, it can shape learning and "make some options for military change possible, and others impossible."[774] Nevertheless, the allies made the decision to undertake the ISAF mission in April 2003 after a significant shift in the Alliance's strategic culture—the first major adaptation after 9/11. It was an open-ended, out-of area decision that was unprecedented in the organization's history.

As noted earlier, the decision was based on a perception of the character of the conflict that turned out to be flawed. As the conflict changed ISAF struggled to find the right way to fight it. The coalition had to repeatedly reconsider what it was doing and how it was doing it. In the end, ISAF seemed to demonstrate it was a multinational coalition capable of learning as it successively changed and adapted its organizational structures and operations and incrementally expanded its activities. Furthermore, all of the NATO allies stayed engaged throughout the campaign (cohesion endured) and twenty-two partner nations joined the coalition even as ISAF eventually engaged in a wide range of unanticipated activities that included counterterrorism, counterinsurgency, and counternarcotics operations, as well as training and mentoring activities. This process of change and adaptation was persistently challenged by a multitude of fraying forces that worked to undermine cohesion.

The fact that cohesion endured is surprising. Given the negative historical experiences of alliances and coalitions, the low stakes involved in the war for the allies and partners, the inconclusive nature of the conflict against the Taliban, the fact that today for many European countries war is considered an illegitimate means for resolving international differences, one could argue the ISAF coalition should have fallen apart. The forces fraying cohesion included intra-alliance tensions over burden-sharing; disagreements about what ISAF should do; concerns about US unilateralism; and reluctance to get involved in combat operations or remain engaged over the long term. Also, operational inefficiencies (from restrictive national caveats to resource, training, and doctrinal shortfalls) led to inconclusive tactical operations, which produced a widespread perception the international effort was a failure. However, unexpectedly, the coalition did not fracture and cohesion endured under adversity.

Since NATO is not an autonomous security organization, there must be a convergence in political will among the members in order for action to occur. In this case, the allies eventually reached consensus on the proposal for NATO to take over the ISAF mission. As noted earlier, finding volunteers for the first three ISAF rotations was not easy or straightforward. In the spring of 2003, nations were not eagerly lining up to lead a rotation. However, the allies shared a view of the dangers posed by transnational Islamic terrorism. The sanctuary provided by Afghanistan to Islamic terrorists had facilitated a multitude of attacks in Europe and around the world by al-Qaeda and its affiliates. Combined with the large number of foiled plots and the extensive, interconnected terrorist networks uncovered by European police and security services in almost every country in Western Europe, allied governments understandably concluded that they were under attack. The security threat was potentially real and this was a major influence in generating the Alliance decision. Preventing Afghanistan from reverting back to a safe haven for transnational Islamic terrorists was an objective the allies agreed with, but this would require nation-building, of which ISAF was a key part. Engaging NATO solved the problem of ISAF and it meant the coalition's mission became a collective effort rather than an individual effort.

However, political will was not only based on the assessment of the jihadist threat. Ultimately, political will was derived from a variety of influences. In fact, national reasons to contribute to the coalition, and to stay engaged, eventually seemed to develop into a complex mosaic based on intertwined domestic and Alliance politics. Many countries had more than one reason to contribute. While the mission was seen as legitimate from a moral and humanitarian perspective—it was the right thing to do, especially since Afghanistan had been abandoned after the Soviet-Afghan war—participation in the coalition was also a means to achieve other objectives for both allies and partner nations. For many countries, their reputation in NATO mattered. So they joined the ISAF coalition and then stayed through the tough period because they wanted to be seen as reliable allies. They did not want to be seen as quitters or shirkers. For example, the reasoning for Canada's decision to deploy into Kandahar was articulated by a senior Canadian foreign affairs official who stated, "The decision to go to Kandahar was a collective one . . . We didn't do it because someone in NATO wanted us to do it, or because the Americans made us do it . . . We did it because Afghanistan was a serious issue, we were a serious country . . . and we were determined to behave accordingly."[775] Countries like Canada, Italy, and Spain wanted to be taken seriously as top-tier nations in the international community. NATO aspirants wanted to show their value to the Alliance in order to improve their chances of membership and new members wanted to fulfill the obligations of membership and show they would not be free riders. Some countries joined or stayed out of a desire to improve their relations with the United States or just out of loyalty to America. Loyalty to NATO and to the allies and partners operating together in Afghanistan was widespread. Members of the coalition wanted ISAF to succeed and, more important, they came to believe that ISAF could not afford to be defeated by the insurgent coalition. The credibility of the Alliance was on the line, especially after tens of thousands of troops had been committed and after ISAF had demonstrated it could defeat large, organized Taliban attacks in 2006. Premature withdrawal and defeat after the investment of so much blood and treasure would be taken by the jihadists as a strategic victory against the international community on par with the Soviet-Afghan war and it would lead to worsening instability in the region. The mutually reinforcing reasons for enduring political will, in the face of often acrimonious tensions among the allies and partners, provided a degree of top-down cohesion to the coalition—but they did not prevent many countries from skimping on resources. Most of the countries were reluctant or unable to increase troops and material capabilities as the conflict escalated, which made it much more difficult for the coalition to achieve its operational objectives.

Political will and national commitment were sustained by organizational capacity. The ISAF coalition was deeply multinational, with most units and all major operations comprised of multiple nations. The interweaving of units and specialist capabilities forced the allies to rely on each other. Over time, as the forces gained experience from training and operating together, familiarity, mutual trust, and confidence increased among the coalition partners. As one allied officer said, "It's a matter of professional pride that you deliver success" and the allies and partners "are key" to that. "There's absolutely a bottom-up drive that binds your fighting force . . . From the tactical level, there's absolutely trust in those you fought with for a long time." He acknowledged among the different contributing nations "there are slightly different cultures . . . slightly different ways of doing things, but professionally there is trust. When you're in the fight, when you've got those [other nations] around you, there is absolute trust, there is real glue there. And that drives that binding further up."[776] This tactical- and operational-level bonding generated the norms and practices that partners do not abandon each other, especially in adversity. "The heat of battle" acted as an incubator of cohesion. In addition, NATO's strategic-level consultation and planning bodies developed forums and processes for multinational coordination that reinforced the norm against abandonment. National decisions to increase, withdraw, or reposition forces were announced in advance, which allowed deliberate planning within ISAF to position forces where they were most needed or to fill gaps when necessary. In addition, the coalition's experiences on the ground facilitated its learning.

In general, learning occurred within the coalition, at NATO, and within national militaries as the character of the conflict shifted. Some nations learned faster than others, which ensured that wide gaps in capabilities endured among the partners and allies. This contributed to the persistent tensions over burden-sharing. Nevertheless, military change and adaptation efforts from learning and experience generated new operating procedures and new organizational structures as the coalition slowly expanded its operations from the initial limited stabilization and reconstruction activities centered in Kabul and the PRTs. As the coalition recognized it had a real fight on its hands in 2006, it undertook counterinsurgency operations and expanded its training and advising activities. It also eventually undertook unexpected missions, such as counternarcotics operations. The change and adaptation efforts produced operational results. ISAF forces were successful in every engagement against the Taliban coalition, which helped to sustain political-level confidence in the deployed forces. However, force levels were often only just sufficient in the years between 2006 and 2008 to combat the insurgency and commanders were forced to rely extensively on overwhelming direct and indirect fire support. This resulted in levels of collateral damage that eroded Afghan support. This in turn led senior level commanders to press for more resources and more forces in order to sustain the hard-won gains achieved by the troops and to build on them. This bottom-up pressure sustained cohesion and ultimately influenced national policy, the most visible decision being the US surge which carried the coalition through the transition and withdrawal.

The interaction of political will and organizational capacity went through three phases between 2003 and 2014. The first phase was 2003–05. The convergent political will that generated the allied decision to take over ISAF and then expand its footprint around the country was based on a set of perceptions and assumptions about the conflict. Because violence levels were generally low, the allies perceived the conflict as largely over. Most of the existing violence and combat activity were in the east, but the US-led OEF operation was taking care of it. The ISAF coalition therefore assumed all it had to do was help the Afghans get on their feet and it could do it through stabilization and reconstruction activities that would include securing Kabul, assisting security sector reform activities, and taking over and expanding the number of PRTs in the regions. The mission, therefore, was similar to the peace operations the Alliance had undertaken in Bosnia and Kosovo in that military efforts were meant to provide a safe and secure environment so that political, civil, economic, and reconstructions activities could proceed. What came to be called ISAF's comprehensive approach at the Riga Summit in 2006 had long been practiced in NATO operations in the Balkans where civil and military authorities endeavored to coordinate security, economic, and governance lines of effort. However, despite the massive involvement of governmental and nongovernmental organizations in Afghanistan, the ISAF coalition found it had to engage in nonmilitary lines of effort. This led to an expansion in ISAF's activities that ultimately went far beyond what the Stabilization Force and Kosovo Force had done. In addition, the successive command headquarters rotations in Bosnia and Kosovo gave the Alliance's standing military formations operational experience that was useful for, and was repeated in, ISAF. For ISAF and Afghanistan, therefore, the Alliance seemed to have a well-developed organizational capacity, based on its prior experiences and operations in the Balkans, to take over what seemed to be a relatively straightforward mission. This organizational capacity gave the coalition confidence it could execute the mission and reinforced political will and commitment, thus generating cohesion. However, the perception of the conflict was wrong. Violence levels were low during this period because the Taliban coalition was reconstituting itself in Pakistan. Coalition force levels, in both ISAF and OEF, were insufficient to secure the population. Generation of Afghan security forces, both army and police, was also insufficient to provide security. The ensuing security vacuum throughout the country proved beneficial to the Taliban coalition as it executed its own campaign to return to Afghanistan. Its ability to launch offensive operations in 2006 changed entirely the character of the conflict and put tremendous pressure on the ISAF coalition.

The second phase for the coalition, 2006–08, was thus driven by the Taliban. The uncontested and methodical nature of ISAF's expansion into RC-North and RC-West, in 2004 and 2005, was nothing like what the coalition encountered as it expanded around the rest of the country in 2006. Contrary to coalition expectations that it would carry on with stabilization, reconstruction, and development activities, the allies and partners that deployed into RC-South in 2006 found themselves facing a full-blown conflict against a well-established enemy which meant they could not avoid combat operations as the Taliban coalition launched large organized attacks. The unexpected shift in the character of the conflict caught the ISAF coalition off guard and it spent the next three years trying to catch up. An allied officer who deployed repeatedly into Helmand between 2006 and 2013 described the situation. Members of the British brigade task force that deployed into Helmand as ISAF took over command of RC-South "very rapidly got involved in a pretty serious fight and very rapidly discovered that [they] didn't have the combat power to do what [they] were [going there] to do." They had expected "to bring governance and security" but "it became obvious pretty rapidly . . . that actually they were going to end up fighting." He added, "The fighting was proper infantry rampart, *Zulu Dawn*, stuff. Waves of people coming at us . . . Taliban throwing themselves against the ramparts. Counterinsurgency? Not really. War fighting? Absolutely." The coalition realized it needed to increase force numbers in the region. For the United Kingdom that meant "the subsequent history of 2007, 2008, 2009 [was] then one of build up, build up, build up to the high point of 9,500 soldiers in a small pocket of Helmand Province as the Marines came in." He concluded, "We stumbled into Helmand Province. I think from 2006 right through until about 2009–10 we were just gradually trying to catch an error, make up for what we did. And not until about 2009–10 did we start having the correct force densities, and then we actually start delivering some quite good stuff." As the coalition took over RC-South, the officer also described problems with command and control. He said the British initially established a split command structure. The commander of the brigade task force also served as the national contingent commander. As such, the one-star general established himself in Kabul with ISAF headquarters. The task force headquarters in Lashkar Gah had "a full colonel who was not part of the brigade running the operation. It was a mess, a huge mess." The officer attributed the unusual command structure to the pressures of another theater, Iraq. He said Afghanistan was a compromise because "we did not have the force structure, and the reason we didn't have the force structure going in was because Iraq was still going and the British army can only produce so much."[777] Other allies and partners had similar experiences.

Overall the shock of combat in 2006 shattered the perceptions and assumptions of the allies and partners. It presented an operational crisis to ISAF and a test of political will to national governments. The grind of escalating conflict through 2008 put further pressure on the coalition. This was a critical time when cohesion could have been strained beyond the breaking point, causing the coalition to unravel. Multiple factors contributed to the stress. The ISAF coalition was forced to acknowledge that the character of the conflict had changed—it could not just engage in stabilization and reconstruction. It had to be ready to engage in complex counterinsurgency operations, but its effectiveness was undermined by political decisions regarding national caveats and where governments were willing to deploy their forces. In addition, reluctance to commit significant forces to Afghanistan, in combination with competing international operational demands, meant ISAF never had sufficient resources to achieve its ambitious objectives across the governance, development, and security domains. This increased risk for the coalition, which in turn translated into casualties. The shortfalls in troops and enabling capabilities forced commanders to rely extensively on overwhelming direct and indirect fire support. This in turn resulted in collateral damage that eroded Afghan support. The political and operational stresses produced intense intra-alliance acrimony about burden-sharing as the conflict turned out to be longer, harder, and costlier than expected. Disagreements on the role and purpose of OEF and ISAF and the disjointed nature of their command and control relationships, despite their functional and geographic overlapping, hindered the coherent execution of the comprehensive approach. Furthermore, the decentralized execution of operations within the regions led to short-term tactical gains. This produced frustrations among the forces on the ground and a widespread perception that the international effort was a failure.

The pressures militating *against* cohesion were significant. However, the coalition did not fracture because the pressures militating *for* cohesion outweighed them. ISAF held together due to the interaction of the two drivers. Political will endured and was derived from multiple Alliance and domestic political influences. These included humanitarian and moral aspirations, solidarity in the face of a shared terrorist threat, and the overriding belief that ISAF's defeat by the Taliban would be fatal for NATO as a security institution. As such, national governments incrementally made critical decisions which reduced strategic and operational pressures. Political will was sustained by cautious optimism that ISAF could prevail over the Taliban because the incremental adaptations in organizational capacity at the strategic and operational levels seemed to make the coalition more effective. This top-down cohesion was supported by the bottom-up cohesion produced by bonding at the operational and tactical levels through shared adversity. Moreover, the Taliban were defeated whenever they attacked. Together, the drivers produced continuing cohesion even as the differences in national strategic culture, availability of military resources, and variation in operational competence made knitting together the coalition extremely complex.

Surprisingly, the hard phase of 2006–08 led to further commitments by a number of the allies and partners. ISAF force levels increased from 9,000 in spring 2006 to 51,100 by November 2008. Operationally, ISAF demonstrated it was a learning organization as it fought back, shifted its operational approach, and undertook new missions in training, mentoring, and counterinsurgency. In short, both ISAF and NATO learned and adapted to the changed character of the conflict as NATO got into the game. However, the major shortfall in ISAF's coalition operations was the continued national unwillingness to commit sufficient resources to ensure success, contributing to the "catching-up" nature of its activities. The multiple inefficiencies and weaknesses of the coalition needed to be addressed, but it took until 2009 for further change to occur.

The third phase, 2009–14, developed as the coalition recognized something needed to change. It was in an untenable position as violence continued to escalate. In the course of intensive consultations and strategic reviews at the operational, strategic, and national levels in 2008–09, the allies and partners thought through what changes needed to be made. The change in US administration and the drawdown of forces in Iraq provided the opportunity and the means for significant changes in the ISAF coalition. For domestic political reasons, the new

US administration decided to massively increase troops and material resources and take a leading role. America's decision to assume the preponderance of the operational burden was the most critical binding agent that held the coalition together and ensured cohesion would not be strained beyond the breaking point after 2009. The US surge was accompanied by increases in allied and partner forces and a major effort to generate ANSF forces. For ISAF, the years of experience gained from operating together under difficult conditions and the ability to learn from mistakes generated a multitude of adaptations once resources started to increase. The surges enabled ISAF to fundamentally improve its command and control configuration, overhaul its operating procedures, and expand its activities as the allies and partners agreed to fully merge OEF and ISAF. In addition, the president's announcement that the surge was only temporary and that combat operations would end by 2014 opened the door for the allies and partners to start overtly thinking about withdrawal. Taken together, the national decisions to surge forces, in conjunction with the merging of OEF and ISAF and the creation of the intermediate commands of ISAF Joint Command and NTM-A, finally gave ISAF the capacity to execute a comprehensive civilian-military campaign plan that brought together the counterterrorism, counterinsurgency, stabilization and reconstruction, and training and mentoring efforts in a coherent way. These improvements in the coalition's organizational capacities also gave it the ability to execute operations that were orders of magnitude larger than all previous operations. They produced results—the Taliban were beaten back. The enduring political will reflected in the surge of resources was supported by the coalition's capacity to deliver achievements. This helped carry the coalition through the toughest phase of the fighting, the security transition, the gradual drawdown of forces, and the end of the ISAF mission.

The decisions and changes that occurred during the third phase also meant ISAF had significantly transformed over time. From a small multinational coalition with a limited mission in 2003 that was comprised of a small headquarters (240 personnel), a multinational brigade in Kabul, and an airport task force, it had evolved into a massive multinational coalition by 2009–10 with wide-ranging missions. Its operational command and control structures included a much larger headquarters (2,200 personnel) supported by the ISAF Joint Command and NTM-A (another 1,900 personnel) in Kabul, as well as five regional commands, scores of multinational battle groups in the regions, hundreds of army and police training/mentoring teams, and twenty-eight PRTs. Overall, the military changes and adaptations made by the coalition and by NATO were incremental, occurring as conditions changed and learning occurred. While the overall objective remained the same, the way the coalition went about achieving it changed. This included adjustments to the civil, economic, and military lines of effort; the creation of new organizational structures; the adoption of new missions, new ways of fighting, and new operating procedures; and the creation of new doctrine and new exercise, training, and educational programs.

In the end, the pressures of the conflict and the various fraying forces were not sufficient to fracture the coalition to the point of dissolution due to the combined interaction of political will and organizational capacity which generated and sustained the cohesion necessary to hold everyone together. While there was no overt free riding (all the allies contributed), there was shirking. Many allies contributed just enough to be respectable. This produced the catching-up character of ISAF operations through much of the conflict and meant combat operations were harder for the allies. Still, the unprecedented commitment ultimately led to a fifty-nation coalition working to achieve a hugely ambitious objective in Afghanistan. It could even be argued that given all the negative pressures, the allies and partners stayed engaged much longer than anyone could have expected.

NATO's extensive commitment in Afghanistan does not mean it will continue to undertake this type of mission in the future. The exhaustive effort in Afghanistan may have been a factor in NATO not getting involved in Libya after Operation Unified Protector and the fall of Muammar Gaddhafi's regime or in the disintegrating Middle East in general.

As the ISAF mission concluded, the international security environment continued to evolve. The dangers posed by nonstate actors, transnational Islamic terrorists, failed states, and ungoverned spaces were joined by the reemergence of Russia as a security threat. NATO secretary general Jens Stoltenberg noted in his 2014 *Annual Report* that "Russia has used military force to annex Crimea, destabilise eastern Ukraine, and intimidate its neighbors."[778] Furthermore, it utilized a hybrid form of warfare in Ukraine, integrating proxies, the separatists in eastern Ukraine, and a sophisticated information/propaganda campaign with the deployments of conventional forces to achieve its security interests. This made it harder for NATO (and the European Union) to respond. So while NATO might not be willing to get involved in another state-building operation in North Africa or the Middle East, it cannot revert to a strategy that prepares for defensive conventional war against its former enemy in the event deterrence fails. It will have to continue to adapt if it is to remain useful and relevant to its members. Its history indicates that this is possible.

Appendix 1: Command Structures (OEF and ISAF), 2001–2012

2001

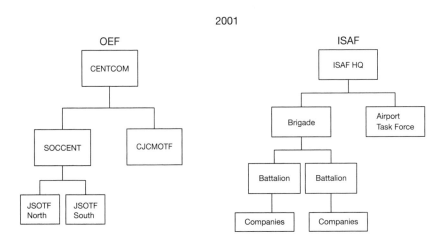

- All diagrams show only the major command structures of OEF and ISAF. They also show overall lines of command and control; they do not distinguish between operational control (OPCON) or tactical control (TACON) relationships.
- The JSOTFs (Joint Special Operations Task Force) conducted combat operations.
- CJCMOTF (Combined Joint Civil-Military Operations Task Force) established December 2001; conducted humanitarian assistance.
- ISAF established December 2001; assisted Afghan Interim Authority; secured Kabul; and facilitated reconstruction.
- SOCCENT means Special Operations Command CENTCOM.

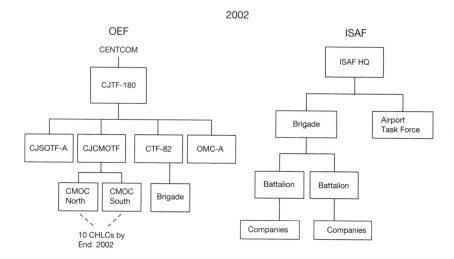

- JSOTF North and South subsumed into CJSOTF-A (Combined Joint Special Operations Task Force–Afghanistan).
- OMC-A (Office of Military Cooperation–Afghanistan) established February 2002; responsible for security sector reform; conducted training and mentoring of Afghan National Army.
- CJTF-180 (Combined Joint Task Force–180) established May 2002; command responsible for security, stabilization, reconstruction, and training.
- CTF-82 (Combined Task Force–82) established summer 2002; conducted security operations.
- CJCMOTF started conducting reconstruction as well as humanitarian assistance via ten CHLCs (Coalition Humanitarian Liaison Cell).
- PRT (Provincial Reconstruction Team) concept proposed to President Karzai fall 2002; plan developed fall 2002.
- December 2002: Afghan government and coalitions agree on goal of creating 70,000 Afghan army and 62,000 Afghan police by 2006.

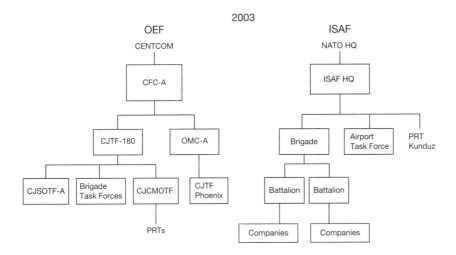

2003

- NATO took over ISAF in August 2003; began expansion by taking over PRT Kunduz in December 2003.
- CJTF Phoenix (Combined Joint Task Force Phoenix) established June 2003; conducted Afghan National Army (ANA) training and mentoring.
- CFC-A (Combined Forces Command–Afghanistan) established October 2003; started conducting counterinsurgency in fall 2003.
- CMOCs (Civil-Military Operations Center) and CHLCs deactivated since PRTs created.
- Afghan Central Corps (201st Corps) activated in Kabul.
- 8 PRTs by end 2003.

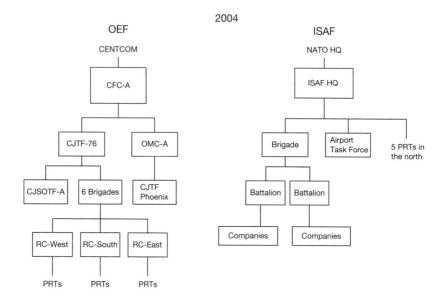

- CJCMOTF deactivated when PRTs came under RC control.
- CJTF-180 renamed CJTF-76 with HQ rotation in April 2004.
- RC-South and RC-East headquarters established May 2004; RC-West established September 2004.
- ISAF expanded into the north by taking over 5 PRTs.
- 19 PRTs by end of 2004.
- Four regional Afghan National Army Corps activated: 203rd in Gardez, 205th in Kandahar, 207th in Herat, and 209th in Mazar-e-Sharif.

2005

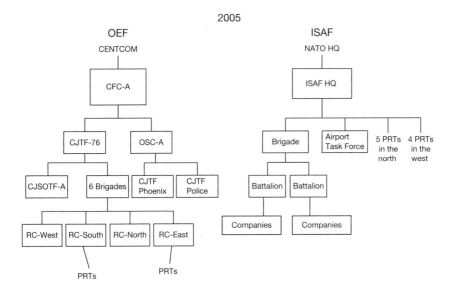

- OMC-A renamed OSC-A (Office of Security Cooperation–Afghanistan) in July 2005 when it started Afghan National Police (ANP) training.
- RC-North established by CJTF-76.
- ISAF expanded into the west by taking over 4 PRTs.
- 23 PRTs by end of 2005.

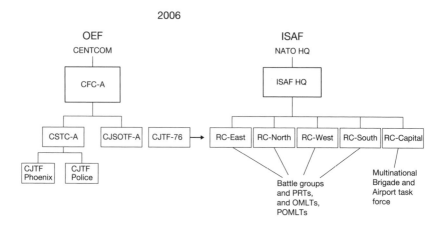

- OSC-A renamed CSTC-A (Combined Security Transition Command–Afghanistan).
- June 2006, Germany took over command of RC-North bringing it into ISAF.
- ISAF expanded into the south (July) and east (October); took over command of RC-South and RC-East; all forces in these regions came under ISAF command; CJTF-76 became RC-East headquarters.
- ISAF established RC-Capital and Italy took over command of RC-West.
- 25 PRTs by end of 2006.

2007

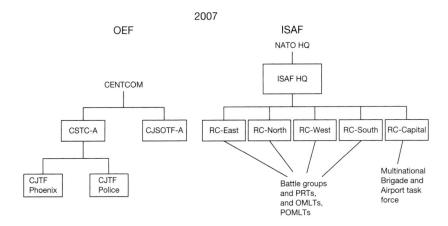

- CFC-A deactivated in January 2007.
- 25 PRTs (no new PRTs in 2007).

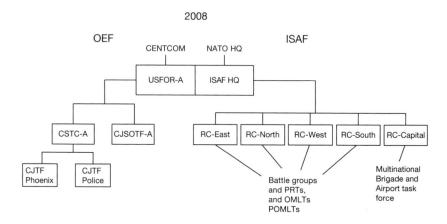

- General McKiernan assumed command of ISAF in June 2008; he also assumed command of USFOR-A (US Forces–Afghanistan) in October 2008.
- USFOR-A established in October 2008.
- 26 PRTs by end of 2008.

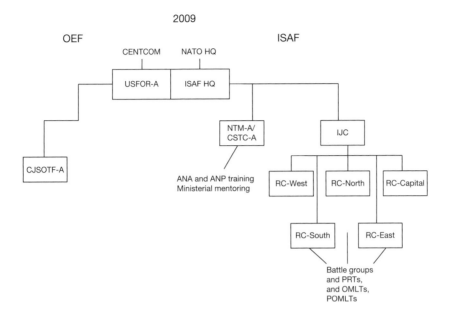

- IJC (ISAF Joint Command) and NTM-A (NATO Training Mission–Afghanistan) established in November 2009.
- CSTC-A merged into NTM-A.
  CJTF Phoenix and CJTF Police deactivated when OMLT/POMLT mission moved to IJC control.
- 26 PRTs (no new PRTs in 2009).

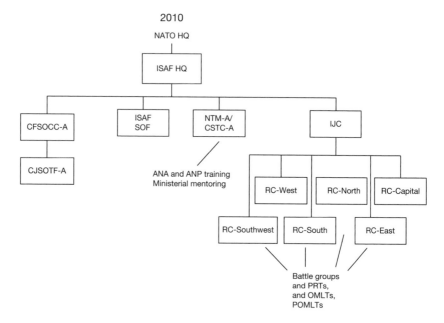

- CJSOTF-A merged into ISAF and subsumed under a new command, CFSOCC-A (Combined Forces Special Operations Component Command–Afghanistan).
- ISAF SOF established.
- RC Southwest established in June 2010.
- 5th regional Afghan National Army Corps, the 215th, activated in Lashkar Gah.
- 28 PRTs by end of 2010.

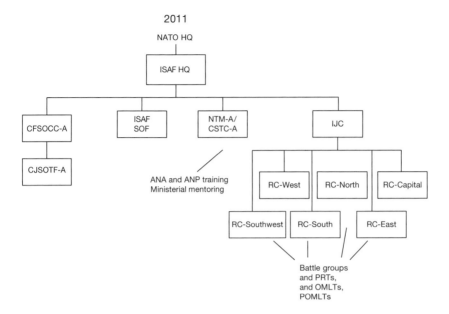

- There were no organizational or mission changes for ISAF in 2011.
- The security transition process (Inteqal) began, whereby Afghan military and police forces took over responsibility for security. The transition process occurred in five phases, each called a tranche.
- Tranche one began in March 2011. All of Bamiyan, Kabul, and Panjshayr provinces came under Afghan control, as well as the cities of Mazar-e-Sharif, Herat, Lashkar Gah, and Mehtar Lam.
- Tranche two began in November 2011. All of the Herat, Nimroz, Sar-e-Pul, Balkh, Samangan, and Takhar provinces transitioned. Portions of Helmand, Daykundi, Ghor, Jowzjan, Wardak, Parwan, Kapisa, Nangarhar, and Badakhshan provinces transitioned.

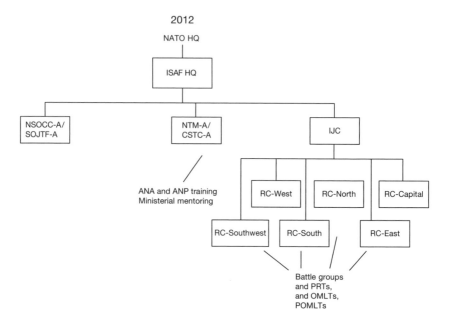

- All special forces elements (CFSOCC-A and ISAF SOF) merged together into a new command, NSOCC-A/SOJTF-A (NATO Special Operation Component Command–Afghanistan/Special Operations Joint Task Force–Afghanistan) in August.

Appendix 2: ISAF Rotations and Commanders

ISAF I	Dec 2001– Jun 2002	UK lead with augmentation	Major General John McColl, UK
ISAF II	Jun 2002– Feb 2003	Turkey lead with augmentation	Major General Hilmi Akin Zorlu, Turkey
ISAF III	Feb 2003– Aug 2003	1 (German/NL) Corps	Lieutenant General Norbert Van Heyst, Germany
ISAF IV	Aug 2003– Feb 2004	Joint Command Center, Heidelberg, with augmentation	Lieutenant General Götz Gliemeroth, Germany
ISAF V	Feb 2004– Aug 2004	Canada lead with augmentation	Lieutenant General Rick Hillier, Canada
ISAF VI	Aug 2004– Feb 2005	Eurocorps	General Jean-Louis Py, France
ISAF VII	Feb 2005– Aug 2005	NATO Rapid Deployable Corps-Turkey	General Ethem Erdagi, Turkey
ISAF VIII	Aug 2005– May 2006	NATO Rapid Deployable Corps-Italy	General Mauro de Vecchio, Italy
ISAF IX	May 2006– Feb 2007	Allied Rapid Reaction Corps (ARRC)	General Sir David Richards, UK
ISAF X & ISAF XI	Feb 2007– Jun 2008	NATO Rapid Deployable Corps-Stettin (first half); Allied Force Command, Heidelberg (second half)	General Dan McNeill, US
ISAF	Jun 2008– Jun 2009	Composite command that included NATO Rapid Deployable Corps-Italy	General David McKiernan, US
ISAF	Jun 2009– Jun 2010	Composite	General Stanley McChrystal, US

ISAF	Jun 2010–Jul 2010	Composite	Lieutenant General Sir Nick Parker, UK
ISAF	Jul 2010–Jul 2011	Composite	General David Petraeus, US
ISAF	Jul 2011–Feb 2013	3 HQ rotations: Allied Force Command, Heidelberg; Eurocorps; Allied Force Command, Madrid	General John Allen, US
ISAF	Feb 2013–Aug 2014	Composite	General John Dunford, US
ISAF	Aug 2014–Dec 2014	Composite	General John Campbell, US

Appendix 3: Coalition Force Levels

April 2002
OEF: 6,500
ISAF: 4,500 (18 nations)

October 2002
OEF: 14,000
ISAF: 5,000 (21 nations)

August 2003
OEF: 11,000
ISAF: 6,100 (31 nations)

June 2004
OEF: 20,000
ISAF: 6,500 (34 nations)

June 2005
OEF: 20,000
ISAF: 8,682 (37 nations)

December 2005
OEF: 18,000
ISAF: 9,000 (37 nations)

Spring 2006
OEF: 19,000
ISAF: 9,000 (37 nations)

September 2006
OEF: 17,000
ISAF: 19,500 (37 nations)

January 2007
OEF: 9,000
ISAF: 35,460 (37 nations)

December 2007
OEF: 8,000
ISAF: 41,741 (39 nations)

February 2008
OEF: 17,000
ISAF: 43,250 (40 nations)

November 2008
OEF: 19,000
ISAF: 51,100 (41 nations)

June 2009
OEF: 24,000
ISAF: 61,130 (42 nations)

February 2010
ISAF: 85,795 (43 nations)
*OEF and ISAF effectively merged

November 2010
ISAF: 130,930 (48 nations)

July 2011
ISAF: 132,457 (48 nations)

December 2011
ISAF: 130,408 (50 nations)

December 2012
ISAF: 102,011 (50 nations)

December 2013
ISAF: 84,271 (49 nations)

November 2014
ISAF: 28,360 (48 nations)

The 50 nations in the ISAF coalition as of December 2011 were:

Albania	Latvia
Armenia	Lithuania
Australia	Luxembourg
Austria	Macedonia
Azerbaijan	Malaysia
Bahrain	Mongolia
Belgium	Montenegro
Bosnia-Herzegovina	Netherlands
Bulgaria	New Zealand
Canada	Norway
Croatia	Poland
Czech Republic	Portugal
Denmark	Republic of Korea
El Salvador	Romania
Estonia	Singapore
Finland	Slovakia
France	Slovenia
Georgia	Spain
Germany	Sweden
Greece	Tonga
Hungary	Turkey
Iceland	Ukraine
Ireland	United Arab Emirates
Italy	United Kingdom
Jordan	United States

Appendix 4: Provincial Reconstruction Teams

PRT	Province	Region & Opening Date	Lead Nation	Contributing Nations
1. Gardez	Paktia	East Jan 2003	US	
2. Bamiyan	Bamiyan	East Mar 2003	US, then New Zealand	Malaysia, US
3. Kunduz	Kunduz and Takhar	North Apr 2003	US, then Germany	Belgium, Hungary, US
4. Mazar-e-Sharif	Balkh, Sar-e-Pol, Samangan, and Jowzjan	North Jul 2003	UK, then Sweden	Denmark, Finland, Romania, Croatia, US
5. Bagram	Kapisa	East Nov 2003	US	Republic of Korea
6. Herat	Herat	West Dec 2003	US, then Italy	France, US
7. Jalalabad	Nangarhar	East Dec 2003	US	
8. Kandahar	Kandahar	South Dec 2003	US, then Canada, then US	US
9. Asadabad	Kunar	East Feb 2004	US	
10. Khowst	Khowst	East Mar 2004	US	
11. Ghazni	Ghazni	East Mar 2004	US, then Poland	Poland, US
12. Qalat	Zabul	South Apr 2004	US	Romania
13. Feyzabad	Badakhshan	North Jul 2004	Germany	Belgium, Czech, Denmark, US

14. Meymaneh	Faryab	North Jul 2004	UK, then Norway	Finland, US, Latvia, Macedonia, Germany, Sweden
15. Lashkar Gah	Helmand	South (west) Sep 2004	US then UK	Denmark, Estonia, US
16. Farah	Farah	West Sep 2004	US	
17. Sharan	Paktika	East Sep 2004	US	
18. Tarin Kowt	Uruzgan	South Sep 2004	US, then Netherlands, then Australia	Australia, Slovakia, US, NL
19. Pol-e-Khomri	Baghlan	North Oct 2004	Netherlands, then Hungary	Croatia, Bulgaria, Albania, US, Montenegro
20. Mehtarlam	Laghman	East Apr 2005	US	
21. Qala-i-Naw	Badghis	West Jul 2005	Spain	US
22. Chaghcharan	Ghowr	West Aug 2005	Lithuania	Croatia, Denmark, Iceland, US
23. Bazarak	Panjshir	East Oct 2005	US	
24. Kala Gush	Nuristan	East Nov 2006	US	
25. Maidan Shar	Wardak	East Nov 2006	Turkey	
26. Pul-e-Alam	Lowgar	East Mar 2008	Czech Republic	US
27. Shibirghan	Jowzjan	North Jul 2010	Turkey	
28. Charikar	Parwan	East Jul 2010	South Korea	

- In 2011, one PRT closed: Bazarak.
- In 2012, five PRTs closed: Bagram, Feyzabad, Jalalabad, Mehtarlam, Meymaneh.
- In 2013, 18 PRTs closed: Asadabad, Bamiyan, Chaghcharan, Charikar, Farah, Gardez, Ghazni, Kala Gush, Kandahar, Khowst, Kunduz, Pol-e-Khomri, Pul-e-Alam, Qala-i-Naw, Qalat, Sharan, Shibirghan, Tarin Kowt.
- In 2014, final four PRTs closed: Herat, Lashkar Gah, Maidan Shar, Mazar-e-Sharif.

Glossary

ANSF: Afghan National Security Forces. These consist of the national armed forces (army and air force) and the national police forces.

DDR: Disarmament, demobilization and reintegration. A UN effort under the auspices of the Afghanistan New Beginnings Program to encourage members of Afghan militias to hand over their weapons, leave their militias, and then join the national armed forces or return to civilian life.

ETT: Embedded training team. Teams of American officers and NCOs embedded in Afghan army units from battalion to garrison level to conduct collective training, advising and mentoring; they also accompanied Afghan army units on actual combat missions.

IJC: ISAF Joint Command. An intermediate command, established in 2009, between the ISAF headquarters and the regional commands that generated overarching civilian-military campaign plans, synchronized the operational activities of combat forces, and provided command and control of the training/mentoring teams and provincial reconstruction teams.

ISAF: International Security Assistance Force. A UN-mandated force, created in December 2001 by UN Security Council Resolution 1386, to assist Afghan authorities to create a secure environment and support the reconstruction of Afghanistan. NATO took command of ISAF in August 2003.

NATO: North Atlantic Treaty Organization. Also referred to as the North Atlantic Alliance, or simply the Alliance.

NTM-A: NATO Training Mission–Afghanistan. An intermediate command, established in 2009, between the ISAF headquarters and the regional commands. Its mission was to help the Afghan ministries of defense and interior build professional, self-sustaining security forces. Its activities included training, mentoring, and operationally supporting the Afghan army and police and mentoring ministry and general staff officials.

OEF: Operation Enduring Freedom. The US-led effort in Afghanistan that began in October 2001; it conducted security, stabilization and reconstruction, and training activities.

OMLT: Operational mentoring and liaison team. The NATO equivalent of American ETTs. They were embedded in Afghan army units from battalion to garrison level to conduct collective training, advising and mentoring; they also accompanied Afghan army units on actual combat missions.

POMLT: Police operational mentoring and liaison team. The NATO name for police training teams; they coached, taught, mentored, and, when necessary, supported the Afghan national police units to which they were partnered.

PRT: Provincial reconstruction team. Teams led by individual ISAF nations that were composed of a mix of military and civilian personnel; their overall mission was to contribute to reconstruction and development efforts. The military component focused on building security sector capacity and increasing stability. The civilian component focused on political, governance, economic, humanitarian, and social aspects.

SACEUR: Supreme Allied Commander Europe. The commander of Allied Command Europe, which was one of the two major military commands in NATO; this person's headquarters is called Supreme Headquarters Allied Powers Europe (SHAPE). Allied Command Europe was transformed into Allied Command Operations in 2003.

Note: Both the OEF and ISAF commands and their operations were "combined" and "joint." Combined (C) means they were multinational; joint (J) means they were multiservice (that is, included army, navy, air force, and marine forces).

NOTES

Chapter 1. Setting the Stage

1. Anders Fogh Rasmussen, "The Secretary General's Annual Report 2011," NATO Public Diplomacy Division, 2012: 8. The Kosovo Force mission began under a UN Security Council mandate (1244) in June 1999 with a force of 50,000 troops. By the start of 2011, the force was 10,000 troops and it was reduced to 5,500 troops in March.

2. Ibid. During its seven years of execution (August 2004–December 2011), NTM-I "trained over 5,200 commissioned and non-commissioned officers of the Iraqi Armed Forces and around 10,000 Iraqi Police."

3. Rasmussen, "The Secretary General's Annual Report 2011," 2.

4. "International Security Assistance Force," ISAF Placemat, December 1, 2011, accessed March 15, 2019, https://www.nato.int/isaf/placemats_archive /2011-12-01-ISAF-Placemat.pdf.

5. Rasmussen, "The Secretary General's Annual Report 2011," 4–6. Also, NATO, "International Security Assistance Force (ISAF): Key Facts and Figures," January 9, 2012, accessed March 15, 2019, http://www.nato.int/isaf/docu/epub /pdf/placemat.pdf.

6. NATO, "Transition to Afghan lead: *Inteqal*," December 2011. Also, NATO, "Mazar after Transition," November 18, 2011, accessed March 15, 2019, http:// www.nato.int/cps/en/natolive/news_81069.htm.

7. Hanson, *A War Like No Other*, 18–19, 291–93.

8. Wedgwood, *The Thirty Years War*, 178, 191, 329, 348, 501–05.

9. Rothenberg, *The Art of Warfare*, 34–58.

10. Nord, *France 1940*, 118–32.

11. Barr, *Eisenhower's Armies*, 1–5, 458–70.

12. Mueller, *Quiet Cataclysm*, 6, 112, 121–26. Sheehan, *Where Have All the Soldiers Gone?* xvi–xvii, 221, 223.

13. Downie, *Learning from Conflict*, 22.

14. Hitchcock, *The Struggle for Europe*, 48.

15. Lord Ismay, *NATO: The First Five Years, 1949–1954*, chap. 1, "Origins of the North Atlantic Treaty," North Atlantic Treaty Organization, 1955.

16. Kaplan, *NATO and the United States*, 4.

17. Hitchcock, *The Struggle for Europe*, 16–18.

18. Judt, *Postwar*, 86, 87, 123, 130–33; Kaplan, *NATO and the United States*, 19–21.

19. Hitchcock, *The Struggle for Europe*, 63, 88–91. Ryan Hendrickson argues that the United Kingdom made the first move to create a permanent transatlantic security alliance. He references a classified 1944 British study that suggested a collective security organization comprised of the United Kingdom, United States, and European allies was in the British long-term interest after the war. Hendrickson, *Diplomacy and War at NATO*, 8–9.

20. Kaplan, *NATO and the United States*, 26–29.

21. Article 3 states the members "separately and jointly, by means of continuous and effective self-help and mutual aid, will maintain and develop their individual and collective capacity to resist armed attack." Article 5 essentially states that an armed attack against any member would be considered an attack on all members and as such they would assist the attacked member and take "such action as [they] deem necessary, including the use of armed force." Article 2 commits the members to "the further development of peaceful and friendly international relations by strengthening their free institutions." It also calls for promoting stability and well-being by seeking "to eliminate conflict in their international economic policies" and encouraging "economic collaboration" among the members. NATO, *NATO Handbook* (Brussels: NATO Office of Information and Press, 2001), 527–28.

22. US Department of State, "North Atlantic Council Communiqué," September 17, 1949.

23. NATO Research Section, *Monograph on "The evolution of NATO political consultation 1949–1962,"* May 2, 1963.

24. Gregory W. Pedlow, ed., *NATO Strategy Documents, 1949–1954* (Brussels: SHAPE Historical Office, 1997), 8–9.

25. Hitchcock, *The Struggle for Europe*, 149.

26. Kaplan, *NATO and the United States*, 42–48, 56–60.

27. Pedlow, *NATO Strategy Documents*, 17–20.

28. Ibid., 15.

29. NATO, "A Short History of NATO," accessed March 15 2019, http://www.nato.int/history/index.html.

30. Kaplan, *NATO and the United States*, 97–98. According to Kaplan, the French government opposed the principle of an integrated military command structure because it infringed on French sovereignty and French political control over French armed forces; France disliked the US prominence in the Alliance; and France opposed a common nuclear policy. The nuclear issue had two facets: the French government insisted on dual-key control arrangements for any NATO nuclear weapons deployed on French soil (which the US refused) and it also wanted an independent nuclear capability (called the *force de frappe*). Ibid., 85–87.

31. NATO, *NATO Handbook* (Brussels, NATO Office of Information and Press, 1995), 176.

32. Kaplan, *NATO and the United States*, 105.

33. NATO, *NATO Handbook* (1995 edition), 182.

34. Ismay, *NATO*, chap. 5, "Counting the Cost."

35. Ismay, *NATO*, chap. 9, "The Increase in Strength."

36. A. W. Deporte noted the changes in threat perceptions during NATO's first forty years. He noted the generally shared high level of fear in the 1940s and 1950s and then the relatively limited reduction and divergence in threat perceptions in the late 1960s through the 1980s; A. W. Deporte, "The First Forty Years," in *NATO in the 1990s*, ed. Sloan, 55–59.

37. Kaplan, *NATO and the United States*, 105–09, 122. The Warsaw Pact was a military alliance created in May 1955 when the Soviet Union, Albania, Bulgaria, Czechoslovakia, East Germany, Hungary, Poland, and Romania signed the Warsaw Treaty. Its impetus was West Germany's membership in NATO. Albania withdrew from the treaty in 1968; Douglas L. Clarke, "The Military Institutions of the Warsaw Pact," *Report on Eastern Europe* 1, no. 49 (December 7, 1990): 28–29.

38. Ismay, *NATO*, chap. 8, "The Annual Review."

39. Kaplan, *NATO Divided, NATO United*, 27, 45, 61–62, 85, 88, 103. Deporte, "The First Forty Years," in *NATO in the 1990s*, ed. Sloan, 55–57, 64, 69.

40. Hendrickson, *Diplomacy and War at NATO*, 16–37.

41. Ferdinand J. M. Feldbrugge, "Gorbachev's Reforms," *NATO Review* 36, no. 6 (December 1988): 16–21; and Ronald Linden, "The Dynamics of Change in Eastern Europe," *Report on Eastern Europe* 1, no. 1 (January 5, 1990): 1–3.

42. Gorbachev announced in a speech to the UN General Assembly on December 7, 1988, that "Freedom of choice is a universal principle. There should be no exceptions." This was widely understood to mean that Moscow would no longer use force against the Soviet satellite states to impose its version of socialism, as it had done previously. Gorbachev reiterated the policy in July 1989 in a speech to the Council of Europe and he told President Bush directly in December 1989 that he would not use force to retain Communist regimes in Eastern Europe; Judt, *Postwar*, 604, 632.

43. Douglas L. Clarke, "Soviet Troop Withdrawals from Eastern Europe," *Report on Eastern Europe* 1, no. 13 (March 30, 1990): 43.

44. Henning Wegener, "The Management of Change: NATO's Anniversary Summit," *NATO Review* 37, no. 3 (June 1989): 2–6.

45. Judt, *Postwar*, 605–27.

46. Hundreds of thousands of Eastern Europeans rushed west as the Iron Curtain disintegrated. Ronald Linden, "Introduction," *Report on Eastern Europe* (December 1, 1989): 1–2; also Barbara Donovan, "East Germany in 1989," and Alfred Reisch, "Hungary in 1989: A Country in Transition," *Report on Eastern Europe* 1, no. 1 (January 5, 1990): 15, 16, 22.

47. Zelikow and Rice, *Germany Unified and Europe Transformed*, viii, 366, 367.

48. Judt, *Postwar*, 646–57.

49. Kjell Engelbrekt, "Redefining National Security in the New Political Environment," *Report on Eastern Europe* 2, no. 30 (July 26, 1991): 4.

50. Michael Alexander, "NATO's Role in a Changing World," *NATO Review* 38, no. 2 (April 1990): 1–2; and Manfred Wörner, "The Atlantic Alliance in the New Era," *NATO Review* 39, no. 1 (February 1991): 5–7. The security concerns were shared by the transitioning countries in Central Europe; Vladimir V. Kusin, "Security Concerns in Central Europe," *Report on Eastern Europe* 2, no. 10 (March 1991): 25–26, 29, 34; and Alfred A. Reisch, "Foreign-policy Reorientation a Success," *Report on Eastern Europe* 2, no. 51/52 (December 20, 1991): 15–16, 18.

51. Manfred Wörner, "NATO Transformed: The Significance of the Rome Summit," *NATO Review* 39, no. 6 (December 1991): 5.

52. NATO, "Declaration of the Heads of State and Government Participating in the Meeting of the North Atlantic Council in Brussels (2–3 March 1988)," *NATO Review* 36, no. 2 (April 1988): 30–31.

53. NATO, "Declaration of the Heads of State and Government Participating in the Meeting of the North Atlantic Council in Brussels, 29–30 May 1989," *NATO Review* 37, no. 3 (June 1989): 28–30.

54. "1989: Malta Summit Ends Cold War," BBC, December 3, 1989.

55. Manfred Wörner, "Final Communiqué," NATO, December 14–15, 1989.

56. NATO, "London Declaration on a Transformed North Atlantic Alliance," *NATO Review* 38, no. 4 (August 1990): 33. A number of multinational formations were created in the 1990s: German-Dutch Corps, Multinational Division Centre, Eurofor, Euromarfor, and Eurocorps; King, *The Transformation of Europe's Armed Forces*, 40–42.

57. Douglas Stuart and William Tow argued that out-of-area debates have been an enduring element in NATO's history. They identified thirty-one major out-of-area disputes that spilled over into the NATO forum between 1949 and 1989. See Stuart and Tow, *The Limits of Alliance*, 3, 8–18.

58. Cogan, *Oldest Allies, Guarded Friends*, 182.

59. Allied Command Operations, "NATO's Operations, 1949–Present," accessed March 15 2019, http://www.aco.nato.int/resources/21/NATO%20 Operations,%201949-Present.pdf.

60. William H. Taft, "European Security: Lessons Learned from the Gulf War," *NATO Review* 39, no. 3 (June 1991): 7–8, 10.

61. NATO, "Rome Declaration on Peace and Cooperation," North Atlantic Council, November 8, 1991.

62. John R. Galvin, "From Immediate Defence Towards Long-Term Stability," *NATO Review* 39, no. 6 (December 1991): 14–17.

63. Kusin, "Security Concerns in Central Europe," 26.

64. Jan B. de Weydenthal, "The Cracow Summit," *Report on Eastern Europe* 2, no. 43 (October 25, 1991): 28.

65. Robert Weaver, "NACC's Five Years of Strengthening Cooperation," *NATO Review* 45, no. 3 (May/June 1997): 24.

66. G. von Moltke, "NATO Takes Up Its New Agenda," *NATO Review* 40, no. 1 (February 1992): 6–7.

67. Weaver, "NACC's Five Years of Strengthening Cooperation," 24. The initial nine members were Bulgaria, Czechoslovakia, Estonia, Hungary, Latvia, Lithuania, Poland, Romania, and the Soviet Union. In March 1992, Armenia, Azerbaijan, Belarus, Kazakhstan, Kyrgyzstan, Moldova, Tajikistan, Turkmenistan, Ukraine, and Uzbekistan joined. In June 1992, Albania and Georgia joined.

68. Ibid., 24–25.

69. John Kriendler, "NATO's Changing Role—Opportunities and Constraints for Peacekeeping," *NATO Review* 41, no. 3 (June 1993): 20–21.

70. Les Aspin, "New Europe, New NATO," *NATO Review* 42, no. 1 (February 1994): 12.

71. Manfred Wörner, "Shaping the Alliance for the Future," *NATO Review* 42, no. 1 (February 1994): 5–6. Richard Vincent, "The Brussels Summit—A Military Perspective," *NATO Review* 42, no. 1 (February 1994): 9.

72. "Partnership for Peace: Framework Document," *NATO Review* 42, no. 1 (February 1994): 29. George A. Joulwan, "NATO's Military Contribution to Partnership for Peace: The Progress and the Challenge," *NATO Review* 43, no. 2 (March 1995): 3–4. PfP requirements further institutionalized some processes the democratizing countries had already undertaken such as appointing civilian defense ministers and adopting defensive doctrines as they began depoliticizing, downsizing, and transforming their Soviet-model armies to institutions that could respond to emerging security challenges and that were subordinate to national political authority.

73. NATO, *NATO Handbook* (Brussels: Public Diplomacy Division, 2006), 196.

74. Joulwan, "NATO's Military Contribution to Partnership for Peace," 3–5; Nick Williams, "Partnership for Peace: Permanent Fixture or Declining Asset?" in *NATO's Transformation*, ed. Gordon, 228.

75. North Atlantic Treaty Organization, "Peace Support Operations in Bosnia and Herzegovina," November 23, 2017, accessed March 15, 2019, http://www.nato.int/cps/en/natolive/topics_52122.htm.

76. Sergio Balanzino, "A Year After Sintra: Achieving Cooperative Security through the EAPC and PfP," *NATO Review* 46, no. 3 (Autumn 1998): 4, 6–7.

77. The Czech Republic, Hungary, and Poland joined in 1999; Bulgaria, Estonia, Latvia, Lithuania, Romania, Slovakia, and Slovenia joined in 2004; and Albania and Croatia joined in 2009.

78. Luthar, ed., *The Land Between*, 508–13.

79. Silber and Little, *Yugoslavia*, 169–74, 190–204; Malcolm, *Bosnia: A Short History*, 230–35.

80. Silber and Little, *Yugoslavia*, 261, 274.

81. Moltke, "NATO Takes Up Its New Agenda," 3–6; and Wörner, "The Atlantic Alliance in the New Era," 8.

82. Silber and Little, *Yugoslavia*, 159.

83. Quoted in Jeffrey Gedmin's testimony before the US Senate, "North Atlantic Relations Talk with the Senate Foreign Relations Committee," March 24, 1999.

84. Kaplan, *NATO Divided, NATO United*, 117.

85. Silber and Little, *Yugoslavia*, 244–52, 258, 276, 303, 319, 335, 364.

86. Colonel S. Nelson Drew, "Post-Cold War American Leadership in NATO," in *NATO and the Changing World Order*, ed. Thompson, 8–9.

87. Kriendler, "NATO's Changing Role," 17–20; and "Statement on 15 July by the Secretary General on Monitoring by NATO Forces of Compliance with the UN Embargo on Serbia and Montenegro," *NATO Review* 40, no. 4 (August 1992): 8; and Allied Command Operations, "NATO's Operations, 1949-Present."

88. Kriendler, "NATO's Changing Role," 16, 19.

89. NATO, *NATO Handbook: 50th Anniversary Edition* (Brussels: Office of Information and Press, 1999), 116–17.

90. Silber and Little, *Yugoslavia*, 366; and Allied Command Operations, "NATO's Operations, 1949–Present."

91. Silber and Little, *Yugoslavia*, 343, 345, 353–56, 366–67.

92. Kriendler, "NATO's Changing Role," 16. The partner nations were Albania, Austria, Bulgaria, Czech Republic, Egypt, Estonia, Finland, Hungary, Jordan, Latvia, Lithuania, Malaysia, Morocco, Poland, Romania, Russia, Sweden, and Ukraine.

93. Gregory L. Schulte, "Bringing Peace to Bosnia and Change to the Alliance," *NATO Review* 45, no. 2 (March 1997): 23.

94. Allied Command Operations, "NATO's Operations, 1949–Present." Some of the troops in the Implementation Force remained in country for the subsequent Stabilization Force mission. The new partners were Argentina, Ireland, Slovakia, and Slovenia.

95. NATO, "Peace Support Operations in Bosnia and Herzegovina," November 23, 2017, accessed March 15, 2019, http://www.nato.int/cps/en/natolive/topics_52122.htm.

96. Leighton Smith, "The Pillars of Peace in Bosnia," *NATO Review* 44, no. 4 (July 1996):12–13.

97. Greg Schulte, "SFOR Continued," *NATO Review* 46, no. 2 (Summer 1998): 27–30.

98. "CIMIC Reconstruction," *NATO Review* 49 (Spring 2001): 21.

99. Milan Andrejevich, "The Yugoslav Army in Kosovo: Unrest Spreads to Macedonia," *Report on Eastern Europe* 1, no. 8 (February 23, 1990): 38.

100. Milan Andrejevich, Patrick Moore, and Duncan M. Perry, "Croatia and Slovenia Declare Their Independence," *Report on Eastern Europe* 2, no. 28 (July 12, 1991): 27; and Milan Andrejevich, "Kosovo: A Precarious Balance

between Stability and Civil War," *Report on Eastern Europe* 2, no. 42 (October 18, 1991): 23, 26–28.

101. Judah, *Kosovo: War and Revenge*, 102–03, 117–20, 128–45, 155–80.

102. Nation, *War in the Balkans*, 228–44.

103. Wesley K. Clark, "When Force Is Necessary: NATO's Military Response to the Kosovo Crisis," *NATO Review* 47, no. 2 (Summer 1999): 15–18.

104. NATO, "Statement on Kosovo Issued at the Ministerial Meeting of the North Atlantic Council Held in Luxembourg on 28 May 1998," *NATO Review* 46, no. 3 (Autumn 1998): D5.

105. NATO, "Statement on Kosovo Issued at the Ministerial Meeting of the North Atlantic Council in Defence Ministers Session, Brussels, 11 June 1998," *NATO Review* 46, no. 3 (Autumn 1998): D12.

106. NATO, "Statement on Kosovo Issued at the Ministerial Meeting of the North Atlantic Council Held in Luxembourg on 28 May 1998," D5; and NATO, "Statement on Kosovo Issued at the Ministerial Meeting of the North Atlantic Council in Defence Ministers Session, Brussels, 11 June 1998," D12.

107. Nation, *War in the Balkans*, 236–37.

108. Clark, "When Force Is Necessary," 15–18.

109. Some, like NATO spokesman Jamie Shea, have argued that NATO undermined its credibility and resolve at the start of the air campaign by ruling out the use of ground forces. It was not until NATO escalated the air campaign and began considering the use of ground forces in May that Milošević decided resistance was futile. See Jamie Shea, "Instant History: Jamie Shea Reflects on Continued Interest in NATO's Kosovo Campaign and Reviews Five Books which Have Already Appeared on the Subject," *NATO Review* 49 (Summer 2001): 21.

110. Clark, "When Force Is Necessary," 18.

111. NATO, *NATO Handbook* (2001 edition), 128.

112. NATO, "NATO's Role in Kosovo," November 29, 2018, accessed March 15, 2019, http://www.nato.int/cps/en/natolive/topics_48818.htm.

113. Klaus Reinhardt, "Commanding KFOR," *NATO Review* 48 (Summer/Autumn 2000): 17–19.

Chapter 2. September 2001–July 2003: NATO Absence

114. A number of scholars have documented the political, economic, and social changes within Afghanistan. Two comprehensive accounts are Ewans, *Afghanistan: A Short History of Its People and Politics*, 110–87; and Barfield, *Afghanistan: A Cultural and Political History*, 164–224.

115. It is estimated that by the end of the 1990s there were some 3.6 million refugees dispersed into camps in Pakistan (2 million), Iran (1.5 million), Russia (20,000), India (17,000) and the Central Asian states (9,000); Kenneth Katzman, "Afghanistan: Current Issues and U.S. Policy," Congressional Research Service,

August 27, 2003, 29. The destruction of traditional tribal structures has been ana-
lyzed by scholars such as Kilcullen, *The Accidental Guerrilla*, 235; also Thomas
H. Johnson and M. Chris Mason, "No Sign until the Burst of Fire: Understanding
the Pakistan-Afghanistan Border," *International Security* 32, no. 4 (Spring 2008):
53–54, 66, 70–71.

116. Tanner, *Afghanistan: A Military History*, 255, 266, 277.

117. This was because the Soviets left behind weapons and equipment they
did not need to cover their withdrawal and because the Soviet government
continued to supply the Najibullah government with food, fuel, ammunition, and
military equipment until 1991. Tanner, *Afghanistan: A Military History*, 271; and
Braithwaite, *Afgantsy: The Russians in Afghanistan*, 296.

118. Katzman, "Afghanistan," 28.

119. Tanner, *Afghanistan: A Military History*, 277–78. Also, Barfield,
Afghanistan, 248–53.

120. Ewans, *Afghanistan: A Short History*, 253–60; Barfield, *Afghanistan: A
Political and Cultural History*, 255–60; and Tanner, *Afghanistan: A Military History*,
279–87.

121. According to USAID, by mid-2001 half of Afghanistan's population lived
in absolute poverty and virtually all of the country's economic infrastructure and
governing institutions were destroyed; USAID Press Office, "USAID Assistance
to Afghanistan 2002–2008," March 27, 2008. The United Nations ranked it 173
out of 178 countries on its Human Development Index, calling it "not just one
of the poorest countries in the world, but [it] also has the worst human development indicators" (human mortality, poverty, illiteracy, disease); UN Development
Program, "Millennium Development Goals in Afghanistan," 2005.

122. Nojumi et al., *After the Taliban*, 198.

123. Ewans, *Afghanistan: A Short History*, 262, 267–68; also Barfield,
Afghanistan: A Political and Cultural History, 261.

124. The group had its origins in the Soviet-Afghan war when Osama bin
Laden and Abdullah Azzam, a Jordanian-Palestinian Muslim Brother, created
the Afghan Service Bureau (MAK) in 1984 to support the foreign mujahedin. It
operated in both Afghanistan and Pakistan. They created al-Qaeda out of it in
1988 as the Soviets began withdrawing from Afghanistan. Bin Laden took over
the organization in 1989 after Azzam was killed. He turned it into a global jihadist front to destroy America and Israel and reestablish the Caliphate by global
jihad. Bin Laden moved the organization to Sudan in December 1991 and began
supporting radical Islamic groups that engaged in guerrilla warfare and terrorism
against apostate Muslim regimes. Al-Qaeda also began attacking the United States
and its allies in 1993. Western pressure forced the organization out of Sudan in
May 1996; Gunaratna, *Inside Al Qaeda*, xxii-xxiii, 14, 24–30, 40.

125. Ibid., 11, 41, 54, 55.

126. Ibid., 54, 78, 82.

127. Gunaratna describes the Wahhabist and Muslim Brotherhood influences on al-Qaeda; Gunaratna, *Inside Al Qaeda*, 22, 24, 26–36. Various scholars have described the Deobandist, Muslim Brotherhood, and Wahhabist influences on the Taliban: Ewans, *Afghanistan: A Short History*, 265; Barfield, *Afghanistan: A Political and Cultural History*, 255–57, 261; and Zeyno Baran, "Radical Islamists in Central Asia," in *Current Trends in Islamist Ideology*, Vol. 2, ed. Hillel Fradkin, Husain Haqqani, and Eric Brown (Washington, DC: Hudson Institute, 2005), 41–42, 47.

128. Bar, *Warrant for Terror*, 105.

129. Shmuel Bar, "The Conflict between Radical Islam and the West" (working paper, submitted for the Herzliya Conference, Lauder School of Government, Diplomacy and Strategy, Institute for Policy and Strategy, Herzliya, January 2007), 4, 6–8, 13, 14.

130. Shmuel Bar and Yair Minzili, "The Zawahiri Letter and the Strategy of al-Qaeda," in *Current Trends in Islamist Ideology*, Vol. 3, ed. Hillel Fradkin, Husain Haqqani, and Eric Brown (Washington, DC: Hudson Institute, 2006), 2, 3, 6, 7.

131. Isby, *Afghanistan, Graveyard of Empires*, 85–86.

132. Kilcullen, *The Accidental Guerrilla*, 235–36.

133. The Durand Line literally cuts Pashtun villages and houses in half. It is also not recognized by the tribes. On the Pakistani side of the line, the Pashtun tribal areas are located in the North West Frontier Province (NWFP), the Federally Administered Tribal Areas (FATA), and Baluchistan. The FATA is unique because it is divided into tribal agencies: Khyber Agency, Orakzai Agency, Kurram Agency, Mohmand Agency, Bajaur Agency, South Waziristan Agency, and North Waziristan Agency. These agencies are not governed by the Pakistani state but are autonomous regions with local administration. This autonomy greatly complicated coalition and Pakistani efforts to combat insurgents and terrorists after 2001 since they established new sanctuaries in the FATA.

134. Goodson, *Afghanistan's Endless War*, 15–16.

135. Gunaratna, *Inside Al Qaeda*, 67.

136. The Article 5 invocation did not become official until October 2. The September NAC declaration stipulated that the attacks against the United States would be regarded as an action covered under Article 5 if it was determined that the attacks were directed from abroad. US officials briefed the NAC on October 2 after which Secretary General Lord Robertson stated, "The facts are clear and compelling. The information presented points conclusively to an Al-Qaeda role in the 11 September attacks . . . and [the attacks] shall therefore be regarded as an action covered by Article 5 of the Washington Treaty." NATO Speeches, "Statement by NATO Secretary General, Lord Robertson," October 2, 2001.

137. The security alliance was formally named the Australia-New Zealand-US (ANZUS) Treaty, but it became a security pact between only Australia and

the United States after New Zealand closed its ports to US nuclear-armed and nuclear-powered ships in 1984. Invocation of the treaty served as the basis for Australia's subsequent participation in the war on terror, which included military contributions to operations in Afghanistan. Information provided by Colonel Shane Gabriel, Australian army (served as the commander of an ISAF battle group battalion in Uruzgan Province, Afghanistan, October 2008–June 2009), interview with author at Carlisle Barracks, PA, April 16, 2013.

138. Luc de Barochez et Philippe Gélie, "Les Quinze légitiment la riposte américaine," *Le Figaro*, September 22, 2001.

139. Barry James and Thomas Fuller, "EU Backs U.S. Drive to Replace Taliban," *International Herald Tribune*, October 20–21, 2001.

140. The eight actions were: intelligence sharing; assisting allies and partners to defend against terrorist attacks; providing increased security for US and allied facilities; backfilling allied assets that deployed to fight terrorism; providing blanket overflight clearances; providing port and airfield access to all allies; deploying naval forces to the eastern Mediterranean; and deploying AWACS to the continental United States.

141. The 1991 Strategic Concept identified fundamental alliance tasks as: dialogue, cooperation, collective defense, and crisis management and conflict prevention, "Rome Declaration on Peace and Cooperation." The 1999 Strategic Concept identified: security, consultation, deterrence and defense, crisis management, and partnership, "The Washington Declaration."

142. Feith, *War and Decision*, 51, 86, 90.

143. Rice, *No Higher Honor*, 79.

144. Nicholas Burns, "NATO: Now More Than Ever" (speech, Aspen Institute, Berlin, November 12, 2001).

145. "NATO Reaffirms Treaty Commitments in Dealing with Terrorist Attacks against the US," September 12, 2001, accessed March 15, 2019, http://www.nato.int/docu/update/2001/0910/e0912a.htm.

146. "Europe Cautious over US Response," BBC, September 17, 2001.

147. George W. Bush, "Presidential Address to a Joint Session of Congress, September 23, 2001," in *We Will Prevail: President George W. Bush on War, Terrorism, and Freedom*, selected and edited by *National Review* (New York: The Continuum International Publishing Group, 2003), 14–15. Dick Cheney, *In My Time*, 330–31. Rumsfeld, *Known and Unknown*, 353–55.

148. Lord Robertson, "NATO After September 11" (speech to the Pilgrims of the United States, New York, January 31, 2002). Also, Osman Yavuzalp, "On the Front Line," *NATO Review* 49 (Winter 2001/02): 24.

149. Brian Knowlton, "U.S. and U.K. Bomb Targets in Afghanistan," *International Herald Tribune*, October 8, 2001. Also, John Vinocur, "Schroeder 'Ready' to Provide Anti-Bioterror Forces," *International Herald Tribune*, October 18, 2001; and "Europe's Foreign Policy: Guess Who Wasn't Coming to Dinner?" *The Economist*, November 10, 2001.

150. Steve Erlanger, "Germany Offers Troops to Help U.S," *International Herald Tribune*, November 7, 2001.

151. Micheletti, *Special Forces in Afghanistan*, 115, 118, 128, 142, 150, 157, 160.

152. Feith, *War and Decision*, 90. Also, personal papers of the author; information from EUCOM Public Affairs background paper, dated April 2002.

153. Myers, *Eyes on the Horizon*, 166, 171, 173.

154. Author experience in coordinating French, Belgian, and Dutch contributions while she served as the country desk officer for France, Belgium, Luxembourg, and the Netherlands at the US European Command (EUCOM), 2001–03.

155. Feith, *War and Decision*, 90–91.

156. Personal papers of the author. Information is from a EUCOM Public Affairs background paper that listed coalition contributions to the war on terrorism through the winter of 2002.

157. Wright, *A Different Kind of War*, 127–28, 136–37.

158. Personal papers of the author. Information is from a EUCOM Public Affairs background paper that listed coalition contributions to the war on terrorism as of April 2002.

159. The assistance was not inconsequential. Belgium volunteered to lead the largest multinational humanitarian assistance mission in history (it included Spain, the Netherlands, and Norway). The mission delivered ninety metric tons of UNIMIX (a high protein food supplement) in a matter of weeks to feed starving children in Afghanistan and 250,000 vaccinations for children. The mission set the standard for follow-on humanitarian assistance missions. Personal papers of the author; information is from a EUCOM Public Affairs background paper dated April 2002.

160. As of spring 2002, twenty-seven nations had sent liaison teams to work at CENTCOM headquarters. Personal papers of the author; information is from a EUCOM Public Affairs background paper dated April 2002.

161. Rice, *No Higher Honor*, 90, 108–9. NATO shared this overall objective and it remained the Alliance's objective through the end of the ISAF mission in 2014; "NATO and Afghanistan," NATO, March 5, 2019.

162. General Richard Myers commented on their relationship: "Political, military, and economic progress . . . You can't ask for just one of those three items to move independently of the others—they have to be linked to advance simultaneously because they are synergistic and build upon and reinforce one another." Myers, *Eyes on the Horizon*, 306. Condoleezza Rice argued a new security concept that linked defense, democracy, and development was needed for a security environment threatened by the combination of failed states and terrorists. Rice, *No Higher Honor*, 148.

163. The international efforts were in a kind of catch-22. Economic and political developments were critical for the long-term viability of a resilient Afghan state, but aid agencies and other governmental and nongovernmental

organizations could not operate in insecure areas. National defense establishments tended to possess a preponderance of national capabilities, so military forces, just as they had in the Balkans, got involved in civil and economic development efforts in the expectation that they could help get the efforts started and then turn them over to others as security took hold.

164. Rice called this an "adopt a ministry" concept in which allied governments (and international institutions) took responsibility for various functions. She also noted that by late 2002 this concept was "already breeding conflict and incoherence." Rice, *No Higher Honor*, 191. Douglas Feith was blunter, declaring the lead nation strategy was a failure; Feith, *War and Decision*, 154. Examples of civilian coalitions were the three diplomatic coalitions represented by UNSCR 1368, EU statements, and NATO's Article 5 declaration, as well as the coalition to freeze terrorist financing and the coalition for reconstruction and development.

165. Taylor, *Global Financial Warriors*, 37.

166. Rice, *No Higher Honor*, 109. Also, Government of Afghanistan, "Government—Afghan Bonn Agreement: Agreement on Provisional Arrangements in Afghanistan Pending the Re-establishment of Permanent Government Institutions."

167. Bush, *Decision Points*, 207.

168. Wright, *A Different Kind of War*, 42–43, 131. President Bush also commented in his memoir that he did not want the coalition to repeat past mistakes or be perceived as occupiers. However, he also admitted force levels were too low: "But in retrospect, our rapid success with low troop levels created false comfort, and our desire to maintain a light military footprint left us short of the resources we needed. It would take several years for these shortcomings to become clear." Bush, *Decision Points*, 207.

169. Peter W. Rodman, "Post-Conflict Afghanistan," statement by the assistant secretary of defense of international security affairs before the Senate Foreign Relations Committee, February 12, 2003.

170. Wright, *A Different Kind of War*, 238–39. Also, Sherwood McGinnis, US State Department (served as the political adviser of the US mission to NATO, Brussels, Belgium, August 2004 to mid-2006 and as political adviser of the commander of ISAF, Kabul, Afghanistan, June 2008 to July 2009), interview with author at Carlisle Barracks, PA, April 2, 2013.

171. Wright, *A Different Kind of War*, 181–84, 200–01.

172. Rodman, "Post-Conflict Afghanistan."

173. Wright, *A Different Kind of War*, 184–86, 211. The major named operations after *Anaconda*, conducted by US, Australian, British, Canadian, Romanian, and Afghan forces, were: *Operation Mountain Lion* (April–July 2002), *Operation Mountain Sweep* (August 2002), *Operation Alamo Sweep* (September 2002),

Operation Village Search (October 2002), *Operation Mongoose* (January 2003), *Operation Viper* (February 2003), and *Operation Valiant Strike* (March 2003).

174. Ibid., 211.

175. Ibid., 216.

176. Taylor, *Global Financial Warriors*, 33. The United States was as slow and unreliable as the other aid donors when it came to honoring its commitments. For example, it took more than a year for the United States to start work on the ring road due to a variety of procedural and bureaucratic delays; Jeanne Cummings, "Bush Learns from Afghanistan," *Wall Street Journal Europe*, April 14, 2003.

177. Wright, *A Different Kind of War*, 193–95, 197, 223.

178. Ibid., 226–27.

179. Mark Burton, "New Zealand to Lead Provincial Reconstruction Team in Afghanistan," New Zealand Minister of Defence, July 7, 2003, accessed March 16, 2019, http://www.beehive.govt.nz/node/17264.

180. Information from interviews of officers who led PRTs, including Lieutenant Colonel Mindaugas Steponavicius, Lithuanian army (served as the chief of staff of a multinational Provincial Reconstruction Team in Chaghcharan, Regional Command-West, ISAF, Afghanistan, May–October 2006), interview with author at Carlisle Barracks, PA, January 31, 2014; and author interview at Carlisle Barracks, PA, with Officer A (who served in a Provincial Reconstruction Team in Afghanistan), December 27, 2012.

181. Rodman, "Post-Conflict Afghanistan."

182. Wright, *A Different Kind of War*, 198–99, 229.

183. Lieutenant Colonel Mark Holler, US Army (served as the G3 battle captain in Headquarters, CJTF-180, Bagram, Afghanistan, May–November 2002, and also served as a brigade operations officer of a combat unit in Regional-Command East, ISAF, Afghanistan, January 2007–January 2008), interview with author at Carlisle Barracks, PA, November 15, 2013.

184. Wright, *A Different Kind of War*, 200–01, 230.

185. Afghan Bonn Agreement.

186. Afghanistan's New Beginnings Programme (ANPB).

187. Wright, *A Different Kind of War*, 213, 217.

188. Karl Eikenberry, interview; Brooks, ed., *Eyewitness to War*, 17–18.

189. Wright, *A Different Kind of War*, 231–33.

190. Burke, *The 9/11 Wars*, 303. Also, Bergen, *The Longest War*, 248, 253.

191. Johnson and Mason, "No Sign until the Burst of Fire," 41–42, 55, 59.

192. Burke, *The 9/11 Wars*, 303. One scholar called the Quetta Shura "a national umbrella insurgent movement." Jeffrey Dressler, "The Afghan Insurgent Group That Will Not Negotiate," *Atlantic*, October 2010.

193. Personal papers of the author; information is from a briefing given by Jeffrey Dressler, an analyst at the Institute for the Study of War, entitled "Afghanistan's Insurgent Groups," to students at the US Army War College on January 27, 2011.

194. Wright, *A Different Kind of War*, 228, 239–40. Also, Crews and Tarzi, *The Taliban and the Crisis of Afghanistan*, 283–84.

195. According to RAND Corp. scholars, there were ten attacks of all kinds in the first quarter of 2002, thirty attacks in the fourth quarter of 2002, and nearly forty in the fourth quarter of 2003; Wright, *A Different Kind of War*, 240.

196. Burke, *The 9/11 Wars*, 304, 308–10. Also, Giustozzi, *Koran, Kalashnikov, and Laptop*, 99.

197. Crews and Tarzi, *The Taliban and the Crisis of Afghanistan*, 275, 292.

198. Giustozzi, *Koran, Kalashnikov, and Laptop*, 99; and Burke, *The 9/11 Wars*, 308–10.

199. Al-Qaeda actions were based on Islamic jurisprudence as expressed in modern fatwas by radical clerics. They sanction suicide bombing, mutilation of dead bodies, the killing of noncombatant women, children, and the elderly, and the use of weapons of mass destruction. Shmuel Bar, "Jihad Ideology in Light of Contemporary Fatwas," research monograph, Hudson Institute, Washington, DC, August, 2006, 1, 10–15.

200. NATO, "NATO's Response to Terrorism," news release, December 6, 2001; NATO, "Statement on Combating Terrorism: Adapting the Alliance's Defence Capabilities," news release, December 18, 2001.

201. Gunaratna, *Inside Al Qaeda*, 7, 8.

202. US Department of State, "Country Reports on Terrorism." Also, Emerson, *Jihad Incorporated*, 133, 138, 145–48.

203. Bush, *Decision Points*, 205, 207.

204. Judy Dempsey, "Britain Explores Peacekeeping Role for NATO in Afghanistan," *Financial Times*, March 13, 2002.

205. Alan Sipress, "Turkey Ready to Lead Afghan Peacekeeping Force," *Washington Post*, December 6, 2001.

206. Sean Rayment, "1,000 British Troops to Spearhead Security Role," *The Telegraph*, December 16, 2001.

207. NATO, "History, ISAF—International Security Assistance Force." Also, United Nations Security Council, "Resolution 1386 (2001)," December 20, 2001.

208. Michael Smith, "Turks Plan to Take Over from British," *The Telegraph*, January 3, 2002.

209. "Afghanistan: Turkey Agrees to Take ISAF Command," *IRIN News*, May 1, 2002.

210. "Germans, Dutch Will Take Over Afghan Security Force: Turkey Will Turn Over Command in February '03," *Stars and Stripes*, December 4, 2002.

211. Personal papers of the author; information is from an email dated January 15, 2003, sent to the author from the US Army attaché in The Hague. The email contained an English translation of an article published in the Dutch newspaper *Algemeen Dagblad*. The English translation of the article's title was "US guarantees the safety of Dutch troops in Kabul."

212. Both NATO and partner nations contributed forces to these first three ISAF rotations: eighteen nations in ISAF I (twelve NATO and six partners), twenty-one nations in ISAF II (ten NATO and eleven partners), and twenty-eight nations in ISAF III (thirteen NATO and fifteen partners).

213. Diego A. Ruiz Palmer, "The Road to Kabul," *NATO Review*, June 1, 2003.

214. "Rebuilding Afghanistan; The War against terrorism," *The Economist*, June 8, 2002.

215. "The Invisible Enemy; Afghanistan," *The Economist*, May 18, 2002.

216. Wright, *A Different Kind of War*, 237.

217. Burke, *The 9/11 Wars*, 78.

218. "Stand by Me; America and Afghanistan," *The Economist*, April 20, 2002; "Special Report: So Much Done, So Far to Go—Afghanistan," *The Economist*, June 8, 2002; "How to rebuild a country; Afghanistan," *The Economist*, August 31, 2002.

219. "Stand by Me; America and Afghanistan," *The Economist*; Also, "Unhappy New Year; Afghanistan," *The Economist*, March 23, 2002; "Special Report: So Much Done, So Far to Go," *The Economist*; and "How to rebuild a country," *The Economist*.

220. "Securing the Peace; Afghanistan," *The Economist*, September 14, 2002.

221. "Insecure; Afghanistan," *The Economist*, September 14, 2002.

222. Palmer, "The Road to Kabul."

223. Colonel Phil Evans, US Army (served as chief of operations, Joint Operations Center, HQ ISAF, Kabul, Afghanistan, August 2003–February 2004; he was otherwise assigned to NATO's third tier headquarters in Heidelberg, 2001–05, and helped coordinate the first deployment of a NATO headquarters to Afghanistan after the Alliance took over responsibility for ISAF), interview with author at Carlisle Barracks, PA, December 27, 2012.

224. Dick Cheney, *In My Time*, 372.

225. "Special Report: The Future of NATO; A Moment of Truth," *The Economist*, May 4, 2002.

226. Personal papers of the author; information is from a May 14, 2002, cable from the American embassy in Reykjavik which quotes the text of the final communiqué from the May 14 North Atlantic Council Ministerial meeting in Reykjavik, Iceland.

227. "Special Report: Europe and America; Old Friends and New," *The Economist*, June 1, 2002.

228. Andrew Vallance, "A Radically New Command Structure for NATO," *NATO Review*, September 1, 2003.

229. Palmer, "The Road to Kabul."

230. Robertson, "NATO After September 11." Also, Gregory Piatt, "NATO's Robertson: 'We must adapt.' Sept. 11 Showed Alliance Members that Defense

Budgets Have to Rise, Militaries Must Be Faster, Lighter," *Stars and Stripes*, December 30, 2001.

231. Edgar Buckley, "Attainable Targets," *NATO Review*, September 1, 2002.

232. Michelle MacAfee and Bruce Cheadle, "Afghanistan Decision Changed NATO: Robertson," *St. John's Telegram (Newfoundland)*, May 7, 2003.

233. Denis Staunton, "Aznar Keen to Ensure EU Toes the US Security Line," *Irish Times*, February 5, 2002.

234. Paul Gallis, "The NATO Summit at Prague, 2002," Congressional Research Service, March 1, 2005, 3.

235. Lord Robertson, "Remarks at the Atlantic Council's Salute to the New NATO," May 5, 2003.

236. The January letter was signed by Czech Republic, Denmark, Hungary, Italy, Poland, Portugal, Spain, and United Kingdom. The February letter was signed by Albania, Bulgaria, Croatia, Estonia, Latvia, Lithuania, Macedonia, Romania, Slovakia, and Slovenia. Mark Champion, "Eight European Leaders Sign Letter Backing U.S.," *Wall Street Journal Europe*, January 30, 2003; and "'New Europe' backs EU on Iraq," BBC, February 19, 2003.

237. "Outrage at 'Old Europe' Remarks," BBC, January 23, 2003.

238. "Chirac Upsets East Europe by Telling It to 'Shut Up' on Iraq," *New York Times*, February 18, 2003.

239. Myers, *Eyes on the Horizon*, 240.

240. NATO, "Introduction by NATO Secretary General, Lord Robertson at the Extraordinary Meeting of the Council with the Participation of Bulgaria, Estonia, Latvia, Lithuania, Romania, Slovakia and Slovenia," March 26, 2003.

241. Lansford and Tashev, eds., *Old Europe, New Europe*, 159, 270, 273. Also, Radek Sikorski, "Bush in Krakow, Among True Allies," *Wall Street Journal Europe*, May 30–June 1, 2003.

242. "No Volunteers Yet for Next Afghan Peacekeeping Mission: ISAF Commander," Agence France Presse, April 8, 2003.

243. Sherwood McGinnis, US State Department. Also, NATO, "Press Statement by NATO Secretary General, Lord Robertson: Following the Meeting of the North Atlantic Council at the Level of Foreign Ministers," April 3, 2003. Guy Chazan, "U.S., Turkey Move to Fix Breach," *Wall Street Journal Europe*, April 3, 2003. Christopher Rhoads and Ian Johnson, "Schröder Backs Ouster of Hussein from Iraq: Chancellor Shifts Stance on War in Attempt to Mend Fences in Europe, with U.S.," *Wall Street Journal Europe*, April 4–6, 2003. "MM. Chirac et Bush renouent le dialogue," *Le Monde*, April 15, 2003.

244. Colonel Phil Evans, US Army.

245. "Paris Spring," *Wall Street Journal Europe*, April 17–20, 2003.

246. NATO spokesman Yves Brodeur, press briefing, Brussels, April 16, 2003.

247. Ibid.

248. Palmer, "The Road to Kabul."

249. Wright, *A Different Kind of War*, 182.

250. Eikenberry interview, *Eyewitness to War*, Vol. 3, 36–37.

251. The detachment was called the European Participating Air Forces (EPAF) detachment; J. A. C. Lewis and Joris Janssen Lok, "French Mirages Hand Over Afghanistan Duties," *Jane's Defence Weekly*, October 9, 2002.

252. "Americans in a Strange Land; A New Force in Central Asia," *The Economist*, May 4, 2002.

253. "Chirac: He Sees New Initiatives as Opportunity for Mideast," *International Herald Tribune*, March 20, 2002.

254. "Unhappy New Year," *The Economist*.

255. Luc de Barochez, "Les Quinze en vedette américaines à Gand," *Le Figaro*, October 19, 2001.

256. Luc de Barochez, "Chirac renouvelle son soutien à Bush," *Le Figaro*, November 7, 2001.

257. "Special Report: The Future of NATO." Also, Lansford and Tashev, eds., *Old Europe, New Europe*, 144, 150, 155, 164, 182, 205, 212, 215, 221, 224, 228–29, 244–45, 259, 266–68. Also, Forsberg and Herd, *Divided West*, 71–72.

258. Katzman, "Afghanistan," 12–14.

259. "Not a Dress Rehearsal; Afghanistan," *The Economist*, August 16, 2003.

260. "The Rebirth of a Nation; Afghanistan," *The Economist*, January 11, 2003.

261. "Not a Dress Rehearsal," *The Economist*.

262. Ibid.

263. "The Rebirth of a Nation," *The Economist*.

264. "Not a Dress Rehearsal," *The Economist*.

265. "The Emir of the West; Afghanistan," *The Economist*, July 19, 2003.

266. Ibid. Also, Burke, *The 9/11 Wars*, 306.

267. "Not a Dress Rehearsal," *The Economist*.

268. Wright, *A Different Kind of War*, 261.

269. "It's Not Awful Everywhere; Afghanistan," *The Economist*, July 5, 2003.

Chapter 3. August 2003–September 2008: NATO Gets into the Game

270. Burke, *The 9/11 Wars*, 78.

271. Colonel Phil Evans, US Army.

272. Colonel Horst Busch, German army (served as a battalion commander in ISAF's multinational brigade, Kabul, Afghanistan, August 2004–February 2005, and as a senior mentor and team leader, Operational Mentoring and Liaison Team, Mazar-e-Sharif, Regional Command-North, ISAF, Afghanistan, June 2011–February 2012), interview with author at Carlisle Barracks, PA, April 11, 2013. "General Götz Gliemeroth: ISAF Commander," *NATO Review*, December

2003; Rick Hillier, "Great Expectations," *NATO Review*, April 2004; David Fox, "Italy Becomes International Force in Afghanistan," Reuters, August 4, 2005.

273. Kenneth Katzman, "Afghanistan: Post-War Governance, Security, and U.S. Policy," Congressional Research Service, November 1, 2007, 22.

274. Rice, *No Higher Honor*, 345.

275. The assessment of failure was expressed in articles, speeches, and books, such as Timo Noetzel and Sibylle Scheipers, "Coalition Warfare in Afghanistan: Burden-sharing or Disunity?" briefing paper, Chatham House, London, October 2007, 1, 7; Kurt Volker, "State's Volker's Speech on Afghanistan, NATO— Why Both Matter" (remarks to the Konrad Adenauer Stiftung, Washington, DC, February 4, 2008); Ledwidge, *Losing Small Wars*; and Bird and Marshall, *Afghanistan: How the West Lost Its Way*.

276. King, *The Transformation of Europe's Armed Forces*, 27–28.

277. NATO, "Istanbul Summit Communiqué, Issued by the Heads of State and Government Participating in the Meeting of the North Atlantic Council," June 28, 2004.

278. NATO, "Riga Summit Declaration, Issued by the Heads of State and Government Participating in the Meeting of the North Atlantic Council in Riga on 29 November 2006," news release.

279. Brodeur, press briefing.

280. NATO, "NATO's Senior Civilian Representative in Afghanistan," March 5, 2019. Between 2003 and 2014, there were six SCRs: Hikmet Çetin (Turkey, 2003–06), Daan Everts (Netherlands, 2006–07), Fernando Gentilini (Italy, 2008–10), Mark Sedwill (UK, 2010–11), Simon Gass (UK, 2011–12), and Maurits Jochems (Netherlands, 2012–14).

281. Gentilini, *Afghan Lessons*, 26.

282. Colonel Phil Evans, US Army.

283. "A Radically New Command Structure for NATO." Allied Command Operations developed the operational template for ISAF and Allied Command Transformation provided the training.

284. Colonel Phil Evans, US Army; and Gentilini, *Afghan Lessons*, 56.

285. Colonel Tucker Mansager, US Army (served as executive assistant to the SACEUR, Mons, Belgium, October 2007–July 2009), email exchange with author, May 31, 2016.

286. Sherwood McGinnis, US State Department.

287. Colonel Phil Evans, US Army.

288. "NATO Considers Role in Afghanistan," *St. John's Telegram (Newfoundland)*, September 19, 2003.

289. Sherwood McGinnis, US State Department.

290. Michael Evans, "Nato to Expand Afghanistan Force," *Times (London)*, October 7, 2003; and UN Security Council, Resolution 1510 (2003), October 13, 2003.

291. NATO, "ISAF's Mission in Afghanistan, 2001–2014," September 1, 2015.

292. *ISAF Provincial Reconstruction Team (PRT) Handbook*, Edition 4 (Public Intelligence, 2009), 94–95.

293. NATO, "ISAF's Mission in Afghanistan."

294. Wright, *A Different Kind of War*, 278, 280, 294.

295. Alexander, *The Long Way Back*, xxviii-xxix. Lieutenant Colonel Hugh McAslan, New Zealand army (served as the commander of the military component of the New Zealand Provincial Reconstruction Team in Bamiyan, Regional Command-East, ISAF, Afghanistan, April–October 2011), interview with author at Carlisle Barracks, PA, April 18, 2013.

296. "Ignoring Afghanistan in the 1980s, a Blunder, Says Gates," ANI, February 12, 2007.

297. Ryan Hendrickson, "History: Sweden's Partnership with NATO," *NATO Review*, July 2007.

298. Hillier, *A Soldier First*, 262–63.

299. Colonel Ivar Omsted, Norwegian army (served as commander, Task Force Faryab and Provincial Reconstruction Team Faryab, Meymaneh, Regional Command-North, ISAF, Afghanistan, June 2009–January 2010), interview with author at Carlisle Barracks, PA, January 24, 2014.

300. Lieutenant Colonel Javier Marcos, Spanish army (served as the commander of a Spanish helicopter unit, Herat, Regional Command-West, ISAF, Afghanistan, May–November 2010), interview with author at Carlisle Barracks, PA, January 30, 2014.

301. Lieutenant Colonel Mindaugas Steponavicius, Lithuanian army; and Colonel Denis Tretinjak, Croatian army (served as a senior mentor and team leader, Operational Mentoring and Liaison Team, Mazar-e-Sharif, Regional Command-North, ISAF, Afghanistan, February–August 2008), interview with author at Carlisle Barracks, PA, January 27, 2014.

302. Lieutenant Colonel Timothy Davis, US Army (supported CJTF Phoenix by deploying a mobile training team from the US Army Armor Center, Fort Knox, Kentucky, to Pol-e-Charki to train an Afghan tank battalion, April–September 2003; also served as the commander of a US Stryker battalion in Kandahar Province, Regional Command-South, ISAF, Afghanistan, March 2012–January 2013), interview with author at Carlisle Barracks, PA, April 11, 2014.

303. Sherwood McGinnis, US State Department.

304. Gülner Aybet, "Towards a New Transatlantic Consensus," *NATO Review*, August 2004.

305. Deborah Hanagan, "Militant Islam and the European Security and Defense Policy," civilian research project, US Army War College, 2008: 55–56.

306. Hillier, *A Soldier First*, 290.

307. Nicholas Fiorenza, "NATO Seeks More Troops for ISAF in Afghanistan," *Defense News*, November 8, 2004.

308. Ibid., and Judy Dempsey, "Nato focuses on Afghanistan's security," *Financial Times*, February 5, 2004.

309. Hillier, "Great Expectations."

310. "General Py: ISAF Commander," *NATO Review*, August 2004.

311. *ISAF Provincial Reconstruction Team (PRT) Handbook*, 95.

312. Paul Gallis, "NATO in Afghanistan: A Test of the Transatlantic Alliance," Congressional Research Service, October 23, 2007, 8.

313. Lolita C. Baldor, "Rumsfeld Seeks NATO Role in Afghanistan," Associated Press, September 13, 2005.

314. "German Peacekeepers Assume Command in Afghanistan," *Deutsche Welle*, June 1, 2006.

315. *ISAF Provincial Reconstruction Team (PRT) Handbook*, 95.

316. Mihai Carp, "Building Stability in Afghanistan," *NATO Review*, March 2006.

317. "Hikmet Çetin: Our Man in Kabul," *NATO Review*, June 2006.

318. *ISAF Provincial Reconstruction Team (PRT) Handbook*, 96.

319. "International Security Assistance Force," ISAF Placemat, January 29, 2007, accessed March 16, 2019, http://www.nato.int/cps/en/natolive/107995 .htm.

320. Wright, *A Different Kind of War*, 237, 242, 243.

321. Ibid., 243–47. Barno's campaign plan was based on a questionable assumption. He claimed he was comfortable with the troop levels he had because his approach was not about using coalition troops to physically secure Afghan communities. He believed that with COIN operations, reconstruction activities, intelligence gathering, and information operations the coalition could gain and maintain popular support. With the Afghan people "on side," they would not support insurgent forces. The plan did not account for the complexity of the conflict, which included tribal, cultural, and criminal factors, or its evolving nature.

322. Eikenberry, *Eyewitness to War* Vol. 3, interview, 19, 27, 28, 46. Specialized training for combat support and combat service support elements, such as logistics and intelligence, was incorporated by 2004.

323. Lieutenant Colonel Chris Mueller, US Army (served in the DDR program, assisting with the cantonment of heavy weapons, April–October 2004, then as the leader of an ETT in Kandahar that was embedded in an Afghan infantry *kandak*, November 2004–March 2005), interview with author in Carlisle, PA, May 1, 2014.

324. Robert McMahon, "PRTs Spreading, Though Impact Remains Unclear," RFE/RL, October 20, 2005.

325. William Woodring, *Eyewitness to War* Vol. 3, interview by Combat Studies Institute, 357–58.

326. Security sector reform refers to policies, plans, programs, and activities that improve a government's ability to provide safety, security, and justice to its people. Activities can include defense and armed forces reform; civilian management and oversight of armed forces; justice, police, corrections, and intelligence reform; national security planning and strategy support; border management; and disarmament, demobilization, and reintegration (DDR).

327. Eikenberry, *Eyewitness to War*, Vol. 3, 27, 37, 42–43, 46.

328. Hillier, *A Soldier First*, 293–97. Also, David Bercuson and J. L. Granatstein with Nancy Pearson Mackie, *Lessons Learned? What Canada Should Learn from Afghanistan* (Calgary: Canadian Defence & Foreign Affairs Institute, 2011), 1, 6–8.

329. Giustozzi, *Koran, Kalashnikov, and Laptop*, 174.

330. Wright, *A Different Kind of War*, 301.

331. Michael O'Hanlon and Adriana Lins de Albuquerque, *Afghanistan Index: Tracking Variables of Reconstruction & Security in Post-Taliban Afghanistan* (Washington DC: The Brookings Institution, February 23, 2005), 2. Population number from the CIA World Factbook.

332. Colonel William Braun, US Army (served as director, CJ-7, Training, Education and Force Development/Force Integration, CSTC-A, Kabul, Afghanistan, June 2008–June 2009), interview with author at Carlisle Barracks, PA, January 8, 2013.

333. Wright, *A Different Kind of War*, 301–02.

334. "Policing in Afghanistan: Still Searching for a Strategy," Crisis Group Asia Briefing no. 85, December 18, 2008: 9.

335. Wright, *A Different Kind of War*, 301–02.

336. "Policing in Afghanistan: Still Searching for a Strategy," 2.

337. "Report on Progress toward Security and Stability in Afghanistan, January 2009," US Department of Defense Report to Congress, 2009: 38, 44.

338. McMahon, "PRTs Spreading, Though Impact Remains Unclear."

339. "Policing in Afghanistan: Still Searching for a Strategy," 3, 6, 12.

340. "Report on Progress toward Security and Stability in Afghanistan, January 2009," 44–45. According to Colonel Braun, FDD was originally supposed to be a comprehensive, interagency program that not only trained the district police but also included a broad range of development projects in the district. However, for a variety of reasons, the concept did not work and it devolved into a CSTC-A-only program.

341. Ibid., 45; and "Germany's Support for Police Reform in Afghanistan," German Federal Foreign Office, Task Force Afghanistan-Pakistan/Federal Ministry of the Interior, March 2012: 19.

342. "Report on Progress toward Security and Stability in Afghanistan, January 2009," 45.

343. Colonel William Braun, US Army.

344. "NATO Urges EU to Do More in Afghanistan," Reuters, November 2, 2006.

345. "EU to Give Green Light to Police Mission in Afghanistan," Agence France Presse, February 10, 2007.

346. "Policing in Afghanistan: Still Searching for a Strategy," 9, 10.

347. Ibid., 1, 5, 9, 10, 11, 16. The Interior Ministry itself prioritized counterinsurgency operations over actual policing, Giustozzi, *Koran, Kalashnikov, and Laptop*, 181.

348. "US Troops in Afghanistan Could Come under British Control," *UK Telegraph*, October 3, 2005.

349. Richard Cobbold, "RUSI Interview with General David Richard," *RUSI Journal* 152, no. 2 (April 2007): 26.

350. "Eikenberry Ends Tenure as Head of CFC-Afghanistan," *Stars and Stripes*, January 23, 2007.

351. Ralf Beste, Konstantin von Hammerstein, and Alexander Szandar, "Shrinking Solidarity in Afghanistan? Debate Flares Anew about German Military Mission," *Spiegel Online*, May 28, 2007.

352. Carp, "Building Stability in Afghanistan." The Plan stated ISAF's mission continued to be assisting the government with security, facilitating governance activities, and assisting development and reconstruction. It recognized the threat was greater in the south, but it addressed it only by giving ISAF forces "robust and flexible rules of engagement" so they could defend themselves in the event of attacks.

353. Giustozzi, *Koran, Kalashnikov, and Laptop*, 11, 37, 99–103.

354. Wright, *A Different Kind of War*, 239, 251.

355. Giustozzi, *Koran, Kalashnikov, and Laptop*, 99.

356. Ibid., 53–62.

357. Mike Martin makes a persuasive argument that the Taliban themselves were manipulated in Helmand. He argues that for about the last thirty years most of the violence in Helmand has been due to a civil war among a kaleidoscope of changing factions which involve tribes, clans, and political and religious power centers. Both the international coalition and the insurgents stepped into the middle of it after 2001. Both sides were used by the Helmandi factions to advance and protect their private interests. Martin, *An Intimate War*, 3–6, 112, 151, 155, 158.

358. Giustozzi, *Koran, Kalashnikov, and Laptop*, 52, 55, 56, 60, 61, 64.

359. Wright, *A Different Kind of War*, 250, 277, 281–82.

360. Giustozzi, *Koran, Kalashnikov, and Laptop*, 40–43, 91, 97, 123–24.

361. Isby, *Afghanistan, Graveyard of Empires*, 16.

362. Giustozzi, *Koran, Kalashnikov, and Laptop*, 124–25.

363. Author interview at Carlisle Barracks, PA, with Officer F (who served in combat units in Helmand Province, Regional Command-South, ISAF, Afghanistan), January 16, 2014. Also, Martin, *An Intimate War*, 160–65.

364. Giustozzi, *Koran, Kalashnikov, and Laptop*, 99, 123, 125–26.

365. "Hikmet Çetin: Our Man in Kabul," *NATO Review*.

366. "German Peacekeepers Assume Command in Afghanistan," *Deutsche Welle*.

367. Colonel Doug Mastriano, US Army (served in the HQ, ISAF Joint Intelligence Center (JIC), Kabul, Afghanistan, between 2006 and 2008; his positions included working as an analyst, as the head of the assessments department, and as the director of the JIC), interview with author at Carlisle Barracks, PA, April 3, 2013.

368. Martin, *An Intimate War*, 164.

369. "Afghanistan: NATO Troops Apply 'Robust' New Rules of Engagement," RFE/RL, February 8, 2006.

370. Shuja Nawaz, *Learning by Doing: The Pakistan Army's Experience with Counterinsurgency* (Washington, DC: Atlantic Council, 2011), 3, 6–8, 10, 11, 14, 15.

371. Cobbold, "RUSI Interview with General David Richards," 24–25.

372. David Richards, "The Art of Command in the Twenty-First Century: Reflections on Three Commands," in *The Oxford Handbook of War*, ed. Lindley-French and Boyer, 353.

373. This was not an ISAF-only operation; some of the US special forces involved were from CFC-A. Neumann, *The Other War*, 114. Also, Horn, *No Lack of Courage*, 40–41, 54–58, 72–73, 89, 93–110.

374. Giustozzi, *Koran, Kalashnikov, and Laptop*, 126.

375. Horn, *No Lack of Courage*, 45–46.

376. Richards, "The Art of Command in the Twenty-First Century," 353.

377. Michael A. Coss, "Operation Mountain Lion: CJTF-76 in Afghanistan, Spring 2006," *Military Review*, January–February 2008: 22–29.

378. Graeme Smith, "Doing it the Dutch way in Afghanistan," *Globe and Mail*, December 2, 2006.

379. British fatalities 2002–05 totaled five and Canadian fatalities 2002–05 totaled eight. Jason Campbell and Jeremy Shapiro, *Afghanistan Index: Tracking Variables of Reconstruction & Security in Post-9/11 Afghanistan* (Washington, DC: The Brookings Institution, September 30, 2008), 7.

380. Molly Moore, "NATO Confronts Surprisingly Fierce Taliban," *Washington Post*, February 26, 2008.

381. Simpson, *War from the Ground Up*, 44–45.

382. Martin, *An Intimate War*, 153–55.

383. David Richards, "NATO in Afghanistan: Transformation on the Front Line," *RUSI Journal* 151, no. 4 (August 2006): 11–12.

384. Mills, *From Africa to Afghanistan*, 28–29.

385. Richards, "NATO in Afghanistan," 12; and Richards, "The Art of Command in the Twenty-First Century," 354–55.

386. Ahmed Rashid, "Setback for General Who Put His Faith in Peace Deals," *Daily Telegraph*, February 3, 2007.

387. "Canada presses NATO to Do More in Afghanistan," Reuters, October 18, 2006.

388. Gloria Galloway, "Canada Slams NATO's Afghan Role," *Globe and Mail*, October 10, 2006.

389. Mike Blanchfield, "France Defends Its Military Contribution in Afghanistan," CanWest News Service, February 21, 2007.

390. Sophie Walker and Paul Majendie, "Britain Confirms Sending More Troops to Afghanistan," Reuters, February 23, 2007.

391. "NATO Asks Italy for More Troops for Afghanistan," Agence France Presse, June 10, 2006; Massimiliano Di Giorgia, "Italy Agrees to Keep Troops in Afghanistan," Reuters, June 30, 2006; and Kent Harris, "Italian Forces to Remain in Afghanistan—for Now," *Stars and Stripes*, July 29, 2006.

392. Mark Deen and Robert Hutton, "Blair Says NATO's 'Credibility' Is at Stake in Afghanistan," *Bloomberg*, November 22, 2006.

393. Blanchfield, "France Defends Its Military Contribution."

394. Caren Bohan and Marcin Grajewski, "NATO Leaders Commit to Afghanistan for Long Haul," Reuters, November 29, 2006.

395. Michael Thurston, "Blair to Press NATO Allies over Afghanistan," Agence France Presse, November 27, 2006.

396. "NATO Says Fewer Taliban Attacks in Afghan South," Reuters, October 11, 2006; and Lorna Cook, "NATO Chief Lashes Allies over Afghan Troop Commitments," Agence France Presse, November 28, 2006.

397. "Canada Says Has Broken S. Afghan Taliban Uprising," Reuters, November 7, 2006.

398. Bohan and Grajewski, "NATO Leaders Commit to Afghanistan."

399. Suleyman Kurt, "Ankara Rejects NATO Request to Move Beyond Kabul," *zaman.com*, October 26, 2006.

400. "Suicide bombers Won't Stop Us in Afghanistan: NATO Chief," Agence France Presse, October 19, 2006; Bohan and Grajewski, "NATO Leaders Commit to Afghanistan"; and "New Croatian Contingent to Join ISAF Mission in Afghanistan," International News Network, Pakistan, January 3, 2007.

401. Vaira Viķe-Freiberga, "Reflecting in Riga," *NATO Review*, October 2006.

402. Joseph Giordono, "British General Will Lead Mission in Afghanistan," *Stars and Stripes*, March 11, 2006.

403. Bohan and Grajewski, "NATO leaders Commit to Afghanistan."

404. David S. Cloud, "Europeans Oppose U.S. Plan for NATO in Afghanistan," *New York Times*, September 13, 2005.

405. Sayed Salahuddin, "NATO Head Says Optimistic about Afghan Consensus," Reuters, October 6, 2005.

406. Mark John Thu, "NATO on Target for Afghan Expansion: NATO Official," Reuters, October 27, 2005.

407. "NATO Will Need More Troops Next Year in Afghanistan," Agence France Presse, December 7, 2006.

408. Isby, *Afghanistan, Graveyard of Empires*, 164–66.

409. Gentilini, *Afghan Lessons*, 34–35.

410. "Report on Progress toward Security and Stability in Afghanistan, January 2009," 31.

411. Campbell and Shapiro, *Afghanistan Index*, 4.

412. "Report on Progress toward Security and Stability in Afghanistan, January 2009," 32.

413. The White House, "Fact Sheet: Combating Terrorism Worldwide," August 6, 2007.

414. Lieven, *Pakistan: A Hard Country*, 416–18, 466–67.

415. Nawaz, *Learning by Doing*, 1, 7–11.

416. Colonel Robert Hamilton, US Army (served as the chief, regional engagement, CFC-A, OEF, Kabul, Afghanistan, July 2005–June 2006, and was responsible for coordinating the meetings of the Tripartite Commission), interview with author at Carlisle Barracks, PA, April 2, 2013.

417. "Afghanistan-Pak-US Joint Military Exercises," *Times of India*, April 21, 2006.

418. "Pakistan, Afghanistan, U.S., NATO Review Plans Of NATO-ISAF Expansion," *People's Daily Online*, June 7, 2006.

419. "Interview: General Ray Henault, Chairman of the Military Committee," *NATO Review*, January 2007.

420. "Afghan, Pakistan, NATO Intelligence Hub to Open This Month," *Khaleej Times*, January 17, 2007.

421. James Phillips and Lisa Curtis, "The War in Afghanistan: More Help Needed," April 17, 2008, Heritage Foundation.

422. Colonel Robert Hamilton, US Army.

423. "No Rush for the Exit, Yet: NATO in Afghanistan," *The Economist*, July 14, 2007; and Yves Clarisse, "L'Otan répond en partie aux demandes US sur l'Afghanistan," *Le Monde*, October 24, 2007.

424. Murray Brewster, "Dutch Tally Cost of Afghanistan," *Globe and Mail*, October 28, 2007.

425. "Dutch Under Pressure over Doubts about Afghanistan Mission," Radio Netherlands, January 13, 2006.

426. Cobbold, "RUSI Interview with General David Richards," 32.

427. Officer F, interview.

428. "Steinmeier Reasserts Germany's Pledge to Afghanistan," *Deutsche Welle*, August 21, 2006.

429. Jeffrey Simpson, "Pay Attention to This Voice in the Afghan Wilderness," *Globe and Mail*, October 17, 2006.

430. "Canada Rules Out Troops' Withdrawal," *Pajhwok Afghan News*, February 13, 2007.

431. "New Zealand Assures NATO on Commitment to Afghan Mission," Associated Press, January 24, 2007.

432. Neumann, *The Other War*, 13, 57, 97, 118.

433. Gates, *Duty*, 150.

434. NATO, "Press Conference by NATO Secretary General, Jaap de Hoop Scheffer Following the Informal Meeting with Non-NATO KFOR Contributing Nations," February 7, 2008.

435. NATO, "Bucharest Summit Declaration, Issued by the Heads of State and Government Participating in the Meeting of the North Atlantic Council in Bucharest on 3 April 2008," April 3, 2008.

436. "Press Conference by NATO Secretary General, Jaap de Hoop Scheffer," February 7, 2008.

437. Colonel Uwe Hartmann, German army (served as the deputy chief of staff for stability, HQ, Regional Command-North, Mazar-e-Sharif, ISAF, Afghanistan, September 2012–February 2013), interview with author at Carlisle Barracks, PA, March 14, 2014; and Colonel Horst Busch, German army.

438. Lieutenant Colonel Javier Marcos, Spanish army.

439. Officer F; and Colonel Robbie Boyd, British army (served as commander of the British Theatre Reserve Battalion; the battalion sent elements on multiple deployments to support operations in Helmand Province, Regional Command-South, ISAF, Afghanistan, between June 2009 and November 2010), interview with author at Carlisle Barracks, PA, April 15, 2013.

440. Colonel Johannes Hoogstraten, Netherlands army (served as the deputy chief of staff for operations, HQ, Regional Command-South, Kandahar, ISAF, Afghanistan, October 2008-July 2009), interview with author at Carlisle Barracks, PA, February 12, 2014.

441. Colonel Piotr Bieniek, Polish army (served as the battalion executive officer of the Polish battle group in Paktika and Ghazni Provinces, Regional Command-East, ISAF, March–November 2008; also served as the Polish liaison officer to ISAF SOF, Kabul, Afghanistan, March–October 2010), interview with author at Carlisle Barracks, PA, February 12, 2014. Also, Colonel Dariusz Parylak, Polish army (served as the chief of strategic planning, Task Force White Eagle, Ghazni Province, Regional Command-East, ISAF, Afghanistan, October 2008–May 2009), interview with author at Carlisle Barracks, PA, April 9, 2013.

442. Colonel William Butler, US Army (served in Afghanistan as a brigade executive officer, Regional Command-South, April 2005–February 2006; the Deputy CJ3 in CJTF-76, Bagram, February–May 2006; a battalion commander, Regional Command-East, ISAF, October 2009–November 2010; and a senior observer/controller at the Joint Maneuver Readiness Center, Hohenfels, Germany, June 2011–June 2012, where he trained and certified US battalions and NATO battle groups deploying to Afghanistan, as well as military and police mentoring teams), interview with author at Carlisle Barracks, PA, April 8, 2013

443. Lieutenant Colonel Mark Holler, US Army.

444. Commander Thomas Singleton, US Navy (served as the J5 in ISAF HQ/US Forces–Afghanistan coordinating the missions, arrival schedule, and logistical support for non-NATO force contributions to ISAF, Kabul, Afghanistan, March 2009–February 2010), interview with author at Carlisle Barracks, PA, November 27, 2013.

445. Colonel Shane Gabriel, Australian army.

446. Lieutenant General Mart de Kruif, commander, Royal Netherlands army, remarks at International Fellows Hall of Fame Induction Ceremony, US Army War College, Carlisle Barracks, PA, January 7, 2013.

447. Colonel Horst Busch, German army. Other officers interviewed made similar comments.

448. Colonel Denis Tretinjak, Croatian army.

449. Colonel Piotr Bieniek, Polish army.

450. Colonel Romulusz Ruszin, Hungarian army (served as the commander of a Provincial Reconstruction Team, Baghlan Province, Regional Command-North, ISAF, Afghanistan, August 2011–March 2012), interview with author at Carlisle Barracks, PA, February 10, 2014.

451. Lieutenant Colonel Javier Marcos, Spanish army.

452. Lieutenant Colonel Timothy Davis, US Army.

453. Colonel Horst Busch, German army. This observation was made by others who were interviewed.

454. Lieutenant Colonel Ken Knudsen, Danish army (served both as the commander of the Danish contingent in Afghanistan and as the commander of a battle group battalion, Helmand Province, Regional Command-Southwest, ISAF, Afghanistan, August 2011–February 2012), interview with author at Carlisle Barracks, PA, May 6, 2013.

455. Lieutenant Colonel Javier Marcos, Spanish army.

456. "Daily Afghan Report," Radio Free Europe/Radio Liberty, August 3, 2005.

457. Officer F. This sentiment was expressed by others who were interviewed.

458. David Richards, "A Firm Foundation," *NATO Review*, January 2007.

459. "Admiral Sir Mark Stanhope: DSACT," *NATO Review*, March 2005.

460. Colonel Christopher Cardoni, US Army (served as the chief, Operational Mentoring and Liaison Team training section at the NATO Joint Force Training Center, Bydgoszcz, Poland, September 2007–April 2010), interview with author at Carlisle Barracks, PA, November 15, 2013.

461. Steve Sturm, "Matching Capabilities to Commitments," *NATO Review*, March 2005.

462. NATO, "Workshop on Provincial Reconstruction Teams' Best Practices," news release, November 30, 2005.

463. Wright, *A Different Kind of War*, 324.

464. General Richards stated in an interview after he left command of ISAF that he did not know whether or not NATO actually had a counterinsurgency doctrine. Cobbold, "RUSI Interview with General David Richards," 26.

465. Andrew Gray, "NATO Revamps Measures of Afghan Progress," Reuters, December 5, 2007.

466. Conclusion based on interviews. The officers who served as national contingent commanders in particular noted the dual reporting chains they responded to.

467. Colonel Ivar Omsted, Norwegian army.

468. "No Rush for the Exit, Yet," *The Economist*.

469. Colonel Alberto Vezzoli, Italian army (served concurrently as the senior mentor to the chief of staff of the Afghan 207th Corps and the chief of staff of the OMLT assigned to the 207th Corps, Herat, Regional Command-West, ISAF, Afghanistan, November 2008–July 2009; also served as the deputy commander of a battle group that operated in Shindand and Herat, Regional Command-West, ISAF, Afghanistan, April–October 2010), interview with author at Carlisle Barracks, PA, January 23, 2014.

470. Robin Pomeroy, "Italy to Stay in Afghanistan But No More Troops—PM," Reuters, January 23, 2007.

471. A few of the officers interviewed also quietly acknowledged they would help in extremis in spite of caveats, which is another example of bonding and trust.

472. Jan Angstrom and Jan Willem Honig, "Regaining Strategy: Small Powers, Strategic Culture, and Escalation in Afghanistan," *Journal of Strategic Studies* 35, no. 5 (October 2012): 663, 671, 675–79.

473. Colonel Ivar Omsted, Norwegian army.

474. Office of the Chief of Staff, US Army, "2005 Posture Statement," February 2005: 4.

475. King, *The Transformation of Europe's Armed Forces*, 34–36.

476. Office of the Chief of Staff, US Army, "2012 Army Posture," February 2012: 10.

477. Jon Riley commented on the operational capabilities and competence of allied nations in his testimony to Oxford's Changing Character of War Program; Jon Riley, "NATO Operations in Afghanistan 2008–2009: A Theatre-Level View," in *British Generals in Blair's Wars*, ed. Bailey et al., 240.

478. Colonel William Butler, US Army.

479. Andrew Graham, "Iraq 2004: The View from Baghdad," in *British Generals in Blair's Wars*, ed. Bailey et al., 103, 141.

480. Ibid. Hew Strachan, "British Generals in Blair's Wars: Conclusion," in *British Generals*, 335.

481. Gates, *Duty*, 200, 202.

482. Blanchfield, "France Defends its Military Contribution."

483. Sherwood McGinnis, US State Department; also Lieutenant Colonel Mark Holler, US Army.

484. Colonel Johannes Hoogstraten, Netherlands army.

485. Interviews with Colonel Romulusz Ruszin, Hungarian Army and Lieutenant Colonel Hugh McAslan, New Zealand army.

486. Colonel Ivar Omsted, Norwegian army.

487. Colonel Denis Tretinjak, Croatian army.

488. Information from interviews, including Lieutenant Colonel Chris Mueller, US Army; Colonel Shane Gabriel, Australian army; Colonel Ivar

Omsted, Norwegian army; and Colonel Stephen Maranian, US Army (served as the commander of a US battalion task force, Nuristan Province, Regional Command-East, ISAF, Afghanistan, May 2007–July 2008) interview with author at Carlisle Barracks, PA, April 4, 2013.

489. Colonel Denis Tretinjak, Croatian army.

490. Colonel Keith Detwiler, US Army (served as the director for international security cooperation, NTM-A, ISAF, Kabul, Afghanistan, July 2010–July 2011), interview with author at Carlisle Barracks, PA, June 13, 2012; and Colonel Frederick Gellert, US Army (served as the chief, Police Force Management Division, NTM-A, ISAF, Kabul, Afghanistan, July 2011–June 2012; concurrently served as the senior adviser to the Afghan general director of force management in the Ministry of the Interior), interview with author at Carlisle Barracks, PA, December 17, 2012. Interestingly, driver's training required a diverse mix of multinational trainers. The Afghan tank battalion had T-62 tanks which originated from the Soviet Union. So CJTF Phoenix put together a team of former East Germans and Romanians to train the tank drivers; Lieutenant Colonel Timothy Davis, US Army.

491. Catherine Dale, "War in Afghanistan: Strategy, Operations, and Issues for Congress," Congressional Research Service, March 9, 2011, 41.

492. NATO, "Progress in Afghanistan: Bucharest Summit 2-4 April 2008," NATO Public Diplomacy Division, 2008: 8, 10.

493. "Report on Progress toward Security and Stability in Afghanistan, January 2009," 8, 35.

494. Ibid., 38, 44.

495. Colonel Phil Evans, US Army.

496. Alexander, *The Long Way Back*, 65; and NATO, "Progress in Afghanistan," 8

497. Lieutenant Colonel Chris Mueller, US Army.

498. James Snyder, "NATO Dispatch: Kabul," *NATO Review*, October 2006.

499. Alexander, *The Long Way Back*, 96–97.

500. Richard A. Boucher, "Afghanistan: A Plan to Turn the Tide" (remarks before the Senate Foreign Relations Committee, Washington, DC, January 31, 2008).

501. Sherwood McGinnis, US State Department.

502. Gates, *Duty*, 199; and "Report on Progress toward Security and Stability in Afghanistan, January 2009," 28.

Chapter 4. October 2008–December 2014: NATO Surges

503. NATO, "Press Conference by NATO Secretary General Jaap de Hoop Scheffer after the Informal Meeting of NATO Defence Ministers, with Invitees, with Non-NATO ISAF Contributing Nations," February 19, 2009.

504. "International Security Assistance Force," ISAF Placemat, November 25, 2008, and November 15, 2010, http://www.nato.int/cps/en/natolive/107995.htm.

505. Bush, *Decision Points*, 218; and Alexander, *The Long Way Back*, 199, 203, 213.

506. General McKiernan did not take over command of detainee operations or the most sensitive counterterrorism operations. Detainee operations continued under the direct control of CENTCOM until January 2010 when ISAF stood up Joint Task Force 435. The task force's main mission was to transition detainee operations to the Afghan government; "Report on Progress Toward Security and Stability in Afghanistan, April 2010," US Department of Defense Report to Congress, 2010: 54.

507. Colonel Ingrid Gjerde, Norwegian army (served as the commander of the Norwegian contingent in Afghanistan, Mazar-e-Sharif, Regional Command-North, ISAF, Afghanistan, June 2011–January 2012), interview with author at Carlisle Barracks, PA, April 12, 2013; Lieutenant Colonel Ken Knudsen, Danish army. Author interview at Carlisle Barracks, PA with Officer C (who served as a contingent commander and in a PRT in Afghanistan), May 14, 2013.

508. Personal papers, Lieutenant Colonel Eric Shafa, US Air Force, ISAF liaison to the Afghan Ministry of Mines, Ministry of Urban Development, Ministry of Energy and Water, and Ministry of Public Works, June 2010–May 2011.

509. Colonel George Woods, US Army (served on the CSTC-A staff July–September 2008 and assisted with the establishment of US Forces–Afghanistan; then served as the senior adviser to the Afghan Minister of Defense, NTM-A, ISAF, Kabul, Afghanistan, October 2008–July 2009), interview with author at Carlisle Barracks, PA, December 17, 2012.

510. Gates, *Duty*, 217, 223, 342, 343.

511. NATO, "Press Conference by NATO Secretary General Jaap de Hoop Scheffer after the Informal Meeting of NATO Defence Ministers, with Invitees, with Non-NATO ISAF Contributing Nations;" and NATO, "Press Conference by NATO Secretary General Jaap de Hoop Scheffer after the meeting of the North Atlantic Council with Invitees in Foreign Ministerial Session," March 5, 2009.

512. McChrystal, *My Share of the Task*, 294.

513. Commander, NATO International Security Assistance Force, Afghanistan, "Commander's Initial Assessment," August 30, 2009, 1-1.

514. Gates, *Duty*, 354–84.

515. "International Security Assistance Force," ISAF Placemat, September 10, 2007, and October 25, 2010,

516. Gates, *Duty*, 485–86, 557.

517. "American and Afghanistan: Hug Them Tight," *The Economist*, May 15, 2010.

518. "Fewer Dragons, More Snakes," *The Economist*, November 13, 2010.

519. Alexander Mattelaer, "How Afghanistan Has Strengthened NATO," *Survival* 53, no. 6 (December 2011): 130.

520. Colonel George Woods, US Army.

521. Three of the individuals interviewed talked about the pressures on the ISAF commander: Sherwood McGinnis, US State Department; Colonel George Woods, US Army and Lieutenant Colonel Christopher Moretti, US Army (served as the deputy chief of targets in the J3 of the ISAF headquarters and then in IJC as it was being created, Kabul, Afghanistan, January–July 2009), interview with author at Carlisle Barracks, PA, January 14, 2014.

522. NATO, "Press conference by the NATO Spokesman James Appathurai after the Informal Working Lunch of NATO Defence Ministers, with Invitees," February 19, 2009.

523. Colonel George Woods, US Army.

524. NATO Media Backgrounder, "NATO Training Mission–Afghanistan (NTM-A)," October, 2009.

525. Lieutenant Colonel Jeffrey Dickerson, US Army (served as the J3, CJTF-Phoenix, CSTC-A, Kabul, May–October 2009, then as the chief of future operations, ANSF Development Assistance Bureau, IJC, ISAF, Kabul, Afghanistan, October 2009–March 2010—in both positions he worked assignment of army and police mentoring teams to the regional commands), interview with author at Carlisle Barracks, PA, April 5, 2013. Also, Colonel George Woods, US Army and Colonel Richard O'Donnell, US Army (served as the chief of staff for the deputy commanding general-support, NTM-A/CSTC-A, ISAF, Kabul, Afghanistan, June 2012–June 2013), interview with author at Carlisle Barracks, PA, March 4, 2014.

526. Gates, *Duty*, 345–47.

527. NATO, "Press conference by NATO Secretary General Jaap de Hoop Scheffer," June 12, 2009.

528. "Report on Progress toward Security and Stability in Afghanistan, October 2009," US Department of Defense Report to Congress, 2009: 19.

529. Lieutenant Colonel Jeffrey Dickerson, US Army.

530. Lieutenant Colonel Christopher Moretti, US Army.

531. Interviews with Lieutenant Colonel Christopher Moretti, US Army and Lieutenant Colonel Jeffrey Dickerson, US Army.

532. Colonel Douglas Campbell, US Army (served as the deputy J1, US Forces–Afghanistan, Kabul, Afghanistan, July 2010–July 2011), interview with author at Carlisle Barracks, PA, January 23, 2014.

533. NATO, "ISAF Headquarters," July 9, 2009, accessed March 17, 2019, http://www.nato.int/isaf/structure/hq/index.html.

534. "Report on Progress Toward Security and Stability in Afghanistan, April 2010," 13–14.

535. Lieutenant Colonel Jeffrey Dickerson, US Army.

536. The NGOs operating across the country were not included in this consolidation. Very often they pursued their development projects independently and did not inform or coordinate their activities with the regional commands or the military forces in their regions. Interviews with Lieutenant Colonel Mark Holler US Army; Colonel Stephen Maranian, US Army; and Lieutenant Colonel Brent Grometer, US Air Force (served as the commander of a Provincial Reconstruction Team, Nangarhar Province, Regional Command-East, ISAF, Afghanistan, February–November 2010), interview with author at Carlisle Barracks, PA, April 9, 2013. Also, Michael J. Forsyth, "Tempering Expectations in Afghanistan: Reflections from a Year in Combat" (unpublished manuscript, in the author's possession, June, 2011), 261–62, 276, 297, 366.

537. Interviews with Colonel William Butler, US Army and Lieutenant Colonel Jeffrey Dickerson, US Army.

538. Lieutenant Colonel Jeffrey Dickerson, US Army.

539. "Report on Progress Toward Security and Stability in Afghanistan, November 2010," US Department of Defense Report to Congress, 2010: 14. A number of countries made substantial increases. France, Italy, Poland, Romania, and Turkey sent about 1,000 additional troops each. Australia, Germany, Spain, and the United Kingdom sent about 500 additional troops each. "International Security Assistance Force," ISAF Placemats, October 1, 2009 to December 3, 2012, http://www.nato.int/cps/en/natolive/107995.htm. Also, interview with Colonel Piotr Bieniek, Polish army.

540. Gates, *Duty*, 343, 347–48, 476.

541. "Report on Progress Toward Security and Stability in Afghanistan, November 2010," 15.

542. Max Boot, Frederick W. Kagan, and Kimberly Kagan, "Yes, We Can: In the 'Graveyard of Empires,' We Are Fighting a War We Can Win," *Weekly Standard* 14, no. 26 (March 23, 2009): 16. Also, "Report on Progress Toward Security and Stability in Afghanistan, November 2010," 41–42.

543. Colonel Richard Lacquement, US Army (served as the liaison to the Afghan Independent Directorate of Local Governance (IDLG) as part of the Ministerial Outreach Team, IJC, ISAF, Kabul, Afghanistan, June 2010–July 2011), interview with author at Carlisle Barracks, PA, January 30, 2014.

544. Ann Marlowe, "A Counterinsurgency Grows in Khost: An Unheralded U.S. success in Afghanistan," *Weekly Standard* 13, no. 34 (May 19, 2008): 19–21.

545. McChrystal, *My Share of the Task*, 347, 376; and Gates, *Duty*, 355.

546. Colonel Richard Lacquement, US Army.

547. Author interview at Carlisle Barracks, PA with Officer D (who served in special operations in Afghanistan), November 6, 2013, and Colonel George Woods, US Army.

548. A number of the officers interviewed remarked on the noticeable increase in resources: Officer D; author interview at Carlisle Barracks, PA with

Officer E (who served in the Regional Command-North region in Afghanistan), January 15, 2014; Colonel Piotr Bieniek, Polish army; and Lieutenant Colonel Peter Whalen, US Army (served as chief, Intelligence Collection Management, J2, IJC, ISAF, Kabul, Afghanistan, January–July 2011), interview with author at Carlisle Barracks, PA, December 27, 2013.

549. Gates, *Duty*, 127, 129, 130, 132, 133, 445.

550. "Report on Progress toward Security and Stability in Afghanistan, October 2009," 6, 12.

551. Boot, Kagan, and Kagan, "Yes, We Can," 14–15.

552. Lieutenant Colonel Brent Grometer, US Air Force.

553. Neumann, *The Other War*, 15.

554. Gates, *Duty*, 211.

555. Ann Marlowe, "Policing Afghanistan: Too Few Good Men and Too Many Bad Ones Make For a Grueling, Uphill Struggle," *Weekly Standard* 14, no. 14 (December 22, 2008): 25–26.

556. Lieutenant Colonel Christopher Moretti, US Army.

557. Interviews with Lieutenant Colonel Peter Whalen, US Army and Lieutenant Colonel Christopher Moretti, US Army.

558. Martin, *An Intimate War*, 186–92. Richard Roy, "With Enough Nails: Canadian COIN in Kandahar," in *Afghanistan in the Balance: Counterinsurgency, Comprehensive Approach, and Political Order*, ed. Ehrhart et al., 44–46.

559. Colonel Robbie Boyd, British army; "Report on Progress Toward Security and Stability in Afghanistan, April 2010," 29–30.

560. ISAF Joint Command–Afghanistan, "Operation Moshtarak," news release, February 13, 2010.

561. McChrystal, *My Share of the Task*, 363–69, 375.

562. Colonel Richard Lacquement, US Army.

563. Colonel Robbie Boyd, British army; "Report on Progress Toward Security and Stability in Afghanistan, April 2010," 30.

564. Frederick W. Kagan and Kimberly Kagan, "A Winnable War," *Weekly Standard* 15, no. 40 (July 5, 2010).

565. "The War in Afghanistan: Still Pouring," *The Economist*, December 18, 2010.

566. "Report on Progress Toward Security and Stability in Afghanistan, October 2011," US Department of Defense Report to Congress, 2011: 3.

567. David H. Petraeus, commander, International Security Assistance Force NATO, Statement Before the Senate Armed Services Committee, March 15, 2011: 5.

568. Boot, *Invisible Armies*, 554.

569. Colonel Robbie Boyd, British army.

570. NATO, "Inteqal: Transition to Afghan Lead," January 7, 2015.

571. "International Security Assistance Force," ISAF Placemat, June 7, 2010, accessed March 17, 2019, http://www.nato.int/cps/en/natolive/107995.htm.

572. NATO, "NATO Agrees to Split of Regional Command South, Afghanistan," news release, May 21, 2010.

573. "Report on Progress Toward Security and Stability in Afghanistan, November 2010," 47.

574. McChrystal, *My Share of the Task*, 377.

575. Cassidy, *War, Will, and Warlords*, 122.

576. Kagan and Kagan, "A Winnable War."

577. Lynne O'Donnell, "Petraeus Says Taliban Making 'Overtures' for Peace," Agence France Presse, September 28, 2010.

578. Max Boot, "Surge Protector," *Weekly Standard* 16, no. 15 (December 27, 2010).

579. "Report on Progress Toward Security and Stability in Afghanistan, October 2011," 60, 63–64.

580. "Report on Progress Toward Security and Stability in Afghanistan, April 2012," US Department of Defense Report to Congress, 2012: 3–4; and "Report on Progress Toward Security and Stability in Afghanistan, December 2012," US Department of Defense Report to Congress, 2012: 3–4.

581. Gates, *Duty*, 478. McChrystal, *My Share of the Task*, 343, 366. CJSOTF-A was subsumed into a larger combined headquarters called the Combined Forces Special Operations Component Command–Afghanistan (CFSOCC-A).

582. Officer E, interview.

583. The NATO Special Operations Headquarters originated from the transformation initiatives announced at the Riga Summit in 2006. It was initially called the NATO SOF Coordination Center when it was formally established in 2007. Commander Michelle Winegardner, US Navy (served as director, J4, NATO SOF Coordination Center, SHAPE, Mons, Belgium, December 2006–July 2009; and as the support operations officer for the Afghan National Army in CJ4, NTM-A/CSTC-A, ISAF, Kabul, Afghanistan, November 2010–July 2011), interview with author at Carlisle Barracks, PA, May 2, 2013.

584. "Report on Progress Toward Security and Stability in Afghanistan, October 2011," 67.

585. "Afghanistan: An Orchard of Ills," *The Economist*, January 29, 2011.

586. "Glimmers of Hope," *The Economist*, May 14, 2011.

587. "Taliban Attacks in Afghanistan: On the Front Line," *The Economist*, September 17, 2011; and "What Comes Next," *The Economist*, December 3, 2011.

588. NATO, "Interview with General John R. Allen, Commander ISAF," September 2, 2011, accessed March 17, 2019, http://www.nato.int/cps/en/natohq/opinions_77543.htm.

589. Officer E, interview.

590. Colonel Uwe Hartmann, German army.

591. Ibid.

592. "NATO after the Summit: Harmony—for Now," *The Economist*, November 27, 2010. According to Gates, Karzai had first suggested the 2014

end date for ISAF's combat operations after his 2009 re-inauguration. Obama "embraced" the proposal and included it in his December 2009 speech. The proposal then went to NATO for formal consideration. Gates, *Duty*, 498.

593. NATO, "Afghanistan and NATO's Enduring Partnership," media backgrounder, April 2011.

594. NATO, "Press Conference by NATO Secretary General Anders Fogh Rasmussen at the Lisbon Summit of Heads of State and Government," November 19, 2010, accessed March 17, 2019, http://www.nato.int/cps/en /natolive/opinions_68927.htm.

595. NATO, "2011 Look Ahead; NATO Senior Civilian Representative to Afghanistan, Mark Sedwill," video message, January 2011.

596. "Fewer dragons, More snakes," *The Economist*.

597. Lieutenant Colonel Javier Marcos, Spanish army.

598. Gates, *Duty*, 337, 338, 349, 350.

599. "After McChrystal," *The Economist*, June 26, 2010; and Gates, *Duty*, 373–74, 496.

600. Colonel Romulusz Ruszin, Hungarian army.

601. Lieutenant Colonel Hugh McAslan, New Zealand army.

602. Gary J. Schmitt, "Italian Hard Power: Ambitions and Fiscal Realities," *AEI National Security Outlook*, no. 3 (November 2012): 9.

603. Colonel Alberto Vezzoli, Italian army.

604. Colonel Uwe Hartmann, German army.

605. "Merkel's Caution: Berlin Reverts to Old Timidity on Military Missions," *Spiegel Online*, March 26, 2013.

606. Colonel Uwe Hartmann, German army.

607. Lieutenant Colonel Jürgen Prandtner, German army (served as the commander of battle group battalion in Regional Command-Capital, ISAF, Kabul, Afghanistan, June–December 2007), interview with author at Carlisle Barracks, PA, January 14, 2014.

608. Colonel Uwe Hartmann, German army.

609. Colonel Piotr Bieniek, Polish army.

610. "NATO after the Summit," *The Economist*.

611. "Australian PM Visits Afghanistan," RFE/RL, October 3, 2010.

612. "Danish Prime Minister in Surprise Visit to Afghanistan," Agence France Presse, September 26, 2010.

613. Jim Garamone, "Petraeus Calls for Unity of Purpose, Effort Crucial," *JBAD Journal* 1, no. 2 (July 2010): 2.

614. The document was under development for a number of years and was officially published as AJP-3.4.4, "Allied Joint Doctrine for Counterinsurgency (COIN)," February 2011.

615. Joint Warfare Center, "ISAF," June 29, 2015.

616. Michito Tsuruoka, "Asia, NATO and its Partners: Complicated Relationships?" *NATO Review*, February 2010.

617. Michael Ruhle, "NATO Ten Years After: Learning the Lessons," *NATO Review*, September 2011.

618. Schmitt, "Italian Hard Power," 5, 7, 9.

619. Roy, "With Enough Nails," 40, 41, 44.

620. Officer E, interview.

621. Colonel Uwe Hartmann, German army.

622. Philipp Münch, "The German Approach to Counterinsurgency: Concepts and Practice," in *Afghanistan in the Balance*, 56–58, 59. Also, Konstantin von Hammerstein, Susanne Koelbl, Alexander Szandar, and Sami Yousafzai, "Expanding Violence: Germany Discovers a War in Afghanistan," *Spiegel Online*, September 8, 2008.

623. Alexander Alderson, "Too Busy to Learn: Personal Observations on British Campaigns in Iraq and Afghanistan," in *British Generals in Blair's Wars*, 287–92.

624. NATO, "NATO Welcomes US nomination of Future Commander ISAF," January 18, 2008, accessed March 17, 2019, http://www.nato.int/cps /en/natohq/news_1219.htm; James Appathurai, weekly press briefing, NATO, January 23, 2008, accessed March 17, 2019, http://www.nato.int/cps/en/natohq /opinions_7385.htm.

625. Gates, *Duty*, 344–46, 487–88, 490.

626. Colonel Tucker Mansager, US Army.

627. NATO, "Press conference by NATO Secretary General Anders Fogh Rasmussen and the Incoming Commander of the NATO-led International Security Assistance Force (ISAF), General David Petraeus," July 1, 2010, accessed March 17, 2019, http://www.nato.int/cps/en/natolive/opinions_64783.htm.

628. Colonel Johannes Hoogstraten, Netherlands army.

629. Information from a number of officers who requested their comments about General McChrystal be off the record.

630. Roy, "With Enough Nails," 44–45, 47–48.

631. Boot, Kagan, and Kagan, "Yes, We Can," 17.

632. "Report on Progress Toward Security and Stability in Afghanistan, October 2011," 4.

633. "Report on Progress Toward Security and Stability in Afghanistan, April 2012," 1.

634. "Report on Progress Toward Security and Stability in Afghanistan, December 2012," 7, 46.

635. ISAF Placemat, July 26, 2011, and December 1, 2011, accessed March 17, 2019, http://www.nato.int/cps/en/natolive/107995.htm.

636. ANSF funding sources were the US Afghanistan Security Forces Fund, the NATO ANA Trust Fund, and the UN-administered Law and Order Trust Fund for Afghanistan (LOTFA).

637. Neumann, *The Other War*, 33, 54, 80–83.

638. "Report on Progress Toward Security and Stability in Afghanistan, November 2010," 17.

639. "Report on Progress Toward Security and Stability in Afghanistan, October 2011," 4. The Afghan Air Corps is included in the ANA numbers. Of the 195,000 goal, 187,000 is the army and 8,000 is the air force.

640. The corps headquarters was located near the RC-Southwest headquarters in Lashkar Gah.

641. NTM-A, "Year in Review: November 2009 to November 2010," November 2010: 5; and NATO, "Press Briefing by LtGen William Caldwell, Commander of the NATO Training Mission–Afghanistan (NTM-A)," March 3, 2010.

642. William Caldwell, "No Trainers? No Transition," *NATO Review*, November 2010.

643. William Caldwell, "Teaming, Transparency, and Transition in Afghanistan," *NATO Review*, October 2011.

644. NTM-A, "Year in Review," 3, 4, 6, 7, 10–12; and NATO, "Press briefing by LtGen William Caldwell."

645. NTM-A, "Year in Review," 7, 10, 12, 15–18; and Caldwell, "Teaming, Transparency, and Transition in Afghanistan."

646. NATO, "Press Briefing by the Commander of the NATO Training Mission—Afghanistan," October 13, 2011, accessed March 17, 2019, http://www.nato.int/cps/en/natolive/opinions_79369.htm. Also, Colonel Frederick Gellert, US Army.

647. German Federal Foreign Office, "Germany's Support for Police Reform in Afghanistan," 19.

648. NTM-A, "Year in Review," 24. The ALP program was preceded by the Afghan National Auxiliary Police (ANAP) program. The ANAP was a two-year (2006–08) "short-term stopgap" to provide some security to Afghans in their villages while the ANP was being built. Neumann, *The Other War*, 121–22.

649. NTM-A, "Year in Review," 10–11; and NATO, "Press Briefing by LtGen William Caldwell."

650. NATO, "Press Briefing by the Commander of the NATO Training Mission–Afghanistan."

651. NTM A, "Year in Review," 11.

652. NATO, "Press Briefing by the Commander of NATO's Training Mission in Afghanistan, Lieutenant General William Caldwell," February 23, 2011, accessed March 17, 2019, http://www.nato.int/cps/en/natohq/opinions_70773.htm; and NATO, "Press Briefing by the Commander of the NATO Training Mission–Afghanistan."

653. "Report on Progress Toward Security and Stability in Afghanistan, October 2011," 23.

654. Colonel Keith Detwiler, US Army.

655. NATO, "Press Briefing by the Commander of the NATO Training Mission—Afghanistan."

656. Colonel Paul Mckenney, US Army (served as the leader of an assessment team that deployed to Afghanistan in 2012 to evaluate the instructors and curriculum at the ANA junior staff college in Kabul; at the time he was teaching at the Canadian staff college and he was asked to lead this Canadian team), telephone interview with author, January 14, 2013.

657. Anders Fogh Rasmussen, "The Secretary General's Annual Report 2013," NATO Public Diplomacy Division, 2013: 6.

658. Jens Stoltenberg, "The Secretary General's Annual Report 2014," NATO Public Diplomacy Division, 2014: 7.

659. NTM-A, "Year in Review," 20. Also, Colonel George Woods, US Army.

660. "Report on Progress Toward Security and Stability in Afghanistan, November 2010," 35.

661. Colonel George Woods, US Army; Colonel Robert Lowe, US Army (served as the senior adviser to the commanding general of the Afghan National Civil Order Police (ANCOP), NTM-A, ISAF, Kabul, Afghanistan, July 2011–June 2012), interview with author at Carlisle Barracks, PA, December 20, 2012. Colonel Steven Donaldson, US Army (served as the senior adviser to the Afghan Minister of Interior, NTM-A, ISAF, Kabul, Afghanistan, July 2012– May 2013), interview with author at Carlisle Barracks, PA, January 28, 2014.

662. Information from interviews.

663. Information from interviews.

664. NTM-A, "Year in Review," 22.

665. "Report on Progress Toward Security and Stability in Afghanistan, October 2011," 19. Also, Colonel George Woods, US Army.

666. Two of the officers interviewed gave overall descriptions of the ministerial outreach efforts by the ISAF headquarters and IJC; Colonel Richard Lacquement, US Army. Also, Lieutenant Colonel Eric Shafa, US Air Force (as a member of the Afghanistan-Pakistan Hands Program he was assigned to the ISAF headquarters and served as a liaison to a cluster of Afghan ministries, June 2010– May 2011; also served as the commander of a Provincial Reconstruction Team in Kapisa Province, Regional Command-East, ISAF, Afghanistan, February– September 2012), interview with author at Carlisle Barracks, PA, November 18, 2013.

667. Lieutenant Colonel Eric Shafa, US Air Force.

668. Colonel Richard Lacquement, US Army.

669. Allied nation OMLT and POMLT teams had access to US funding to provide logistical and training support to ANSF formations because CSTC-A embedded US logistical support teams into them. Colonel Denis Tretinjak, Croatian army. Also, Colonel Robert Mundell, US Army (served as commander, Afghan Regional Security Integration Command-North, June–October 2009, then as commander, Regional Support Command-North, November 2009–July

2010, Mazar-e-Sharif, NTM-A/CSTC-A, ISAF, Afghanistan), interview with author at Carlisle Barracks, PA, July 25, 2013.

670. The RSCs were not controlled by IJC and they had been preceded by a similar command structure under CSTC-A called the Afghan Regional Security Integration Commands (ARSIC). As with the RSCs, there had been an ARSIC in each of the five regions. Colonel Robert Mundell, US Army. Also, Major James Cheney, US Army (served as the ANP support officer, Regional Support Command-Capital, February–August 2010, then as executive officer, DCOM-Regional Support, August 2010–February 2011, NTM-A/CSTC-A, ISAF, Kabul, Afghanistan), email interview with author, April 14, 2014.

671. Lieutenant Colonel Jeffrey Dickerson, US Army.

672. Lieutenant Colonel Arjan Hilaj, Albanian army (served as the commander of an Albanian-US OMLT, Regional Command-Capital, ISAF, Kabul, Afghanistan, July 2011–March 2012), interview with author at Carlisle Barracks, PA, April 3, 2013.

673. Colonel Alberto Vezzoli, Italian army.

674. In 2007, the requirement for OMLTs was forty-six; ISAF fielded thirty-two. In mid-2010 the OMLT requirement was 180 (168 fielded) and the POMLT requirement was 470 (327 fielded). In December 2011 the OMLT requirement was 172 (157 fielded) and POMLT requirement was 551 (334 fielded). In December 2012 the total requirement for SFATs was 466 (and 406 were fielded). Sources: NATO, weekly press briefing by NATO spokesman James Appathurai, October 17, 2007, accessed March 17, 2019, http://www.nato.int/cps/en/natohq/opinions_8514.htm; NATO Fact Sheet, "NATO's Operational Mentor and Liaison Teams (OMLTs)," June 2010; NATO Fact Sheet, "NATO's Police Operational Mentor and Liaison Teams (POMLTs)," June 2010; NATO Media Backgrounder, "Afghan National Security Forces (ANSF): Training and Development," December 2011; "Report on Progress Toward Security and Stability in Afghanistan, October 2011," 40; and "Report on Progress Toward Security and Stability in Afghanistan, December 2012," 10.

675. Lieutenant Colonel Arjan Hilaj, Albanian army; and Colonel Michael Peeters, US Army (served as PMT team leader and adviser to an Afghan Uniformed Police provincial police chief, Ghazni Province, Regional Command-East, ISAF, Afghanistan, July 2011–June 2012), email interview with author, August 23, 2012.

676. The commander's unit assessment tool (CUAT) assessed units on a scale of 1 to 5. A capability milestone score of 5 meant the unit was newly formed and could barely function even with partner assistance.

677. Colonel Christopher Cardoni, US Army.

678. NATO, "Afghan National Security Forces (ANSF): Training and Development," media backgrounder, April 2012.

679. NATO, "Afghan National Security Forces (ANSF): Training and Development," media backgrounder, December 2012.

680. "Report on Progress Toward Security and Stability in Afghanistan, July 2013," US Department of Defense Report to Congress, 2013: 104.

681. A number of the officers interviewed described PRT activities; Colonel Ivar Omsted, Norwegian army; Colonel Romulusz Ruszin, Hungarian army; Lieutenant Colonel Hugh McAslan, New Zealand army; Lieutenant Colonel Mindaugas Steponavicius, Lithuanian army; Lieutenant Colonel Eric Shafa, US Air Force; Lieutenant Colonel Brent Grometer, US Air Force; and First Sergeant Robert Browne, US Army (served as the first sergeant of a Provincial Reconstruction Team, Laghman Province, Regional Command-East, ISAF, Afghanistan, April 2006–April 2007), interview with author at Carlisle Barracks, PA, December 20, 2012; and Officer A.

682. Colonel North Charles, US Army (served as the deputy commander of an Agri-business Development Team, Nangarhar Province, Regional Command-East, ISAF, Afghanistan, July 2010–June 2011), interview with author at Carlisle Barracks, PA, December 21, 2012.

683. Lieutenant Colonel Brent Grometer, US Air Force. Also, Colonel Ingrid Gjerde, Norwegian army and Lieutenant Colonel Hugh McAslan, New Zealand army.

684. Colonel Romulusz Ruszin, Hungarian army.

685. Colonel Ivar Omsted, Norwegian army.

686. Colonel Uwe Hartmann, German army.

687. Interviews with Lieutenant Colonel Eric Shafa, US Air Force; Colonel Ivar Omsted, Norwegian army; Lieutenant Colonel Hugh McAslan, New Zealand army; and Colonel Ingrid Gjerde, Norwegian army.

688. "Berlin Extends German Forces' Mandate in Afghanistan…Though Germans to Avoid Counternarcotics Operations," Radio Free Europe/Radio Liberty, September 29, 2005, https://www.rferl.org/a/1143490.html.

689. Christopher M. Blanchard, "Afghanistan: Narcotics and U.S. Policy," Congressional Research Service, December 6, 2007, 9.

690. NATO, "Press Briefing by Hikmet Çetin, NATO Senior Civilian Representative in Afghanistan and Mr. Habibullah Qaderi, Minister for Counter Narcotics of Afghanistan," January 20, 2005, accessed March 17, 2019, http://www.nato.int/cps/en/natohq/opinions_21943.htm.

691. NATO, "Afghanistan Briefing: Helping Secure Afghanistan's Future," NATO Public Diplomacy Division, 2008: 9. Mike Martin describes in detail the involvement of police forces and provincial and district leaders in Helmand in the illicit opium economy. The provincial governor, Sher Mohammed, who was removed on the insistence of the British, for example, was the target of a raid by Afghan narcotics police in June 2005. They found nine tons of opium in his office. Martin, *An Intimate War*, 119–24, 133–34.

692. Gretchen Peters, "The New Killing Fields?" *NATO Review*, Summer 2009. Also, Gretchen S. Peters, "The Taliban and the Opium Trade," in *Decoding the New Taliban*, ed. Giustozzi, 9–11.

693. NATO, "Afghanistan Briefing," 9.

694. NATO, "ISAF's Strategic Vision: Declaration by the Heads of State and Government of the Nations Contributing to the UN-mandated NATO-led International Security Assistance Force (ISAF) in Afghanistan," news release, April 3, 2008.

695. General John Craddock, "SACEUR's Address to the Royal United Services Institute for Defence and Security Studies: NATO Operations—Internal and External Challenges," October 20, 2008.

696. NATO, press briefing by NATO spokesman James Appathurai and video teleconference by General Robert W. Cone, commander of the Combined Security Transition Command—Afghanistan, September 3, 2008, accessed March 17, 2019, http://www.nato.int/cps/en/natohq/opinions_46441.htm.

697. Craddock, "SACEUR's Address."

698. NATO, press conference by NATO secretary general Jaap de Hoop Scheffer, June 12, 2009, accessed March 17, 2019, http://www.nato.int/cps/en/natohq/opinions_55630.htm.

699. Hammerstein et al., "Expanding Violence."

700. "Report on Progress Toward Security and Stability in Afghanistan, April 2010," 76.

701. "Report on Progress Toward Security and Stability in Afghanistan, April 2014," US Department of Defense Report to Congress, 2014: 81.

702. Colonel Paul Phillips, US Army (served as the chief, ISAF Coordination Element in Pakistan, Islamabad, September 2009–August 2010), interview with author at Carlisle Barracks, PA, December 18, 2012.

703. Daveed Gartenstein-Ross and Bill Roggio, "Descent into Appeasement," *Weekly Standard* 13, no. 37 (June 9, 2008): 16–17.

704. Michael Rubin, "Sixty Miles from the Capital," *Weekly Standard* 14, no. 32 (May 11, 2009): 10.

705. Brigadier General Ahsan Gulrez, Pakistan army (briefing given as a noon-time lecture, US Army War College, Carlisle Barracks, PA, January 13, 2014). The briefing stated that in 2005 there were 61,000 army and Frontier Corps troops deployed along the Pakistan-Afghan border. This increased to 112,000 in 2008, 148,000 in 2010, and topped out at 158,000 in 2013.

706. Petraeus, "Statement Before the Senate Armed Services Committee," 6.

707. "Report on Progress Toward Security and Stability in Afghanistan, April 2010," 32. "Report on Progress Toward Security and Stability in Afghanistan, November 2010," 50. "Report on Progress Toward Security and Stability in Afghanistan, December 2012," 146.

708. Gulrez, briefing.

709. "Pakistan's Border Badlands: Double Games," *The Economist*, July 12, 2014; and "Pakistan's Militants: Taliban Tumult," *The Economist*, October 25, 2014.

710. "Report on Progress Toward Security and Stability in Afghanistan, October 2011," 3.

711. McChrystal, *My Share of the Task*, 329, 334, 347.

712. NATO, "Phase 4: Transition to Afghan Ownership and Leadership in Security," media backgrounder, October 2009.

713. Barbara Starr, "Smooth Transition Will Be Key to Bringing Troops Home from Afghanistan," CNN, October 31, 2010.

714. NATO, "Transition," media backgrounder, April 2010.

715. Ibid., and NATO, "Transition to Afghan Lead: *Inteqal*," media backgrounder, December 2011.

716. NATO, "Transition: *Inteqal*," media backgrounder, October 2010.

717. NATO, "Transition to Afghan lead: *Inteqal*." Also, "Report on Progress Toward Security and Stability in Afghanistan, October 2011," 55.

718. NATO, "Declaration by the Heads of State and Government of the Nations Contributing to the UN-mandated, NATO-led International Security Assistance Force (ISAF) in Afghanistan," November 20, 2010.

719. NATO, "Final communiqué: Meeting of the North Atlantic Council at the Level of Foreign Ministers Held at NATO Headquarters, Brussels," December 3, 2008.

720. Barbara Starr, "In Afghanistan, Small-scale Security Handovers Quietly Ensue," CNN, November 8, 2010.

721. Colonel Uwe Hartmann, German army.

722. Lieutenant Colonel Joe Burger, US Army (served as the chief, Campaign Assessment Section, IJC, ISAF, Kabul, Afghanistan, July 2011–June 2012), interview with author at Carlisle Barracks, PA, November 12, 2013.

723. NATO, "Transition to Afghan lead: *Inteqal*"; also NATO News, "Mazar after Transition."

724. Edward Cody and Karen DeYoung, "France Will Speed Up Troop Withdrawal from Afghanistan By One Year," *Washington Post*, January 27, 2012.

725. NATO, "Press Conference by NATO Secretary General Anders Fogh Rasmussen Following the Meeting on Afghanistan in Heads of State and Government Format," May 21, 2012.

726. "Report on Progress Toward Security and Stability in Afghanistan, December 2012," 15.

727. Lieutenant Colonel Charles Freeman, US Army (served as the deputy director of staff, ISAF, Kabul, Afghanistan, November 2011–January 2012), interview with author at Carlisle Barracks, PA, November 13, 2013.

728. Colonel Lawrence Brown, US Army (served as the CJ2 for NTM-A/CSTC-A and then as the chief of staff, NTM-A, ISAF, Kabul, Afghanistan, July 2013–July 2014), interview with author at Carlisle Barracks, PA, August 7, 2014.

729. NATO, "Resolute Support Mission Placemat," June 2015, https://www.nato.int/cps/en/natolive/107995.htm.

730. Colonel Romulusz Ruszin, Hungarian army. Other officers interviewed agreed.

731. Lieutenant Colonel Jürgen Prandtner, German army. Almost all of the officers interviewed stated their tours in Afghanistan were the most satisfying in their careers.

732. Interviews with Lieutenant Colonel Chris Mueller, US Army and Colonel Robbie Boyd, British army; Marlowe, "A Counterinsurgency Grows in Khost," 23, 24; Gates, *Duty*, 492.

733. Interviews with Colonel Shane Gabriel, Australian army; Colonel Ingrid Gjerde, Norwegian army; Colonel Denis Tretinjak, Croatian army; Colonel Alberto Vezzoli, Italian army; and Colonel Robbie Boyd, British army.

734. Lieutenant Colonel Timothy Davis, US Army.

735. Gates, *Duty*, 561.

736. Ibid., 480, 492.

737. Ibid., 497.

738. "Report on Progress Toward Security and Stability in Afghanistan, December 2012," 46.

739. Ibid., 11.

740. "Report on Progress Toward Security and Stability in Afghanistan, July 2013," 13.

741. NATO, "Transition to Afghan Lead: Inteqal."

742. "Report on Progress Toward Security and Stability in Afghanistan, October 2011," 6, 56–57, 59; "Report on Progress Toward Security and Stability in Afghanistan, April 2012," 5; "Report on Progress Toward Security and Stability in Afghanistan, December 2012," 1–5, 11, 18; "Report on Progress Toward Security and Stability in Afghanistan, July 2013," 1–2.

743. "International Security Assistance Force," ISAF Placemat, December 3, 2012, December 1, 2013, and November 7, 2014.

744. Author observation of media reporting in the United States, United Kingdom, and France over the years. Also, Lieutenant Colonel Jürgen Prandtner and Colonel Uwe Hartmann of the German army stated there was very little media coverage of Afghanistan in Germany.

745. NATO, "Transition to Afghan lead: Inteqal."

746. "International Security Assistance Force," ISAF Placemat, June 24, 2013, April 1, 2014, and November 7, 2014.

747. Colonel Robbie Boyd, British army.

748. Nicolas Delaunay, "Dutch Troops to Leave Afghanistan," Agence France Presse, July 28, 2010.

749. Rob Gillies, "Canada Considering Staying in Afghanistan," *foxnews.com*, November 7, 2010.

750. Laura King, "Canada's Exit Highlights Afghanistan Challenges," *Los Angeles Times*, July 16, 2011.

751. Martijn Kitzen, Sebastiaan Rietjens, and Frans Osinga, "Soft Power, the Hard Way: Adaptation by the Netherlands' Task Force Uruzgan," in *Military Adaptation in Afghanistan*, ed. Farrell et al., 160.

752. Stephen M. Saideman, "Canadian Forces in Afghanistan: Minority Government and Generational Change while under Fire," ibid., 229.

753. International Security Assistance Force, ISAF Placemats between 2011 and 2014.

754. NATO, "Press Conference by NATO Secretary General Jaap de Hoop Scheffer," June 12, 2009.

755. Interviews with Colonel Keith Detwiler, US Army and Lieutenant Colonel Jeffrey Dickerson, US Army. The official term for the manning requirements of a specific mission, like ISAF or Kosovo Force, was Combined Joint Statement of Requirements (CJSOR).

756. Lieutenant Colonel Roman Nahoncik, "The Czech Provincial Reconstruction Team: Civil-Military Teaming in Logar Province," strategy research project, US Army War College, 2013: 8–9.

757. Interviews with Colonel Shane Gabriel, Australian army and Lieutenant Colonel Arjan Hilaj, Albanian army.

758. Interviews with Colonel Phil Evans, US Army, Colonel Doug Mastriano, US Army, and Lieutenant Colonel Christopher Moretti, US Army.

759. Information from Colonel Christopher Cardoni, US Army and interviews of officers who deployed as part of the ISAF or RC headquarters or in battle groups or OMLTs.

760. Interviews with Colonel Piotr Bieniek, Polish army, Officer D, and Officer E.

761. "Report on Progress Toward Security and Stability in Afghanistan, October 2011," 8.

762. "Report on Progress Toward Security and Stability in Afghanistan, December 2012," 12.

763. Officer D, interview.

764. Lieutenant Colonel Eric Shafa, US Air Force. Also, McChrystal, *My Share of the Task*, 307, 385–86.

765. Interviews with Colonel Doug Mastriano, US Army and Colonel Piotr Bieniek, Polish army.

766. Ibid. Also, interviews with Lieutenant Colonel Peter Whalen, US Army and Lieutenant Colonel Douglas Woodall, US Army (served as commander, 109th Military Intelligence Battalion, Regional Command-East, ISAF, Afghanistan, May 2012–February 2013), interview with author at Carlisle Barracks, PA, August 6, 2013.

767. Peter Bergen, "What Went Right?" *Foreign Policy*, March 2013.

768. Lieutenant Colonel Douglas Woodall, US Army; Gordon Lubold, "Are We Winning in Afghanistan?" *Foreign Policy*, September 5, 2012; "Local Uprising

Against Taliban Proving Effective," *Washington Free Beacon*, March 21, 2013; and Bill Gertz, "Anti-Taliban Movement Gaining Strength in Afghanistan, US Says," *Washington Free Beacon*, July 12, 2013.

769. Jens Stoltenberg, "The Secretary General's Annual Report 2014," NATO Public Diplomacy Division, 2014: 7.

770. "The Election in Afghanistan Has Delivered a Powerful Message at Home and Abroad," *The Economist*, April 12, 2014; "Afghanistan's Presidential Election: Stuffed," *The Economist*, July 12, 2014; "Democracy, Afghan-style," *The Economist*, September 27, 2014.

771. "Report on Enhancing Security and Stability in Afghanistan, June 2015," US Department of Defense Report to Congress, 2015: 5, 57–58.

772. Stoltenberg, "The Secretary General's Annual Report 2014," 8–9.

Chapter 5. Why Cohesion Endured under Adversity

773. Anders Fogh Rasmussen, "The Future of the Alliance: Revitalizing NATO for a Changing World" (remarks at Brookings Institution, Washington, DC, March 19, 2014).

774. Farrell, "Introduction," in *Military Adaptation in Afghanistan*, ed. Farrell et al., 3–5, 15.

775. Bercuson et al., *Lessons Learned?*, 21.

776. Officer F, interview.

777. Officer F, interview.

778. Stoltenberg, "The Secretary General's Annual Report 2014," 3.

References

Personal Papers

Papers of Colonel (retired) Phil Evans. US Army. Chief of Operations, Joint Operations Center, Headquarters, ISAF, Kabul, Afghanistan.

Papers of Colonel (retired) Deborah Hanagan. US Army. Country Desk Officer for France, Belgium, Luxembourg and the Netherlands, Plans and Policy Directorate (J5), US European Command, Vaihingen, Germany.

Papers of Lieutenant Colonel Eric Shafa. US Air Force. ISAF Liaison to the Afghan Ministry of Mines, Ministry of Urban Development, Ministry of Energy and Water, and Ministry of Public Works, ISAF, Kabul, Afghanistan.

Interviews

Bieniek, Colonel Piotr. Polish Army. 2014. Interview with author. Carlisle Barracks, PA. February 12.

Boyd, Colonel Robbie. British Army. 2013. Interview with author. Carlisle Barracks, PA. April 15.

Braun, Colonel (retired) William. US Army. 2013. Interview with author. Carlisle Barracks, PA. January 8.

Brown, Colonel Lawrence. US Army. 2014. Interview with author. Carlisle Barracks, PA. August 7.

Browne, First Sergeant (retired) Robert. US Army. 2012. Interview with author. Carlisle Barracks, PA. December 20.

Burger, Lieutenant Colonel Joe. US Army. 2013. Interview with author. Carlisle Barracks, PA. November 12.

Busch, Colonel Horst. German Army. 2013. Interview with author. Carlisle Barracks, PA. April 11.

Butler, Colonel William. US Army. 2013. Interview with author. Carlisle Barracks, PA. April 8.

Campbell, Colonel Douglas. US Army. 2014. Interview with author. Carlisle Barracks, PA. January 23.

Cardoni, Colonel Christopher. US Army. 2013. Interview with author. Carlisle Barracks, PA. November 15.

Charles, Colonel North. US Army. 2012. Interview with author. Carlisle Barracks, PA. December 21.

Cheney, Major James. US Army. 2014. Email interview with author. April 21.

Davis, Lieutenant Colonel Timothy. US Army. 2014. Interview with author. Carlisle Barracks, PA. April 11.

Detwiler, Colonel Keith. US Army. 2012. Interview with author. Carlisle Barracks, PA. June 13.

Dickerson, Lieutenant Colonel Jeffrey. US Army. 2013. Interview with author. Carlisle Barracks, PA. April 5.

Donaldson, Colonel Steven. US Army. 2014. Interview with author. Carlisle Barracks, PA. January 28.

Evans, Colonel (retired) Phil. US Army. 2012. Interview with author. Carlisle Barracks, PA. December 27.

Freeman, Lieutenant Colonel Charles. US Army. 2013. Interview with author. Carlisle Barracks, PA. November 13.

Gabriel, Colonel Shane. Australian Army. 2013. Interview with author. Carlisle Barracks, PA. April 16.

Gellert, Colonel Frederick. US Army. 2012. Interview with author. Carlisle Barracks, PA. December 17.

Gjerde, Colonel Ingrid. Norwegian Army. 2013. Interview with author. Carlisle Barracks, PA. April 12.

Grometer, Lieutenant Colonel Brent. US Air Force. 2013. Interview with author. Carlisle Barracks, PA. April 9.

Hamilton, Colonel Robert. US Army. 2013. Interview with author. Carlisle Barracks, PA. April 2.

Hartmann, Colonel Uwe. German Army. 2014. Interview with author. Carlisle Barracks, PA. March 14.

Hilaj, Lieutenant Colonel Arjan. Albanian Army. 2013. Interview with author. Carlisle Barracks, PA. April 3.

Holler, Lieutenant Colonel Mark. US Army. 2013. Interview with author. Carlisle Barracks, PA. November 15.

Hoogstraten, Colonel Johannes. Netherlands Army. 2014. Interview with author. Carlisle Barracks, PA. February 12.

Knudsen, Lieutenant Colonel Ken. Danish Army. 2013. Interview with author. Carlisle Barracks, PA. May 6.

Lacquement, Colonel (retired) Richard. US Army. 2014. Interview with author. Carlisle Barracks, PA. January 30.

Lowe, Colonel Robert. US Army. 2012. Interview with author. Carlisle Barracks, PA. December 20.

Maranian, Colonel Stephen. US Army. 2013. Interview with author. Carlisle Barracks, PA. April 4.

Marcos, Lieutenant Colonel Javier. Spanish Army. 2014. Interview with author. Carlisle Barracks, PA. January 30.

Mastriano, Colonel Doug. US Army. 2013. Interview with author. Carlisle Barracks, PA. April 3.

McAslan, Lieutenant Colonel Hugh. New Zealand Army. 2013. Interview with author. Carlisle Barracks, PA. April 18.

McGinnis, Sherwood. US Department of State. 2013. Interview with author. Carlisle Barracks, PA. April 2.

Mckenney, Colonel Paul. US Army. 2013. Telephone interview with author. January 14.

Millen, Lieutenant Colonel (retired) Raymond. US Army. 2012. Interview with author. Carlisle Barracks, PA. December 21.

Moretti, Lieutenant Colonel Christopher. US Army. 2014. Interview with author. Carlisle Barracks, PA. January 14.

Mueller, Lieutenant Colonel Chris. US Army. 2014. Interview with author. Carlisle, PA. May 1.

Mundell, Colonel Robert. US Army. 2013. Interview with author. Carlisle Barracks, PA. July 25.

O'Donnell, Colonel Richard. US Army. 2014. Interview with author. Carlisle Barracks, PA. March 4.

Omsted, Colonel Ivar. Norwegian Army. 2014. Interview with author. Carlisle Barracks, PA. January 24.

Parylak, Colonel Dariusz. Polish Army. 2013. Interview with author. Carlisle Barracks, PA. April 9.

Peeters, Colonel Michael. US Army. 2012. Email interview with author. August 23.

Phillips, Colonel Paul. US Army. 2012. Interview with author. Carlisle Barracks, PA. December 18.

Prandtner, Lieutenant Colonel Jürgen. German Army. 2014. Interview with author. Carlisle Barracks, PA. January 14.

Ruszin, Colonel Romulusz. Hungarian Army. 2014. Interview with author. Carlisle Barracks, PA. February 10.

Shafa, Lieutenant Colonel Eric. US Air Force. 2013. Interview with author. Carlisle Barracks, PA. November 18.

Singleton, Commander Thomas. US Navy. 2013. Interview with author. Carlisle Barracks, PA. November 27.

Steponavicius, Lieutenant Colonel Mindaugas. Lithuanian Army. 2014. Interview with author. Carlisle Barracks, PA. January 31.

Tretinjak, Colonel Denis. Croatian Army. 2014. Interview with author. Carlisle Barracks, PA. January 27.

Vezzoli, Colonel Alberto. Italian Army. 2014. Interview with author. Carlisle Barracks, PA. January 23.

Whalen, Lieutenant Colonel Peter. US Army. 2013. Interview with author. Carlisle Barracks, PA. December 27.

Winegardner, Commander Michelle. US Navy. 2013. Interview with author. Carlisle Barracks, PA. May 2.

Woodall, Lieutenant Colonel Douglas. US Army. 2013. Interview with author. Carlisle Barracks, PA. August 6.

Woods, Colonel (retired) George. US Army. 2012. Interview with author. Carlisle Barracks, PA. December 17.

Woods, Colonel Tom. US Air Force. 2013. Email interview with author. April 25.

Partially Anonymous Interviews

Officer A. 2012. Interview with author. Carlisle Barracks, PA. December 27.

Officer B. 2013. Interview with author. Carlisle Barracks, PA. April 6.

Officer C. 2013. Interview with author. Carlisle Barracks, PA. May 14.

Officer D. 2013. Interview with author. Carlisle Barracks, PA. November 6.

Officer E. 2014. Interview with author. Carlisle Barracks, PA. January 15.

Officer F. 2014. Interview with author. Carlisle Barracks, PA. January 16.

Published sources

Alexander, Chris. *The Long Way Back: Afghanistan's Quest for Peace.* New York: Harper Collins, 2011.

Bailey, Jonathan, Richard Iron, and Hew Strachan, eds. *British Generals in Blair's Wars.* Burlington, VT: Ashgate, 2013.

Barr, Niall. *Eisenhower's Armies: The American-British Alliance During World War II.* New York: Pegasus Books, 2015.

Bar, Shmuel. *Warrant for Terror: The Fatwas of Radical Islam and the Duty to Jihad.* Lanham, MD: Rowman & Littlefield, 2006.

Barfield, Thomas. *Afghanistan: A Cultural and Political History.* Princeton, NJ: Princeton University Press, 2010.

Bergen, Peter L. *The Longest War: The Enduring Conflict between America and al-Qaeda.* New York: Free Press, 2011.

Bird, Tim, and Alex Marshall. *Afghanistan: How the West Lost its Way.* New Haven, CT: Yale University Press, 2011.

Boot, Max. *Invisible Armies: An Epic History of Guerrilla Warfare from Ancient Times to the Present.* New York: Liveright, 2013.

Braithwaite, Rodric. *Afgantsy: The Russians in Afghanistan, 1979–89.* New York: Oxford University Press, 2011.

Brooks, Michael G., ed. *Eyewitness to War* Vol. 3: *US Army Advisors in Afghanistan.* Fort Leavenworth, KS: Combat Studies Institute Press, 2009.

Burke, Jason. *The 9/11 Wars.* New York: Allen Lane, 2011.

Bush, George W. *Decision Points.* New York: Crown Publishers, 2010.

Cassidy, Robert M. *War, Will, and Warlords: Counterinsurgency in Afghanistan and Pakistan, 2001–2011.* Washington, DC: Marine Corps University Press, 2011.

Cheney, Dick, with Liz Cheney. *In My Time: A Personal and Political Memoir.* New York: Threshold Editions, 2011.

Cogan, Charles G. *Oldest Allies, Guarded Friends: The United States and France Since 1940.* Westport, CT: Praeger, 1994.

Crews, Robert D., and Amin Tarzi. *The Taliban and the Crisis of Afghanistan.* Cambridge, MA: Harvard University Press, 2008.

Downie, Richard. *Learning from Conflict: The US Military in Vietnam, El Salvador, and the Drug War.* Westport, CT: Praeger, 1998.

Ehrhart, Hans-Georg, Sven Bernhard Gareis, and Charles Pentland, eds. *Afghanistan in the Balance: Counterinsurgency, Comprehensive Approach, and Political Order.* Kingston, Ontario: McGill-Queen's University Press, 2012.

Emerson, Steven, and the Investigative Project on Terrorism. *Jihad Incorporated: A Guide to Militant Islam in the US.* New York: Prometheus Books, 2006.

Ewans, Martin. *Afghanistan: A Short History of Its People and Politics.* New York: Harper Perennial, 2002.

Farrell, Theo, Frans Osinga, and James A. Russell, eds. *Military Adaptation in Afghanistan.* Stanford, CA: Stanford University Press, 2013.

Feith, Douglas J. *War and Decision: Inside the Pentagon at the Dawn of the War on Terrorism.* New York: HarperCollins, 2008.

Forsberg, Tuomas, and Graeme P. Herd. *Divided West: European Security and the Transatlantic Relationship.* London: Blackwell, 2006.

Gates, Robert M. *Duty: Memoirs of a Secretary at War.* New York: Vintage Books, 2014.

Gentilini, Fernando. *Afghan Lessons: Culture, Diplomacy, and Counterinsurgency.* Translated by Angela Arnone. Washington, DC: Brookings Institution Press, 2013.

Giustozzi, Antonio. *Koran, Kalashnikov, and Laptop: The Neo-Taliban Insurgency in Afghanistan.* New York: Columbia University Press, 2008.

Giustozzi, Antonio, ed. *Decoding the New Taliban: Insights from the Afghan Field.* New York: Columbia University Press, 2009.

Goodson, Larry P. *Afghanistan's Endless War: State Failure, Regional Politics, and the Rise of the Taliban.* Seattle: University of Washington Press, 2001.

Gordon, Philip H. ed., *NATO's Transformation: The Changing Shape of the Atlantic Alliance.* Lanham, MD: Rowman & Littlefield, 1997.

Gunaratna, Rohan. *Inside Al Qaeda: Global Network of Terror.* New York: Columbia University Press, 2002.

Hanson, Victor Davis. *A War Like No Other: How the Athenians and Spartans Fought the Peloponnesian War.* New York: Random House, 2005.

Hendrickson, Ryan C. *Diplomacy and War at NATO: The Secretary General and Military Action After the Cold War.* Columbia: University of Missouri Press, 2006.

Hillier, General Rick. *A Soldier First: Bullets, Bureaucrats and the Politics of War.* Toronto: HarperCollins, 2009.

Hitchcock, William I. *The Struggle for Europe: The Turbulent History of a Divided Continent, 1945–Present*. New York: Doubleday, 2002.

Horn, Bernd. *No Lack of Courage: Operation Medusa, Afghanistan*. Toronto: Dundurn Press, 2010.

Isby, David. *Afghanistan, Graveyard of Empires: A New History of the Borderland*. New York: Pegasus Books, 2010.

Jabko, Nicolas, and Craig Parsons, eds. *The State of the European Union*, Vol. 7: *With US or Against US? European Trends in American Perspective*. Oxford: Oxford University Press, 2005.

Judah, Tim. *Kosovo: War and Revenge*. New Haven, CT: Yale University Press, 2000.

Judt, Tony. *Postwar: A History of Europe Since 1945*. New York: Penguin Books, 2006.

Kaplan, Lawrence S. *NATO and the United States: The Enduring Alliance*. New York: Twayne Publishers, 1994.

Kaplan, Lawrence S. *NATO Divided, NATO United: The Evolution of an Alliance*. Westport, CT: Praeger Publishers, 2004.

Kilcullen, David. *The Accidental Guerrilla: Fighting Small Wars in the Midst of the Big One*. Oxford: Oxford University Press, 2009.

King, Anthony. *The Transformation of Europe's Armed Forces: From the Rhine to Afghanistan*. Cambridge: Cambridge University Press, 2011.

Lansford, Tom, and Blagovest Tashev, eds. *Old Europe, New Europe and the US: Renegotiating Transatlantic Security in the Post 9/11 Era*. Burlington, VT: Ashgate, 2005.

Ledwidge, Frank. *Losing Small Wars: British Military Failure in Iraq and Afghanistan*. New Haven, CT: Yale University Press, 2011.

Lieven, Anatol. *Pakistan: A Hard Country*. New York: PublicAffairs, 2011.

Lindley-French, Julian, and Yves Boyer, eds. *The Oxford Handbook of War*. Oxford: Oxford University Press, 2012.

Luthar, Oto, ed. *The Land Between: A History of Slovenia*. Frankfurt: Peter Lang, 2008.

Malcolm, Noel. *Bosnia: A Short History*. New York: New York University Press, 1996.

Martin, Mike. *An Intimate War: An Oral History of the Helmand Conflict, 1978–2012*. New York: Oxford University Press, 2014.

McChrystal, General Stanley. *My Share of the Task: A Memoir*. New York: Portfolio/Penguin, 2013.

Micheletti, Eric, trans. Cyril Lombardini. *Special Forces in Afghanistan 2001–2003*. Paris: Histoire & Collections, 2003.

Mills, Greg. *From Africa to Afghanistan: With Richards and NATO to Kabul*. Johannesburg: Wits University Press, 2007.

Mueller, John. *Quiet Cataclysm: Reflections on the Recent Transformation of World Politics*. New York: HarperCollins, 1995.

Myers, General Richard B. *Eyes on the Horizon: Serving on the Front Lines of National Security*. With Malcolm McConnell. New York: Threshold Editions, 2009.

Nation, R. Craig. *War in the Balkans, 1991–2002*. Carlisle, PA: Strategic Studies Institute, 2003.

National Review, ed. *We Will Prevail: President George W. Bush on War, Terrorism, and Freedom*. New York: Continuum International Publishing Group, 2003.

Neumann, Ronald E. *The Other War: Winning and Losing in Afghanistan*. Dulles, VA: Potomac Books, 2009.

Nojumi, Neamatollah, Dyan Mazurana, and Elizabeth Stites. *After the Taliban: Life and Security in Rural Afghanistan*. Lanham, MD: Rowman & Littlefield, 2009.

Nord, Philip. *France 1940: Defending the Republic*. London: Yale University Press, 2015.

Rice, Condoleezza. *No Higher Honor: A Memoir of My Years in Washington*. New York: Crown Publishers, 2011.

Rothenberg, Gunther E. *The Art of Warfare in the Age of Napoleon*. Bloomington: Indiana University Press, 1980.

Rumsfeld, Donald. *Known and Unknown: A Memoir*. New York: Sentinel, 2011.

Sheehan, James J. *Where Have All the Soldiers Gone? The Transformation of Modern Europe*. New York: Houghton Mifflin, 2008.

Silber, Laura, and Allan Little. *Yugoslavia: Death of a Nation*. New York: Penguin Books, 1997.

Simpson, Emile. *War from the Ground Up: Twenty-First-Century Combat as Politics*. New York: Oxford University Press, 2013.

Sloan, Stanley, ed. *NATO in the 1990s*. Washington, DC: Pergamon-Brassey's International Defense Publishers, 1989.

Stuart, Douglas, and William Tow. *The Limits of Alliance: NATO Out-of-Area Problems Since 1949*. Baltimore: Johns Hopkins University Press, 1990.

Tanner, Stephen. *Afghanistan: A Military History from Alexander the Great to the Fall of the Taliban*. Cambridge, MA: Da Capo Press, 2002.

Taylor, John B. *Global Financial Warriors: The Untold Story of International Finance in the Post-9/11 World*. New York: W. W. Norton, 2007.

Thompson, Kenneth W., ed. *NATO and the Changing World Order: An Appraisal by Scholars and Policymakers*. Lanham, MD: University Press of America, 1996.

Wedgwood, C. V. *The Thirty Years War*. New York: Review Books, 2005.

Wright, Donald P. *A Different Kind of War: The United States Army in Operation Enduring Freedom, October 2001–September 2005*. With the Contemporary Operations Study Team. Fort Leavenworth, KS: Combat Studies Institute Press, 2010.

Zelikow, Philip, and Condoleezza Rice. *Germany Unified and Europe Transformed: A Study in Statecraft*. Cambridge, MA: Harvard University Press, 1997.

About the Author

Deborah Hanagan retired from the US Army as a colonel. She was commissioned as a military intelligence officer and subsequently transferred to the foreign area officer functional area. She served in a variety of leadership and staff positions in Germany, Slovenia, Saudi Arabia, and the continental United States. Her army assignments included: chief, Office of Defense Cooperation, Slovenia; political-military staff officer, US European Command, Germany; chief of staff, Defense Language Institute Foreign Language Center, Presidio of Monterey, California; and professor of strategy, US Army War College, Carlisle, Pennsylvania. She was a national security affairs fellow at the Hoover Institution, Stanford University, from 2007 to 2008. Hanagan graduated from the US Military Academy, West Point, and holds a master's degree in French military history from the Institut d'études politiques d'Aix-en-Provence, France, and a PhD in war studies from King's College London. She is the author of "The Sarkozy Revolution?," published in *Hoover Digest* (Hoover Institution, April 2008); and two chapters, "International Order" and "The Democratic Peace," published in *U.S. Army War College Guide to National Security Issues, Volume II: National Security Policy and Strategy* (Carlisle Barracks, PA: Strategic Studies Institute, 2012).

Index